WRITING ASSIGNMENTS ACROSS UNIVERSITY DISCIPLINES

ROGER GRAVES
AND THERESA HYLAND, EDITORS

Order this book online at www.trafford.com
or email orders@trafford.com

Most Trafford titles are also available at major online book retailers.

Print information available on the last page.

ISBN: 978-1-4907-8401-4 (sc)
ISBN: 978-1-4907-8403-8 (hc)
ISBN: 978-1-4907-8402-1 (e)

Library of Congress Control Number: 2017913308

Trafford rev. 12/06/2017

 www.trafford.com

North America & international
toll-free: 1 888 232 4444 (USA & Canada)
fax: 812 355 4082

Contents

Acknowledgements

We would like to dedicate this book to the hundreds of instructors who create, assign, and evaluate the writing of their students every term and whose work is the subject of the studies in this book. Teaching writing is hard work, and it is under-appreciated and under-rewarded in the usual instructor evaluation metrics used to evaluate teaching. More than anything else, we want to express our appreciation for the work you do and hope that something in the studies we have done may help you do this work more effectively.

We would like to acknowledge the Social Sciences and Humanities Research Council of Canada (SSHRC) for funding our work through a Standard Research Grant (410-2011-1845). We would also like to thank the Provost's Office of the University of Alberta for funding the early research studies, and Huron University College and Western University for funding the initial project. Finally, we would like to thank the many research assistants, both graduate and undergraduate, at the various campuses who worked with us to code the data we report here.

This book would not have been possible without the contributions of the many research assistants, graduate students, and undergraduate students who helped with various aspects of these research projects over the years, including Daniel Harvey, Megan Farnel, Taylor Scanlon, Shahin Moghaddasi, Susan Chaudoir, Andy Verboom, Aly Koskela, Alexandria King, Catherine Lee, Melissa Haynes, Graham Shaw, Jack Pender, Kelly McDonald, Stephanie Tolman, Sarah Cloutier, Joan Ellsworth, Jessica Jackson, Allison Enright, and Kathryn Marcynuk.

Introduction

Roger Graves and Theresa Hyland
University of Alberta / Huron University College

This study began, for us, in 2006. The writing program Roger directed at that time offered two versions of the introductory writing course: one for all students, and one (under a different course number) for students in the media or communications programs. As a program development goal, he thought that the sections for the media students could be tailored to the assignments that they would be writing in their subsequent media classes. After all, it was the media unit who requested that we create these sections for them with the idea being that this course would prepare students to write for the media courses; so it seemed to follow that adjusting the course to this end would be beneficial to all. Before we could redesign the writing course, however, it seemed prudent to explore what kinds of writing assignments students would face in their subsequent media courses. What writing assignments did professors give to media students?

We never did find the answer to that question. It turned out that the media instructors would not divulge to us anything about their instructional practices, including anything about the writing assignments they gave to students. But Theresa Hyland, a colleague at Huron University College and co-editor of this collection, was interested in gathering this kind of information from her institution with an eye toward improving the instruction she delivered through the writing centre she ran there. Her colleague, Boba Samuels, who at that time was a graduate student, instructor, and tutor at Western and other institutions, was interested in this research project, too, and so we began with the support of the Dean of the Faculty of Arts and Social Sciences at that time, Dr. Trish Fulton. Using data from nearby institutions, we published our first inventory of writing assignments in 2010 in *Written Communication.*

In that study we reported on all of the writing assignments given out to students in every course that the college offered—179 courses in all. We identified 448 writing assignments unevenly distributed across 17 departments in a wide range of genres—anything from briefing notes to concept maps to feasibility studies. We also found almost half of all assignments were named generically as essays, papers, or "assignments." One surprising finding was that students were not asked to write more as they progressed through their degree: the number of writing assignments given to first year students was very similar to the number of writing assignments given to students in any other year. When instructors specified the length of assignments (about 60% of the time), we found that almost half of the assignments (45%) were less than 4 pages long, and almost three-quarters (73%) were less than 10 pages long. We also found that many instructors (44%) were using the tactic of creating linked or "nested" assignments where one assignment leads to another, subsequent written task. Few instructors gave explanations of grading criteria for their assignments in the syllabus, and few made any mention in the syllabus of giving feedback to students before assignments were handed in for grading. Students in first and second year courses were given the least amount of detail about expectations of instructors for their written work.

That investigation proved fruitful in many ways and lead directly to the work reported in this book. We wanted to know if what we had found in this one small, liberal arts college would be similar to departments at larger, more research-based universities. We also wanted to know if we could replicate the results from one smaller institution at other smaller institutions. Did the wide range of assignments we found also occur within other academic units or was it the product of the liberal arts context? In the second half of our *Written Communication* article we described two program profiles, one from a Humanities department and one from a Social Sciences department. We took our cue from an article by Anson and Dannels (2009) who pointed us toward the idea that students experience a curriculum through their degree progress in an academic program. Consequently, we needed to map the writing assignments according to how different departments organized these degree programs. Put another way, this meant that while overall trends and results were interesting, results that were organized by curricular unit (departments, faculties or colleges, or programs/units) were more significant because students would progress through these courses to a degree.

As we continued to collect data from the course syllabi and present that data to the faculty, we began to realize that we needed to say more about faculty interaction with the research and the researchers and the follow-up measures that were taken or planned as a result of the research. Two chapters deal specifically with this theme: "Conversations in the Attic" questions faculty about how they viewed students' writing, what growth they expected to see in senior writing assignments, and how they conveyed their expectations to the students. This material was then analyzed to look at the differences that exist in the ways that professors talk about writing in the different disciplines, the metaphors they use when they teach students to meet the various tacit and explicit assumptions that they made, and how they vary in their use of external resources to educate students in disciplinary writing. In the chapter "Cross-Talk and Crossed Boundaries," Theresa Hyland turned to Gifford's theories of social dilemma awareness and Stern's values, beliefs, and norms theory to explain how and why faculty resisted some research initiatives and embraced others. These themes also figure in the Parker, Slomp, and McKeown articles. All three researchers worked very closely with the faculty in order to understand the results of the research and to fashion strategies that would address problems that had been uncovered. In Parker's case, more discussions about writing occurred, and the definition of good communication skills for engineers was refined. McKeown worked with faculty in focus groups to not only communicate the findings of the research, but also gauge faculty interest and incite faculty to refine the writing practices in their departments. Departments agreed to have presentations from the writing researchers to look at the data and to determine a course of action for better integration of writing expectations into the course syllabi and the adoption of techniques such as nesting assignments. McKeown also looked to the students to understand the impact of faculty strategies on their writing. Her survey of graduating students confirmed some of the assertions that faculty made about the usefulness of verbal instructions over written instructions and the need for specific audiences for some of the assignments. Williams' article also mentions funding for follow-up studies and plans to develop departmental guidelines for writing assignment design and writing workshops for undergraduate students. Slomp's article uses the course syllabi analysis as a starting point for the redesign of assignments, based on the data analysis of faculty and student comments. He described the process of creating and validating awareness in the faculty for a need for change and described how that change was initiated.

The bulk of this book, then, is devoted to chapters that examine the writing requirements of specific curricular units. In Chapter 1, Roger Graves sets the context for the book by comparing course syllabi of five different curricular units (faculties, departments, and programs) at a large research-based university, in terms of genre in order to understand the challenges undergraduate students face with writing. In Chapter 2, McKeown analyzes all the writing assignments in a small liberal arts college and discovers some similarities but also many differences between the writing challenges at her college and those of students in the first Course Syllabi Study. In Chapter 3, Parker demonstrates how the course syllabi data have been used by her Engineering Faculty to create rubrics and refine assignments to better conform to modern communication needs as defined by the Canadian Engineering Accreditation Board's standardized Attribute 7. In Chapter 4, Williams suggests ways in which the course syllabi project can help institute curricular changes that help students perform scientific writing within a Life Sciences Department. In Chapter 5 Jewinski and Trivett explore ways in which the course syllabi project can help Mechanical Engineering students at an Ontario university conform to CEAB standards while at the same time satisfying the requirements of the university's task force on English competency. In Chapter 6, Slomp and his colleagues use the course syllabi data to explore assignment load in the Faculty of Education in order to help faculty reimagine the Bachelor of Education to encourage deep thinking about educational practices.

Chapters 7 and 8, in exploring writing in the disciplines from the faculty's point of view, look to the future of such research in terms of tacit and explicit iterations of writing theory and how faculty view the value of such research.

Chapter 1

Writing Assignments Across Five Academic Programs

Roger Graves
University of Alberta

Introduction

What do we know about what students write in their undergraduate programs of study? Administrators usually do not have good data in answer to this question even during program evaluation events, often assuming that students write a lot, usually essays or reports. They tend to assume that students come to their institution with a general writing competency and that, perhaps through a required English literature course or even a writing course, generalized ability to write transfers to the demands of writing in all other disciplines of study. But instructors who have direct knowledge of students' failure to produce appropriate written work in their programs of study express puzzlement—or frustration—at the failure of students to transfer their success as writers in previous contexts (at the secondary level, in the required English literature course, or in their English language preparatory courses) to their written work in their major programs of study.

Similarly, those who work to help students develop as writers face the same problem: how can they help students write assignments in response to instructors' prompts? Writing centre tutors, writing course instructors, and writing program administrators generate

1

knowledge about the challenges students face when they leave the tutorial or the course. Many writing centres collect examples of instructor's assignments and develop strategies for helping students with a particular assignment. Some instructors and program directors create courses that take as the subject of study writing in various academic contexts. Many administrators create their own writing support systems (tutors, online documents, workshops, even entire writing centres) in their own faculties to help students perform better as writers. In most instances, these academics lack data about what tasks their students actually face as writers. One of the consequences is writing support that, while well-intended, often misses the mark. Student writing outcomes often do not improve according to instructors in these programs.

My aim in this chapter is to provide data about the challenges students face as writers by describing in detail what they are asked to write. This research responds to the call from Anson and Dannels (2009) to create program profiles of departments in an effort to map the writing demanded of undergraduates onto the curriculums that they encounter. In an earlier study, Graves, Hyland, and Samuels collected a complete sample of syllabi from one college and 17 different departments. This article shows how writing assignments vary within a specific program at one college; that research provided us with a complete picture of writing tasks assigned to students within each of these programs. The broad actions we can take have been described elsewhere (Graves 2013, 2014). This chapter provides data and a more nuanced look at what instructors are actually asking students to write.

Why Do Assignment Genres Matter?

Fuller and Lee (2002) describe the ways that a writing assignment changes the subjectivity of a student as they go through the process of writing that assignment. They point out how "the student essay" as a genre contributes to creating "generic" subjects because of the ritualized nature of the essay as an assignment. Many instructors are unaware of how the assignments they choose to give students lead to this kind of subjectivity, while others create assignments to break from it. This is an important reason for all instructors to attend to the assignments they create: assignments that are too tightly controlled create a lack of agency in students. Tightly-controlled assignments can lead to disengagement from the intellectual tasks and lead to a sense among students that the writing they do is just a hoop to jump through in order to pass the course and complete the degree. For instructors, the results can lead to frustration with student writing and with students who ask the wrong question— "what does the prof want?"—rather than the right question: "What do I have to say about this topic?"

But as this chapter documents, assignments vary considerably from program to program and within programs. While some genres do dominate the lists of assignments—"papers" and presentations occur in all five disciplines reported in this chapter—in some disciplines, papers accounted for as many as 32% of assignments and as few as 10% of assignments. In some programs, we recorded over 50 different genre names given by instructors. Only one program, Nursing, came anywhere near having a dominant set of genres, with only 13 different assignments. In this case, however, the professional nature of the program had as its goal the creation of a professional mindset. Further, many of those assignments belonged to what could be called a "reflective practice" genre family. That the assignments in that group demanded that students reflect on their experiences would seem to counter the concern that they were not engaged in their studies.

Assignment Genres at the Post-Secondary Level: A Review of the Literature

Writing assignments have interested researchers at all levels of schooling since the 1980s (Applebee, Langer & Mullis, 1986; Bridgeman & Carlson, 1984; McCarthy, 1987; Canseco & Bird, 1989). Early work sometimes touched on writing assignments as a side issue (Kelly & Bazerman, 2003; Dias, Freedman, Medway & Paré, 1999; Dias & Paré, 2000; Beaufort, 2007; Brereton, 2007; Carson et al., 1992). At the secondary level, Applebee and Langer have done the most extensive research. In 2006, they reported that students in US schools wrote the following types of documents: narrative, analysis/interpretation, persuasion, log or journal, report on study or research, and summary of reading (Applebee & Langer, 2006). They note that at the grade 12 level only one-third of students write essays more than a few times each year. They also reported that in 1998 40% of Grade 12 students did not write papers longer than 3 pages, and that students in high school did not write long (more than 3 pages) or complex assignments. For Applebee and Langer, this presents two potential problems for high school graduates: students going on to post-secondary education will not be prepared for the demands of writing at that level, and students who go into the workforce will not have the advanced literacy skills needed to succeed there. Writing done in non-English classes decreases from grade 8 to grade 12 with fewer than 20% of math and science students writing even one paragraph each week. In a 2011 study, Applebee and Langer describe a system that has not changed significantly. However, Peterson and McClay (2010) report substantially more writing by grade 4-8 students in their survey of Canadian school teachers, with over half assigning a wide variety of types of writing. I could find no similar study of writing assigned to Canadian high school students, so we have no way of knowing if the trends reported by Applebee and Langer in 2006 extended to Canadian schools.

At the post-secondary level, much work has been done in the last 20 years. Several researchers have published work describing writing assignments across the disciplines (Light, 2001, 2003; Paltridge, 2002; Cooper & Bikowski, 2007; Melzer, 2003, 2009). Light's work on writing and student engagement provides the rationale for administrators to support writing instruction and support because Light's research showed that writing is the most important factor in creating student engagement (intellectual engagement; time spent on the course; or level of interest with the subject matter). But what do they write aside from examinations? Canseco and Byrd (1989) describe the writing assigned in graduate business courses: class-based assignments, case studies, and reports dominated. Moran (2013) found that psychology students wrote in only 25% of their courses the first two years of their degrees; in the third and fourth years, psychology students wrote mostly "summary/reactions to a reading" and "connection of theory with data." She also found that chemistry students wrote lab reports that grew in complexity as students advanced through the degree. Paltridge (2002) summarized the studies of Horowitz's (1986) and Braine's (1995) reports of writing assignments. Horowitz reported that liberal arts students at a small, teaching focused university wrote research essays, assignments that connected theory and data, summaries and reactions to readings, reports of experiences, case studies, research projects, and annotated bibliographies. Braine focused on natural sciences and engineering student assignments and found they clustered around five groups—summary/reactions, lab or experimental reports, design reports, case studies, and research papers—but were dominated by lab or experimental reports (75% of the total).

These studies, while useful, prompted other researchers to search out larger datasets in an effort to see if the results applied more broadly. Melzer's work focuses on writing across the curriculum approaches, identifying courses that have a writing across the curriculum focus and using Britton's (1975) taxonomy of purposes for writing (expressive, poetic, functional). Melzer's studies (2003; 2009; 2014) of assignments drew from syllabi available online at 100 different institutions in the US; this appears to be a convenience sample rather than a representative sample, and that is a significant limitation on his findings. In his studies he found that the overwhelming majority (83%) of assignments had transactional (using Britton's terminology) and informative (66%) as the purpose of the writing. Melzer's findings about the audience for assignments were similar to Britton's and Applebee's: Melzer reports that 64% of assignments were directed to the teacher as examiner (where the goal is to provide the correct answer), while Britton reported 48% and Applebee 55%. Britton reported that the teacher as audience, a more general category, applied to 86% of assignments. Melzer found a wide variety of genres of assignments in his sample, though he declined to categorize them or even list them.

While Melzer declined to classify the genres of writing assigned to students, Nesi and Gardner (2012) did not. They worked with the British Academic Written English (BAWE) corpus to identify the genres of writing students were asked to produce for grades in courses. Their goals were similar to ours: to document which genres tended to appear in which disciplines and at which levels of study; to identify these genres more accurately than instructors' naming conventions; and to give some sense of which genres dominated in particular disciplines. Their method differed from the other studies cited in this review because they examined the actual writing that students produced, and not just the assignment descriptions. They found thirteen genre families total, with only five genre families responsible for more than 5% of the total (Table 1).

Table 1

Genres of written assignments. Data reported by Nesi and Gardner; percentages computed by R. Graves

Genre family	Number	% of total
Essay	12 37	43.3
Methodology recount	361	12.7
Critique	322	11.2
Explanation	214	7.5
Case study	194	6.8

Nesi and Gardner gathered specific genres announced in assignments into genre families, groups of genres linked by a common purpose, function, or structure (pp. 25-26). They identified three main purposes for student writing: demonstrate disciplinary knowledge; produce new disciplinary knowledge; and prepare for post-graduation employment. They organized their book largely by these purposes, exploring the genre families that supported student development towards those ends.

In the first study we completed (Graves, Hyland, & Samuels, 2010), we sought to identify the kinds of writing assignments undergraduates at a small liberal arts college wrote. We collected a complete sample of syllabi from one college (that is, every syllabus from every course in 17 different departments). This approach provided us with a complete picture of writing tasks assigned to students within each of these programs. That research responds to the call from Anson and Dannels (2009) to create program profiles of departments in an effort to map the writing demands of undergraduates onto the curriculums that they encounter. This chapter and the others in this book all respond in some way to the call for examining the writing students do in their programs of study. Each research group identified programs, collected data on the writing assignments required in the program, and then interacted with the program administrators to discuss the results. We began in 2008 with the programs reported in this chapter and expanded our scope as we gained federal funding and shared preliminary results. The results and what they mean are important, but the method is perhaps also significant because it focuses on assessing the programs, not the instructors, and provides a mirror of the curriculum to the people who run these programs. It is the image in that mirror that helps program administrators decide what, if any, changes they wish to make in their programs.

Methods: Developing a Coding Protocol and Guide

This chapter describes the genres of academic writing assignments identified in studies of writing assignments collected in 5 different programs of study (departments, college/faculties, and interdisciplinary programs). Our general process began by collecting syllabi. We communicated with administrators in the academic unit (dean's office, department chair, program director). These contacts then gathered the syllabi for us, compiled them into digital media (USB stick, CD_ROM, Google Drive folder), and forwarded them to our research group. Research assistants then read each syllabus to identify separate writing assignments; each assignment became one record in the database. We defined writing assignments as written assignments (including oral presentations) that were worth 5% or more of the final grade in the course. We did not code exams (mid-term, quizzes, and finals) because we felt these written performances did not contribute to the development of writing ability: they were one-time events, not revisable, and did not allow for preparation activities that lead to writing development. Coders were trained using the coding guide in Appendix A.

Each assignment was coded for genre, length, feedback, topic choice, and other features. Appendix B is a copy of the print-based coding sheet we initially used before developing a web-based application for entering the results directly into a database.

Research assistants read all syllabi twice and identified anomalies which were then discussed and adjudicated; specific issues for each project are described below. The data from the coding sheets was entered directly into a web-based application we developed that compiled the results into spreadsheets that were downloadable. These spreadsheets became the basis for the tables and charts that we created for our reports back to the academic unit that sponsored the research.

To control for reliability, coders flagged syllabi that presented problems for them. The research team met, discussed the anomalies, and created entries in the coding guide to record the decisions about how to handle these cases. We then went back into the database and re-coded the data to reflect the updated method.

Coding these assignments presented challenges of various kinds. In recording the genre of the assignment that the instructor gave, we sometimes encountered instructors who used more than one label to refer to the same assignment in their syllabus (and sometimes 3 or 4 distinct names). For example, an assignment labeled 'research paper' at the head of the assignment description was also called an 'essay' within the details of the assignment, and a 'field report' was labeled as 'literature review' in the assignment details. In these cases we used the first name or the name most often used in the syllabus. When we sought to identify assignments that were "linked" or "nested," we identified assignments that had more than one component (such as a separate mark for an abstract and for the main assignment); we did not code a group of assignments that were the same assignment repeated several times as linked, though we did code each iteration as a separate assignment. In categories such as explicit statements of learning goals, we coded any statement, however brief, as having that characteristic. Similarly, in the audience category we counted any mention, however brief, of the audience for the assignment. For the category of feedback to students, we did not include the offer of informal office hours; if students were required to meet with the instructor, we did categorize that as providing feedback.

Coding Specifics: Nursing Study

The Nursing study was the first one done at this institution and with this research team. Consequently, for this part of the data we made some changes to the initial coding sheet to account for anomalies (such as courses of differing lengths) and the need to train coders to be consistent. Some courses contained writing assignments similar to other courses, so we added another stage to our process where we compared the coding sheets for those assignments to ensure consistency. Because our original coding sheet did not allow for courses of varying lengths, we added "length of course" to our data sheet. Initially there was inconsistency by the coders in coding audience, plagiarism, feedback, references, style, suggested resources, and evaluation criteria. We re-coded the data and created the coding guide in Appendix B to guide coders. We re-examined each syllabus to examine the coding inconsistencies in each category and re-coded the assignments on the assignment sheet.

Coding Specifics: Pharmacy

When an assignment labeled 'research essay' in one section of the syllabus was called 'research project' in another section, we coded the assignments with the exact label written by the instructor in the evaluation section of the syllabus. For pass/fail assignments, the coders needed to decide on the mark value for explicit pass/fail assignments. The mark value category was coded as zero for all pass/fail assignments.

Coding Specifics: Political Science

If the student was able to choose a topic for the assignment and the syllabus did not include an explicit list of topics to choose from, then this was coded as open. For example, the syllabus for one course did not have an explicit list of topics for an assignment called 'major paper,' but on a subsequent page the instructor noted a topic limitation. Therefore, this assignment was coded as yes (i.e., the student had a choice of topic for the assignment) and the topic choice as open because the student could choose any topic within the scope of the course's subject. We found that there were three types of presentation assignments: group project presentations, in-class presentations of the course readings, and individual presentations of a research paper. Group project and individual presentations were embedded or linked assignments. In-class presentations of the course readings, however, were not embedded or linked with another writing assignment. We cross-checked each presentation assignment for consistency.

Limitations

The data we report here are drawn from syllabi. Where possible, we added details from supplementary documents provided to us by instructors or administrators. Nevertheless, interviews with faculty members would have added to our data. Student data, in the form of the texts they wrote and handed in as a response to the assignments, would have given us important data about how students responded to these assignments. Finally, the selection of these five curricular units was essentially a convenience sample: these units had a working relationship with the Writing Across the Curriculum program and so agreed to participate in the study as a form of curriculum assessment and revision.

Assignment Genres

Writing is required in the vast majority of undergraduate courses:

- Nursing required writing assignments in 86% of courses;
- Physical Education and Recreation required at least one writing assignment in 82% of courses;
- Pharmacy required a writing assignment in 83% of courses;
- Community Service-Learning required writing assignments in every course; and
- Political Science courses required a writing assignment in every course.

Table 2 shows the average number of assignments per course at each year in the program. Programs outside the arts and humanities—such as Pharmacy, Nursing, and Physical Education and Recreation—require as many or more written assignments as the one program in a traditional arts area, Political Science, which requires an average of three assignments per course. This is important because many academics and many administrators assume that courses in the arts require more written work than in other disciplines. It is an important research finding to note the prevalence of written assignments across all the curricular areas in this study. Two outliers appear in Table 2: the number of assignments in Year 1 for Community Service-Learning and in Year 4 of Pharmacy. Both numbers are high due to one course in each program that had a weekly writing assignment.

Table 2

The number of assignments per course at each year level

Year	Community Service-Learning	Political Science	Physical Education, Recreation	Pharmacy	Nursing
Overall	6.7	3.0	3.2	5.4	3.7
1.	10.5	1.4	2.5	5.0	1.5
2.	4.0	2.3	3.2	3.8	4.7
3.	5.8	2.4	2.6	4.9	4.1
4.	6.7	4.2	4.6	14.2	4.4

The number of assignments, then, paints part of the overall picture. However, one explanation for the large number of assignments outside of arts might be that the assignments in arts disciplines, for example, might be longer than in other disciplines. There might be fewer of them in arts, as Table 2 shows, but they might be significantly longer. Table 3 shows the length of assignments in each area. Political Science assignments are indeed longer than those in other areas with 46% of all assignments in the 5-10 page range. Community Service-Learning, a largely arts program, has many more 1-4 page assignments and presents a profile much closer to the non-arts disciplines. At the same time, the vast majority of assignments in all studies (78% or more) were less than 11 pages long, and the majority of assignments in all but one discipline were four pages or shorter. Students rarely write assignments longer than 4 pages; most of their writing assignments are short.

Table 3

Length of assignments

Length (pages)	Community Service-Learning (%)	Political Science (%)	Physical Education, Recreation (%)	Pharmacy (%)	Nursing (%)
1-4	**57**	32	**62**	**71**	**75**
5-10	29	**46**	28	16	17
11+	17	22	10	13	8

The only commonly reported genres that appeared across all five disciplinary units, using the instructor's label for the assignment, were papers and presentations (Table 4). Outlines (four times), journals (four times), reports of one kind or another (three times), handouts (three times), and proposals (three times) were the only genres appearing in a majority of disciplinary units. So while there are some genres that extend widely across disciplines, the majority of writing assignments in all disciplines were varied and not dominated by any one genre. Students must write in a wide variety of genres in their undergraduate degree programs.

Table 4

Most common genres by professor's label. Percentages refer to how often this genre was specified within that discipline

Rank	Community Service-Learning	Political Science	Physical Education, Recreation	Pharmacy	Nursing
1.	**Paper** (21%)	**Paper** (32%)	**Presentation/** teaching demonstration (21%)	*Care plan* (12%)	*Self-evaluation* (38%)
2.	**Presentation** (17%)	Essay (21%)	**Paper** (16%)	**Presentation** (12%)	**Paper** (29%)
3.	Journal (10%)	**Presentation** (15%)	*Assignment* (9%)	**Paper** (10%)	Handout (17%)
4.	Essay (6%)	Proposal (7%)	*Log* (5%)	*Documentation* (9%)	*Personal goals* (12%)
5.	Outline (5%)	Draft (4%)	Summary (4%)	*Consultation* (9%)	Journal (12%)
6.	Draft (5%)	Handout (4%)	Lab report (3%)	*Medical reconciliation* (6%)	Report (12%)
7.	*Field report* (5%)	Journal (4%)	Proposal (3%)	Note (2%)	*Peer evaluation* (11%)
8.	*Online discussion/ blog* (4%)	Outline (3%)	*Lesson plan* (3%)	Journal (1%)	*Group email* (11%)
9.	Email (4%)	*Book review* (4%)	*Analysis* (3%)	Lab report (1%)	**Presentation** (8%)
10.	Proposal (3%)	Other (2%)	Outline (3%)	Handout (1%)	Outline (3%)

If we combine Table 4 with Table 5, we get a sense of how common the dominant genres are across the curriculum. Notable by its absence is the essay, which was reported only in Community Service-Learning and Political Science, two arts-based disciplines. Instead, two non-specific genres—'paper' and 'presentation'—appear as the most common genres. These labels provide little detail to students about what kind of written text to prepare or what kind of presentation to give.

Table 5

Most common genres across the sample set (genres that occur in at least three disciplines)

Genres assigned	Percentage reported (average over 5 academic units)	Percentage reported (average over units where assigned)
Paper	21.6	21.6
Presentation	14.6	14.6
Outline	2.8	4.7
Journals	5.4	9.0
Reports	4.2	5.3
Handouts	4.4	7.3
Proposals	2.6	4.3

Some genre families dominated the syllabi of academic units: *self evaluation* and *papers* for nursing; *presentations* and *papers* for physical education and recreation; *papers, essays,* and *presentations* for political science; and *papers* and *presentations* for Community Service-Learning. In some academic programs, however, the lists of genres announced on syllabi are very long: we counted 54 different genres in physical education and recreation and 58 in pharmacy. Nursing appears to be the outlier here: those syllabi listed only 13 genres. Most academic programs require a lot of writing in a great variety of forms.

Genres were not distributed evenly across all four years of the undergraduate programs. In the Physical Education faculty, lab reports, journals, and handouts dominated the first two years; summaries, reports, proposals, and critical thinking problems dominated the upper years. In Pharmacy, discipline-specific genres dominated fourth year: documentation (of various kinds), medical reconciliations, care plans, and assessments. In Nursing, annotated bibliographies, proposals, field notes, and reports dominate fourth year, while self-evaluations occur throughout all years. In Community Service-Learning, papers, presentations, and field reports dominate the upper years. In general, the assignments that dominate the upper years of undergraduate programs seem the ones most likely to draw on the higher ends of Bloom's taxonomy: analysis, synthesis, and evaluation.

One final point from this data relates to the naming of genres by instructors in their syllabi. Table 6 shows the large number of different genres that instructors listed in their syllabi. The creativity instructors showed in naming assignments creates problems for students (Shaver 2007). Students infer assignment requirements from the names; multiple names for an assignment within one syllabus creates confusion. At the program level, using the proliferation of names for similar assignments leads to even greater confusion, at least in part because students use past experience to guide their next writing attempts. If instructors in early courses in a program use one name for an assignment, but instructors in senior courses use another name, students may not be cued to the similarity of expectations that the two seemingly dissimilar assignments require.

Table 6

Genres listed by instructors in syllabi

Academic unit	Number of announced genres
Pharmacy	58
Physical Education, Recreation	54
Community Service-Learning	21
Political Science	18
Nursing	13

Students Write Frequently in Degree Credit Courses

We found that writing assignments occur very frequently across all five academic programs in this study, ranging from 3.0 to 6.7 assignments per course. In two programs (Political Science and Community Service-Learning), students wrote in every course in the program. It seems clear from the data gathered in these studies and reported in Graves, Hyland, and Samuels (2010), where we found an average of 2.5 assignments per course, that students write frequently. While the Graves, Hyland, and Samuels (2010) study reported two programs with no writing assignments (mathematics and economics), neither of these disciplines is represented in the current study. As an aside, however, I have worked with an economics program that does have extensive writing assignments in its program; it remains unclear if the 2010 sample is an exception for economics programs. Elsewhere in this volume, McKeown reports that students in her study wrote an average of 64 pages per semester in seven assignments, an amount similar to what Light (2001) reported. Parker (this volume) reports students in mechanical engineering write an average of 3.9 assignments per course; she could not, however, determine the length of the assignments from her data. Williams (this volume) also found an average of 4 writing assignments per course, with students moving from less than 1500 words per assignment in the first two years to much longer, 6500 word assignments in the third and fourth years. Slomp et al. (this volume) report over 6 assignments per course.

Despite increasing class sizes at some institutions in response to budget reductions or budget increases that fail to match inflation, the amount of writing assigned to students remains high. A second research question intrigued us, though: what are they writing? What genres do instructors assign? The data we found suggest that students are asked to write a wide variety of assignments, ranging from 77 assignments in Education (see Slomp et al., this volume) to 13 in Nursing. In some programs, there appears to be little coordination among instructors in the naming of assignments. Shaver (2007) points to the problems this causes for students, and the data we gathered suggest that the idiosyncratic naming conventions used in some programs would likely create confusion for students. A related problem in the data is the prevalence of generic names for assignments: paper, essay, report, and even the word "assignment." These names are too general to indicate what genre of document students must produce, and in some fields (and certainly between disciplines) what is meant by a "paper" can vary significantly from one course to another. The data also show the prevalence of specific genres in most fields: medical reconciliations, field reports, and personal goals statements, for example.

Audience for Assignments

When coding assignments, we assumed the instructor as audience unless otherwise indicated. For every discipline except Pharmacy, the instructor or peers (academic audiences) dominated writing assignments (see Table 7 below). In each case, over 90% of assignments were written for academic audiences. The exception is Pharmacy. In this discipline, instructors specified a wide range of audiences outside the academic classroom. These are the groups that practising pharmacists need to communicate to. In the case of Nursing, all of the instructors were licensed nurses, so they stood in for or closely resembled the professional audiences that students would eventually be communicating with.

Table 7

Percentage of assignments written to academic or non-academic audiences

Community Service-Learning (%)	Political Science (%)	Physical Education, Recreation (%)	Pharmacy (%)	Nursing (%)
Instructor or peers (91%)	Instructor or peers (92%)	Instructor or peers (97%)	Instructor or peers (59%)	Instructor or peers (99%)
Outside of class (9%)	Outside of class (8%)	Various other professional groups (3%)	Preceptor (16%)	Outside of class (1%)
			Standardized patient (11%)	
			Public/ community (4%)	
			Healthcare audience (3%)	
			Peer student (3%)	
			Various other (4%)	

Who do students write for? Researchers have consistently been interested in the audiences for student writing. Results of this study deviate from the results reported by Melzer (2003; 2009; 2014) of 64%; Britton (1975) of 48%; and Applebee (2006) of 55% for the teacher as examiner audience. Britton (1975), however, also reported a finding similar to this study for "teacher as audience"—86% of assignments—a number much more in line with this study.

The major departure from this data comes from the Pharmacy faculty, who assigned a wide variety of audiences other than the teacher. Writing for different audiences matters because it is associated with advanced student writing. Thaiss and Zawacki (2006) identify a complex understanding of audience with their third-stage student writers, students who have formed a sophisticated understanding of the writing they are asked to do in their disciplines. When students write only for the instructor, they must deal with the contradictions inherent in that rhetorical situation. Soliday (2011) points to the problems in asking students to write for the instructor: instructors also want students to write for "know-nothing readers" to encourage students to include full explanations of procedures; however, an expert reader (the instructor) would not require a full explanation. A related problem occurs when the instructor stands in or simulates another audience. Soliday (2011) and Nesi and Gardner (2012) point to research in genre studies that questions the wisdom of simulating workplace genres. In the pharmacy data reported here and in other professional faculties, however, the instructors are often both academics and professionals in their fields. In addition, many of the professional fields employ adjunct instructors who are primarily working professionals rather than academics. These people are not what some genre studies researchers are referring to as simulated audiences. Popham (2005) established the case for what she called "boundary objects" or genres that addressed audiences from different disciplines, or in the case of academic and professional audiences, those two distinct audiences. These kinds of assignments, while challenging, help students prepare for the complexities of writing beyond their degree programs.

Nested or Scaffolded Assignments

A previous study (Graves, Hyland, & Samuels, 2010) noted that some assignments can be profitably broken down into sub-assignments, sometimes called nested or scaffolded (Bean, 2011) assignments. The pedagogical rationale for separating steps of a larger project is clear: this separation allows for feedback between the steps of the larger project and thus allows students to make adjustments in their approaches. The 2010 study found that 44% of all assignments were nested or scaffolded, and that instructors used this technique more often in upper year courses (59% of all assignments in fourth year were nested). In the five follow-up studies described in Table 8, three of the programs (Pharmacy, Nursing, and Community Service-Learning) showed even higher rates of nested or scaffolded assignments, while two had lower rates (Political Science and Physical Education).

Table 8

Percentage of assignments that were linked to other assignments

Nested	Community Service-Learning (%)	Political Science (%)	Physical Education, Recreation (%)	Pharmacy (%)	Nursing (%)
Yes	68	37	30	60	71
No	32	63	70	40	29

The three programs that used nested or scaffolded assignments—Pharmacy, Nursing, and Community Service-Learning—share an orientation to the purpose for writing that Nesi and Gardner call "preparing for professional practice" (2012). While Community Service-Learning does not have a profession to point towards, those students must all apply their knowledge and reflect upon their experiences in light of their interactions with the community. Applying newly created knowledge to a novel context for writing is a difficult, strenuous task for most undergraduates. Scaffolding or nesting assignments is one way that instructors can mitigate these difficult tasks and provide feedback or guidance to students.

In-Process Feedback on Writing Assignments

In addition to nested or scaffolded assignments, which embed opportunities for feedback into the structure of these assignments, we coded the assignments for feedback opportunities on an individual assignment. Our rationale was that we wanted to see if opportunities for revision were part of the process of completing an assignment; revision is key to improvement in student writing quality. We looked for any sign that students would have an opportunity for feedback from either the instructor or from peers before handing the assignment in for grading. In our 2010 study, we found that only 14% of assignments provided a structured opportunity for feedback.

Practices on this item for the five programs in this study were widely divergent (see Table 9 below). Nursing provided feedback on an almost universal scale, with students receiving feedback on almost every assignment. At the other end of the scale, very few written assignments in Physical Education received feedback before being evaluated.

Table 9

In-process feedback on writing assignments

Feedback	Community Service-Learning (%)	Political Science (%)	Physical Education, Recreation (%)	Pharmacy (%)	Nursing (%)
Yes	41	21	7	22	96
No	59	79	93	78	4

The exceptionally high rate in Nursing can be traced to the structure of the courses. Students in larger lecture classes were also members of small (12 student) tutorial groups. The feedback on student work occurred in these tutorial groups. It should also be noted that reflecting on practice is a core value in Nursing courses. Students are encouraged to continually think about their practices, and reflecting on their writing is part of that overall bias toward metacognitive awareness.

Evaluation Criteria or Rubrics

Good instructional design principles require that assessment procedures be made transparent to learners. For writing assignments in these syllabi, we expected to encounter some mention of how they would be evaluated. For the purposes of coding, we counted any mention of criteria by which the instructor would evaluate the assignments. This could be as little as one sentence in the syllabus, or it could include a formal rubric. This did not have to be a formal rubric or scoring guide; any kind of statement, however brief, was counted as "yes." In our 2010 study, we found that 70% of assignments made no reference to how the assignments would be evaluated. In the five programs reported in this chapter, Nursing is again the outlier, with almost 60% of syllabi including references to how the written work would be evaluated (Table 10).

Table 10

Reference to evaluation criteria for assignments

Scoring guides	Community Service-Learning (%)	Political Science (%)	Physical Education, Recreation (%)	Pharmacy (%)	Nursing (%)
Yes	13	25	27	30	59
No	87	75	73	70	41

Three other programs reported levels similar to what we found in the 2010 study—around 30% of syllabi provided some explanation of how writing would be evaluated. In speaking to members of the Nursing faculty about these results, their concern was that 40%

of their syllabi did not provide some guidance to students about assessment. Their goal was that all syllabi should do this.

Implications

These studies show that students write a lot in each of these areas of study. Instructors require students to write in a wide variety of genres over the course of their degree programs; in the studies discussed here, we do not even account for the genres students must produce in the courses they take in their non-major programs. If we were to do so, the range of genres any one student would face would increase above what we reported here. They are not challenged, by and large, to write for non-instructor audiences, and they usually do not get feedback on their writing prior to grading. Instructors have tried to provide some guidance by nesting or scaffolding their assignments, however. Evaluation criteria, in most cases, cannot be found in the syllabus or the supporting documents that we were able to access. In short, students face a daunting task to write well in most undergraduate programs, and instructors can take several steps to make the experience more productive.

These studies have created a means of communicating with the faculty about how instructors transmit their expectations about writing to their students. In essence, as consultants we hold a mirror up to the faculty that shows an image of their work back to them. This method of communicating works because it takes statistics from their own syllabi about the kind of information they give regarding genres of assignments, audiences, nesting or scaffolding of assignments, grading criteria, and length of assignments. These research projects form the basis of a self-assessment for each unit that participates, and that work can then be used in unit reviews. Faculty can then choose to act on this information as a group, or individually, within departments and programs. Uptake on this information is indicated in subsequent chapters in the book (see in particular chapters by Jewinski and Trivett and Parker's on engineering).

These studies also suggest how university administrators and teaching support units might make changes both within programs and across programs. One clear cross-program implication centres on the issue of genre within disciplines, and specifically the naming of assignments. That Nursing lists only 13 genres but 58 are listed in Pharmacy suggests that there is a greater consensus in the Nursing faculty around naming assignments, but it also speaks to a clearer sense about which genres are necessary to the field. This may simply mean that the Pharmacy faculty needs to have a discussion to explore how they name assignments, and what those assignments are meant to teach students about writing within the profession. Such a discussion has the potential to reduce the number of genres named in the syllabi and cause less confusion among students about what and how they write. Within programs, we often found considerable variation in the number and length of assignments, use of audience other than faculty, and use of rubric and scaffolding. It would be useful for faculties to discuss how much of this variation is due to individual differences between faculty members or to something inherent in the subject matter of the course. Are some instructors asking their students to do much more than others? Are there workload implications for students when we see the total amount of writing they are required to produce in one term? Again, these issues have been taken up in subsequent chapters (see in particular Hyland, MacDougall, and Howell).

Finally, research is needed around how students are impacted by changes to in-process feedback, genre naming, scaffolding, and more explicit detailing of expectations and rubrics on the syllabi. Do these written changes translate into changed strategies in the classroom? Do they generate useful discussions around writing in the disciplines between faculty and students? Answers to these questions emerge in subsequent chapters of the book (Slomp and Williams about writing in Education and Biology), and future studies may provide even more sense of the effectiveness of better writing pedagogies.

References

Anson, C. A., & Dannels, D. (2009). Profiling programs: Formative uses of departmental consultations in the assessment of communication across the curriculum [Special issue on Writing Across the Curriculum and Assessment]. *Across the Disciplines, 6*. Retrieved from http://wac.colostate.edu/atd/assessment/anson_dannels.cfm

Applebee, A. N., & Langer, J. A. (2006). *The state of writing instruction in America's schools: What existing data tell us*. Albany, NY: Center on English Learning and Achievement.

Applebee, A. N., & Langer, J. A. (2011). A snapshot of writing instruction in middle schools and high schools. *English Journal, 100*(6), 14-27.

Beaufort, A. (2007). *College writing and beyond: A new framework for university writing instruction*. Logan, UT: Utah State University Press.

Brereton, J. (2007). Trends in American research on college composition, 1960-2005. *L1-Educational Studies in Language and Literature, 8*(2), 35-45.

Bridgeman, B., & Carlson, S. B. (1984). Survey of academic writing tasks. *Written Communication, 1*, 247-280.

Britton, J., et al. (1975). *The development of writing abilities (11-18)*. London: Macmillan Education.

Canseco, G., & Byrd, P. (1989). Writing required in graduate courses in business administration. *TESOL Quarterly, 23*, 305-316.

Carson, J. G., Chase, N. D., Gibson, S. U., & Hargrove, M. F. (1992). Literacy demands of the undergraduate curriculum. *Reading Research and Instruction, 31*(4), 25-50.

Cooper, A., & Bikowski, D. (2007). Writing at the graduate level: What tasks do professors actually require? *Journal of English for Academic Purposes, 6*(3), 206-221.

Dias, P., Freedman, A., Medway, P., & Paré, A. (1999). *Worlds apart: Acting and writing in academic and workplace contexts*. Routledge.

Dias, P., & Paré, A. (Eds.). (2000). *Transitions: Writing in academic and workplace settings*. Hampton Press.

Garbati, J., McDonald, K., Meaning, L., Samuels, B. M., & Scurr, C. (2015). *Writing assignments and instruction at Ontario's publicly funded universities: A view from three disciplines.* Toronto: Higher Education Quality Council of Ontario.

Gardner, S., & Nesi, H. (2012). A classification of genre families in university student writing. *Applied Linguistics, 34*(1), 25-52. doi:10.1093/applin/ams024

Graves, R. (2013). Why students struggle with writing: What to do about it. *University Affairs, 54*(8), 37.

Graves, R. (2014). Five strategies to improve writing in your courses. *University Affairs.* Retrieved from http://www.universityaffairs.ca/five-strategies-to-improve-writing-in-your-courses.aspx

Graves, R., Hyland, T., & Samuels, B. M. (2010) Undergraduate writing assignments: An analysis of syllabi at one Canadian college. *Written Communication, 27*(3).

Kelly, G. J., & Bazerman, C. (2003). How students argue scientific claims: A rhetorical–semantic analysis. *Applied Linguistics, 24*(1), 28-55.

Light, R. J. (2001). *Making the most of college: Students speak their minds.* Cambridge, MA: Harvard University Press.

Light, R. J. (2003). Writing and students' engagement. *Peer Review, 6*(1), 28-31.

McCarthy, L. (1987). A stranger in strange lands: A college student writing across the curriculum. *Research in the Teaching of English, 21,* 233-265.

Melzer, D. (2003). Assignments across the curriculum: A survey of college writing. *Language and Learning Across the Disciplines, 6*(1). Retrieved from http://wac.colostate.edu/atd/archhives.cfm

Melzer, D. (2009). Writing assignments across the curriculum: A national study of college writing. *College Composition and Communication, 61,* W240-261.

Moran, K. E. (2013). *Exploring undergraduate disciplinary writing: Expectations and evidence in psychology and chemistry* (Dissertation). Georgia State University. Retrieved from http://scholarworks.gsu.edu/alesl_diss/24

Paltridge, B. (2002). Genre, text type, and the English for Academic Purposes (EAP) classroom. In A. Johns (Ed.), *Genre in the classroom: Multiple perspectives* (pp. 73-90). Mahwah, NJ: Lawrence Erlbaum.

Peterson, S. S., & McClay, J. (2010). Assessing and providing feedback for student writing in Canadian classrooms. *Assessing Writing,* 15(2), 86-99.

Popham, S. L. (2005). Forms as boundary genres in medicine, science, and business. *Journal of Business and Technical Communication,* 19(3), 279-303. Retrieved from http://journals.sagepub.com/doi/abs/10.1177/1050651905275624

Russell, D. R. (2001). Where do the naturalistic studies of WAC/WID point? A research review. In S. McLeod, E. Miraglia, M. Soven, & C. Thaiss (Eds.), *WAC for the new millennium: Strategies for continuing writing-across-the-curriculum programs* (pp. 259-298). Urbana, IL: National Council of Teachers of English.

Shaver, L. (2007). Eliminating the shell game: Using writing-assignment names to integrate disciplinary learning. *Journal of Business and Technical Communication,* 21(1), 74-90.

Soliday, Mary. (2011). *Everyday genres: Writing assignments across the disciplines.* Carbondale: Southern Illinois UP.

Appendix A: Writing Assignments Coding Guide

In general, many of the categories are self-explanatory ("Name of course"; "Explicit rubric provided") and so are not commented on below. The entries below clarify the issues that we considered to be problematic when coding.

Genre (prof's label)

- The "prof's label" will often seem inconsistent with the genre. Write the assignment <u>exactly</u> as it appears in the syllabus.
  - If syllabus states that the assignment is "Weekly Reflective Note Cards" write this as is.

- Assignment title appearing in a bulleted list of the course evaluation section differed from the title appearing at the head of a lengthier description of the assignment. In such cases, we coded the first title appearing in the syllabus, under the course evaluation section.

"Is this component part of a larger assignment (>=2 different components)?

- Nested assignments were coded Yes
  - Example of a nested assignment: research paper with a separate abstract of 150 words to be submitted with the paper.

Mark value

- Pass/fail assignments
- Nested assignments with no mark value
- Alternative marking schemes. Examples included things like:
  - the student has the choice to drop 1 of the 5 lab assignments; coded as 5 assignments

- o the student has the choice to do (A) field project (30%) + final exam (70%); or (B) journal (10%) + literature review (20%) + final exam (70%); coded each element as an individual assignment with the percentage given
  - o the instructor will drop the lowest mark of the 3 short essays (only 2 will count): coded as two assignments

- Total mark value for more than one assignment with no breakdown for each assignment
  - o 500-word journal is due each week of the semester and the total mark value is 30%. There is no mark value given to each week's journal assignment. We coded this as 12 assignments each worth 2.5%.

Description/information provided

- We coded anything more than just the name of the assignment as Yes.

Length in words

- We converted pages to words using 250 words = one page.
- Assignments were often given a "range" of word length or page length. We recorded the middle number of pages or words.

Choice of topics

- In the case of nested assignments, this category was coded consistently with the first component. For example, if a paper and presentation are nested assignments, and the syllabus states that the paper has an 'open choice' of topics, then the presentation should also be coded consistently with 'open choice' of topics unless it is otherwise explicitly stated in the syllabus.
- "Yes Open" category means that there is choice but that the instructor did not give a list of topics to choose from but instead gave the student the option to choose anything.

Time to complete in weeks

- Weekly assignments were recorded as one assignment. The breakdown of the weekly assignment, due dates, and final submission date(s) were recorded in 'Notes'.
- Where journals have been assigned every week, we recorded 1 week as the time to complete.

Audience

- Coded Yes if a specific audience other than the instructor is identified

Feedback provision

- In order for this to be coded Yes, the feedback must be mandatory rather than optional or voluntary. "Students may consult with the professor while developing their topic" would be coded No. "Student must schedule a meeting with the professor…" would be coded Yes.

References required/specified

- This category was coded Yes when the syllabus explicitly stated the number of references required for the assignment(s) and coded No when there was no explicit statement of required references.

Style manual specified

- Coded only when the style was explicitly stated. Statements such as "use a consistent style" were not considered a specified manual of style. Examples are: MLA, APA, CMS, ASA, and AMA.

Resources/sources suggested

- Coded 'Yes' when any suggested or required text is anywhere in the syllabus or handout.

Appendix B: Sample Coding Sheet

Date: _____ Coder:_____

1. **Course name/number:** _____ Project Course #: _____
Full Name of Course: _____

2. **Assignment coding #:** _____ (assigned when entered into database)
An "assignment" is any written text required to be handed in <u>separately</u> to the instructor. It must be evaluated either on its own OR as part of a larger assignment unit.
a) Genre (prof's label): _____

b) Component type: ☐ Journal ☐ Essay ☐ Proposal ☐ Paper ☐ Bibliography ☐ Report ☐ Presentation ☐ Project ☐ Handout (class discussion) ☐ Other: _____

c) Is this component part of a larger assignment ($\geq$2 different components)?   Y   N
d) Mark value: _____

3. **Assignment description**
a) Description/information provided   Y   N   Syllabus Separate:_____
b) Explicit statement of learning goal/objective   Y   N
c) Length/# words: _____
d) Choice of topics   Y   N   U if yes, ☐ list ($\geq$2) ☐ open
e) Time to complete in weeks: _____
f) Course length in weeks: _____
g) Audience specified (not class/prof/TA):   Y   N   who?_____
h) Plagiarism Warning (in syllabus)   Y   N
i) Feedback provision (within larger assign process)   Y   N
j) References required/specified   Y   N   # of refs: _____
k) Style manual specified   Y   N   _____
l) Resources/sources suggested   Y   N   ☐ restrictions_____
                                                      ☐ content ☐ style

4. **Rubric/Marking scheme**
a) Exemplar/prototype/sample text provided   Y   N
b) Formal explicit rubric provided   Y   N
   Format of rubric: ☐ written statement ☐ weighted values/table ☐ other _____
c) Number of evaluation criteria: _____

5. **Final exam:** ☐ No ☐ Yes If yes, ☐ Written ☐ M/C ☐ Take Home ☐ Not specified

Notes: _____

Chapter 2

Gathering and Assessing Writing Assignments in the Arts Faculty of a Small University: Process and Product

Marion McKeown

Royal Military College

Reactions to "Undergraduate Writing Assignments: an Analysis of Syllabi at One Canadian College" (Graves, Hyland, & Samuels, 2010) suggested that widening the field would give valuable data for those investigating the teaching of academic writing in Canada. This article analyzed the syllabi and assignment sheets from every course offered at a small Canadian college (College A) during 2006-2007, giving a complete snapshot of the writing required of its students at one post-secondary institution. The intense focus, consistency of terminology, and completeness of material accepted from neutral sources were designed to avoid some of the possible biases of the professors' self reporting or incomplete web-sampling that were decried by Melzer (2003 and 2009), and to provide a more complete and balanced view of writing assignments than had been given by earlier surveys, such as the wide sampling of the first year experience found in Bridgeman and Carlson (1984).

At the 2010 Montreal conference of the Canadian Association for Studies in Language and Learning (CASLL), Roger Graves requested contributions to an expanded writing project based on the original study. The addition of at least one other small liberal arts college of similar size was suggested as an initial step to give depth by providing a comparative database. The addition of two medium-sized and two large universities was also proposed, to give the breadth needed to be truly useful in Canadian research. Since that initial conference, colleges, departments, and programs from eleven universities across Canada have joined the team. Theresa Hyland's subsequent (2012) presentation to the Canadian Association for the Study of Discourse and Writing (CASDW) recorded faculty reactions to the data collected for "Undergraduate Writing Assignments" and suggested that the information had proved useful to the small liberal arts college that was its source. The data had become a valuable platform for generating faculty discussion and some syllabus and curriculum review.

This chapter describes the evolution of the research undertaken in the Arts Faculty of the second small Canadian university which chose to participate in the project (College B). As in the original study, "Undergraduate Writing Assignments," the chapter will begin by describing the gathering of the data. Next, it will summarize the significance of the data by comparing the main points to the data from College A. The chapter will then focus on the results of the study by tracing the series of presentations, reports, focus groups, surveys, and further research that was prompted by the data gathering activity.

Background

Similarities of size and situation initially suggested suitability for participation in the study. College B had 1,250 undergraduate students, not too different from the 1,100 of the original study. It had also a solidly established research base, especially in the Sciences and Engineering, and affiliations with a large research university with which it shared courses. The course offerings in the Arts Faculty were similar to those of College A, although only one third of the students were graduated from the Arts Faculty. In particular, College B also emphasized the importance of critical thinking and writing in all disciplines in mission statements and in the general college culture. It had sponsored a pilot project on student writing in 2001, and a Writing Centre had been given academic recognition in 2005. In contrast to College A, however, College B had no formal policies or strategies concerning student writing, no designated writing intensive courses, and no program for writing across the curriculum. College B agreed to join the project because of a desire to participate in the development of writing studies in Canada by contributing to the building of a national database, and also because of an interest in using the information gathered to become more aware of its own pedagogical behaviours in the teaching of writing.

Gathering the Data

As in the original paper, the overall aim of the College B project was "to discover *how* the writing assignments helped the students understand the distinctive features of disciplinary knowledge and develop ... the broader skills of critical thinking" (Graves, Hyland, & Samuels, 2010, p. 294, emphasis in the original). To this end, the research focused on the directives given to the students in the syllabi and course outlines. This emphasis on the instructional characteristics reflects the thinking of John Bean (2001), and so many others, on the importance of explicitly communicating information crucial to the students' understanding of the work they are to undertake.

The research at this second small college followed the methodology of the original study as closely as possible. Data was derived from a collection of course syllabi supplemented by as many instructor handouts as could be readily obtained in electronic form. As in Graves', Hyland's, and Samuels' initial research, it was recognized that some pertinent documents might be unavailable because they had not been recorded in electronic format. It was accepted also that in most programs, "spontaneous writing assignments, assignments given verbally, or assignments not adequately represented in the syllabi ... were the exceptions rather than widespread practices" (2010, p. 297).

In College B, most syllabi were distributed to the students at the beginning of the year and filed electronically. They gave a general overview of the course, but did not necessarily discuss specific assignments. The details of a writing assignment, guidelines, and rubrics, though often on class websites, were sometimes simply handed out in class. As a result, the cooperation of departments and individual professors was necessary to ensure that the data for this project was as complete as possible.

In 2011, permission to obtain the documents was sought from deans, department heads, and individual professors, with several interested individuals and departments requesting briefings on the aims and methodology of the study. Some departments and individual professors requested feedback in return for participation. The project was fully supported, even anticipated with some interest.

Organization and Analysis

The data from College B were based on all available electronic records of syllabi, course outlines, and assignment sheets from the Arts Faculty in the academic year 2011-2012. Those courses that were exclusively used for online learning were eliminated (although those that used the same syllabus on-campus and online were included). In all, 412 assignments (by definition any written text required to be handed in *separately* to the instructor) were analyzed for this survey.

In College B, the data were grouped and analysed by department rather than by program as they had been in the original study. As course offerings were of similar types in the two colleges, and the structuring of many programs crossed departmental lines, the groupings were not too different. As in College A, College B required specific combinations of courses from several departments in every program, and some programs integrated senior courses from several other departments or even other faculties.

All records were forwarded to a cadre of University of Alberta graduate students trained by Dr. Roger Graves to ensure consistency of interpretation and to avert any imputation of conflict of interest. Using a coding sheet almost identical to that of the original study, each assignment was coded for genre, frequency, and instructional characteristics (Graves, Hyland, & Samuels, 2010, p. 298). In the course of analysis, about fifteen percent of the data was inter-rater verified to ensure that this study was consistent with the methodologies used by other studies in the general project.

Initial Results

In May 2013, an interim report on the second arts project, "First Impressions of a Comparative Analysis of Syllabi at Two Small Canadian Colleges," was circulated to deans and department heads in College B and submitted for presentation to the Canadian Association for Studies in Discourse and Writing (CASDW). This report first demonstrated that there was a sound basis for comparison between the two colleges, then followed the trajectory of the original paper, focusing on the two basic research questions: "What types of writing assignments were given to Canadian university students," and "how much were they expected to write?"

Assignment Types

The data showed that the professors' labelling of the writing assignments was remarkably similar in the two colleges. *Assignments, essays,* and *papers* accounted for 53.7% of the total number of terms used to label assignments. Although patterns of usage could be discerned in that certain terms tended to dominate in particular departments (for example, *papers* in Political Science, *essays* in English), distribution was inconsistent. Many instructors added modifiers, such as *final, major, position, research, response, short,* or *term* to clarify the term *paper,* and although these were useful to discriminate between the assignments within a specific course, they did little to clarify what was expected in the assignment. This might be especially confusing for the students as the expectations of the different disciplines varied even when the terms used to describe the assignment were the same.

The following table presents the findings on the varied use of labels on the assignments:

Table 1

Data on assignment labels

Professor's Label	Frequency in % (*n*=412)	Professor's Label	Frequency in % (*n*=412)
*Abstract**	.5	*Presentation*	3.2
Analysis	3.6	Project	1.5
Annotated Bibliography	1.2	*Proposal*	3.2
Assignment (Group, Lab, Library, Memo, Short, Written, Weekly)	15.6	Report Case, Consulting, Lab (Experimental), Marketing, Project, Research, Short	2.7
Briefing note	.7	Review (Book, Literature Review)	3.4
Draft	2.2	Summary	6.8
Essay (Diagnostic, Final, Large, Reflection, Short, Term)	18.9	Thesis	.5
Journal	8.7	Miscellaneous	
		Film Critique	.25
Memo	2.4	*Library Scavenger Hunt*	.9
Outline	3.2	Mind map	.25
Paper (Final, Major, Position, Research, Response, Short, Term)	19.2	*On-line discussion*	.2
		Self-evaluation	.4
		Seminar discussions	.3
		Write-up	.2

Note that the terms listed in italics were not used in College A

Although the terminology was basically similar in both colleges, the variations were interesting. For example, the labels *comment, comparison, composition, paragraph assignment,* and *review essay,* important terms for College A, do not appear in the College B data, but labels such as *journal entry, presentation,* and *proposal* are introduced (see Table 1, above). These labels were introduced across the disciplines. Although the increase in the number of labels is suggestive of a search for greater precision, it still remained quite difficult to determine from the label just what was expected in a particular assignment in a specific discipline, especially considering the necessary variety of subject matter. Of greater significance is the increase in the appearance of the label *draft,* indicating that College B professors were more frequently including independently-assessed preliminary forms of later assignments in their syllabi as separate assignments, incorporating revision into the pedagogical approach of the courses.

The differences in terminology and type that appear in the records of College A (2006) and College B (2011-12) may be due to differences in collegial culture, an evolution in the writing culture caused by changes in writing pedagogy in the university, or simply by passage of time. In both colleges, however, some of the difficulties faced by a student in clearly ascertaining how to approach a writing assignment can be gathered from the frequency of vague generic terms and broad labels attached to the writing assignments.

Length of Assignments

College B recorded slightly fewer writing assignments per class per semester than did College A, and these assignments were longer and given slightly greater weighting in the courses' marking schemes. Very few assignments were valued under 10%. In addition, the assignments tended to become longer in the third and fourth years in the majority of the departments, although at that level, they were often labelled *seminar papers.* No course was without a writing assignment.

Just how much was to be written in these assignments? College B estimates were calculated in the same way as those from College A, reflecting the course load of a General Arts student with a major in History (the most commonly chosen major in the snapshot year). Five courses are required per semester, although honours students and others may take more. Courses with multiple sections and different assignments were averaged. In Table 2, for example, each cell gives double numbers; the number to the left represents the average number of assignments in each section of the course (2.6 in the first cell), and the number to the right gives the average number of pages assigned (7.8). In the "Totals" column, the first number represents the total number of writing assignments in the semester, and the second gives the total number of pages to be submitted.

Table 2

Average writing requirements for a sample student

Semester	Course					Total No. Assignment/ Pgs
Year 1: Fall Ass/pps	English 2.6 /7.8	History 3 /16.8	Psych 2 /7	Politics assignments*	Math 0	7.6/36
Year 1: Winter	English 2.63 /7.8	History 3 /18	Psych 2 /7	Econ assignments*	Math 0	7.6/38
Year 2: Fall	English 2 / 7.6	History 2/14.8	History 1/ 4.8	History 1/10	Math 0	6 /37.2
Year 2: Winter	English 2 /7.6	History 2/15	History 1/10	History 1/10	(Chem/Bio) 0	6 /42.6
Year 3: Fall	Psych 10 / 9.6+	History 1/12	History 1/20	History 1/10	Geo 1/3	14/54.6
Year 3: Winter	History 1/12	Econ 1/12+	History 7/36	History 1/20	(Physics) 0	10 /80
Year 4: Fall	History 1/40	History 1/ 26	Geo 1/8	Politics 1/4	(Info Tech) 5/20	9 /98
Year 4: Winter	History 1/40	History 1/22.5	Psych 12/16.2 +	History 1/16	Politics 1/22	16/116.7

*indicates that multiple assignments are indicated, but not listed, with no page count supplied

+indicates that the number gives the minimum length

Table 2 demonstrates that every first year Arts student was expected to complete at least seven writing assignments per semester, or 64.4 pages of writing over the year. This figure is very similar to that given by College A which expected the minimum number of pages written per year to be 62.0. These numbers could also be compared to the figures given in Light's (2001) study which suggested that students at Harvard wrote a minimum of 60.0 pages a year.

On the other hand, although the data from College A showed that the assignments in the third and fourth years were not obviously lengthier than the first year assignments, College B assignments became appreciably longer as the years progressed, with the fourth year students producing 214.7 pages per year. Moreover, the overall program average rested at 123.1 pages per year which was considerably longer than College A's "'typical' student taking 7 courses ... [writing] 87.0 pages per year," (Graves, Hyland, & Samuels, 2010, p. 311), and still longer than Harvard's 60.0 (Light, 2001).

Faculty Consultation

This preliminary report also noted that, as in College A, the activity of collecting the data occasioned various reactions among the faculty. For example, several individuals consulted noted that Graves, Hyland, and Samuels excluded written examinations in its data gathering. Although the original protocols were followed in the research at College B, much discussion was generated as College B required written final exams and 50-minute midterms each semester in the first two years of any program. Examinations were generally recognized as "writing assignments" in this college's culture, and very few courses, even at the senior level, eliminated written examinations. For example, the History Department, with 36 courses, had only four senior seminar courses that did not require formal written exams, although several of the upper year courses assigned take-home "essay" exams. The trend of assigning "essays" as exams at the senior level was also marked in Business Administration and Psychology; courses requiring in-hall exams in these departments were generally either statistics or research methodology courses. On the whole, the 3-hour written examinations and 50-minute midterms were such a significant feature at College B that many professors argued that they should be included in any discussion of writing requirements.

Departmental Consultations

During consultations, individual professors expressed interest in the project's progress, and a presentation of one department's data was arranged. The majority of the professors of that department attended the focus group and representatives were sent from two other departments.

The presentation restated the general objectives of the study, and then presented the elements of the data in graphs that focussed on departmental statistics. The elements of the data were broken into three rough groupings to facilitate discussion. The first reported on the presence of practical directives on plagiarism, format, and styles of referencing. The second more pedagogical section recorded types and number of assignments and the presence of learning goals and nested assignments and made comparisons with the data derived from College A. The third section contained those topics that I have found to be the most complex in this study: audience, feedback, and rubrics.

The information on labelling of assignments and on the amount of writing required generated very little discussion. The data gathered on varied "instructional characteristics" were of central interest. The presenters repeatedly referred to the importance of the overall aim of the project, which was "to discover *how* the writing assignments helped the students understand the distinctive features of disciplinary knowledge and develop ... the broader skills of critical thinking" (Graves, Hyland, & Samuels, 2010, p. 294).

Practical Directives

The directives on plagiarism, format, and styles of referencing make an obvious grouping as they are those most likely to be mandated generally by the college or by the individual departments, and they reflect the administrative requirements within the curriculum. For example, College B asked that a warning about academic misconduct appear on every course syllabus. As a result, across the college, most of the 412 assignments accepted for the database came with a warning, with one department ensuring that 100% of the assignments included such warnings. In other departments, most omissions appeared to occur in two well-defined situations: where group or individual work was described as being under the close direction of a supervisor, or where there were multiple assignment handouts for a single course. In the latter case, the warnings were prominent in the separate syllabus or course outline that announced the assignments.

Departments generally agreed on format for the discipline, and directives to consult style manuals seemed to mirror departmental policy. Department A, for example, was uniform in stating that it required the standard formatting and referencing for its discipline on each course outline. The 11 (out of 55) assignments that did not mention the standard were those in which the genres did not require references. Department B less frequently referred to its standard guide, but seemed to do so only when quotations or citations were required for marks. On the other hand, Department C, which required one particular choice of formatting in the first year, generally did not refer to format again except in some assignments where a specific number of references was required. In a number of this department's syllabi, reference was made to "Guidelines for Term Papers and Essays found on the ... [College] Intranet," but this guide did not at that time seem to be generally accessible to college faculty or students. On the whole, many departments seemed to mention formatting or referencing only when they thought the protocols needed to be introduced or reinforced, or when they differed in some way from the general departmental usage (legal protocols for references, for example).

On the whole, in this grouping, where there was collegial or departmental consensus, there was remarkable uniformity and consistency in the direction given to students; otherwise, students were apparently left to rely on their own judgement. This grouping was of interest in the departmental focus group, but did not generate much discussion.

Pedagogical Structuring

Discussions of the second grouping demonstrated the variations in the pedagogical emphases of individual professors and of different departments: variations in the presence of explicit learning goals; assignment types, length, and number; and nesting of assignments.

In one department, every assignment presented a specified learning goal for the student. Other departments' compliance ranged from 97% through to 80%; and 79% to 52.1%. This divergence could represent departmental policies. Certainly, when they were consulted individually, most professors were more than willing to explain their pedagogical philosophy and the rationale behind the specific assignment.

In the same way, the generic terms for assignments, the ubiquitous "essay" or "paper" that seemed to predominate in specific departments, probably echoed the culture of the discipline. Interestingly, the category "draft" appeared to be scattered evenly throughout the departments. "Journal" and "diary entry" appeared in four departments, and "library scavenger hunt" appeared in two departments. In each of these cases, there were two courses that used this assignment type. Again, the data on the labelling of assignments generated very little discussion in the focus group. The group, on the whole, agreed that they clarified their expectations verbally in class.

The data presented for the next pedagogical category, nested assignments, generated much more discussion. These were assignments broken down into components and submitted separately over a term. Here, the data from College B showed some variation from the patterns shown by College A. Although the overall 41.4% of assignments recorded as part of a nested assignment structure at College B seemed comparable to the 44% at College A, the pattern of employment of such assignments was not the same. At College B, use of nested assignments was scattered variously across all year levels, including the first, with no predominance in any one year. There was also a surprisingly wide variation between departments at College B, with two departments nesting over 60% of the assignments and one nesting less than 30%. Those departments that used nested assignments most often also required lengthier assignments in the upper years. As in College A, breaking assignments down into several components that were submitted separately and sequentially was seen as a way of ensuring consistent progress over the length of the term.

The descriptions of some of College B's assignments may have obscured the prevalence of nested assignment structures. As was also noted in College A, several of the assignments, particularly in introductory courses, carried titles that showed that they were designed to teach the research methods of that discipline step by step: "library research assignment," "annotated bibliography," and "research essay" for example. However, the assignment directives gave no indication that the material was connected or that the assignments represented a sequence of steps in one project. Discussions with individual professors clarified the intent to researchers, and the focus group commented on the differences between the actual aims of the assignment sequences and the intent communicated in the course syllabi.

The graphs of the data that generated the most discussion showed the data for *audience awareness, rubrics,* and *feedback.* The discussion on *audience* was prompted by the discovery that very few assignments in any department specified the type of audience for which the assignment was to be written (about 5.5%). The focus group engaged in a thoughtful exchange on the various benefits of making students in different disciplines aware of the demands of a variety of audiences. The discussion resulted in a resolution to study the question further in separate departmental groups.

Part of the discussion on *audience* concerned the assertion that the audience for many assignments was usually designated and described verbally in the classroom when the assignment was being introduced. This point was also raised during the discussions of *rubrics* and *feedback.* For example, the statistics of one department showed that about 45% of the assignments had written rubrics attached, but the focus group pointed out that many of the other assignments were covered generally by the course syllabus that included a marking guide, and that the particular marking of each assignment was always discussed in class, and many times also in individual interviews.

In the same way, when it was shown that no first year course of any department had any record of a feedback mechanism or promise of feedback, and these were present in only 35% of second, third, and fourth year courses, all faculty present declared that they and their colleagues constantly worked one-on-one with numbers of students each term, and several reported that they worked individually with all their upper year students on major assignments. Some required all students to schedule an interview at least once a term. All felt that the opportunity to give students individual direction on writing assignments was one of the most enjoyable and valuable duties and benefits of teaching at a small university.

The discussion then turned to the relative value to students of written instructions versus verbal direction. Although the focus group as a whole acknowledged the value of a written record to the aurally oriented learner and to the Writing Centre, many commented that students tended to ignore written directions as they felt overwhelmed by paperwork. One participant said that he changed his online course quite deliberately, to adapt it to a more aurally oriented classroom setting. Another said that he had discovered that students semi-automatically checked off a "rubric reminder" in their haste to submit the assignment on time. All of the participants again commented on the unique situation of a small college in which the instructors were able to work directly with individual students.

All the data generated caring and intelligent comments. At the end of the session, the discussion was distilled and focussed on two questions: first, whether all of the analyzed elements had equal value in the assignments of every discipline and in every year; and second, whether it was necessary to describe the assignments exhaustively in each assignment sheet when the same material was repeatedly dealt with in the course syllabus, in the classroom, or in individual tutorials. It was resolved that the first question should be discussed further in a departmental forum on writing pedagogy, and that experts in writing pedagogy should be invited to give a presentation at the college, and the answer to the second would be sought after a student survey to verify the impressions of the instructors. All three of these activities were then undertaken and completed in the following months.

Widening Parameters: Student Response

The participants in the group were extremely curious as to whether the impressions given by the data were shared by the students with whom they were working. The researchers, therefore, suggested conducting an exit poll of the students who were graduating that year in Arts, and who had, therefore, written the assignments being discussed. A questionnaire was drawn up reflecting the areas of discussion that most concerned the participants in the focus group. The Dean of Arts approved the draft, and the Ethics Review Board gave consent to the project. With careful preparations to respect anonymity, the questionnaire was sent electronically to each student graduating in Arts about three weeks before convocation. Despite the limited response time, 24% of the students who were contacted responded to the questionnaire, and the numbers were considered sufficient to be a significant indicator of general attitudes (see Appendix A).

The responses were weighted in value: *strongly agree* had a value of 100; *agree*, 75; *neutral*, 50; *disagree*, 25; *strongly disagree*, 0. Most of the students declined to self-identify by department, but those who did were representative of all departments at the college.

In general, the responses to the questionnaire confirmed the data gathered from the Course Syllabi Study and validated the assertions of the focus group. For example, the 61.4% satisfaction rate in question 4 confirmed that many of the students were not aware of the intended audience for each assignment, and 33.3% were not happy that the marking criteria were clearly explained. Only one *strongly disagree* was registered, and that was in question 7 concerning marking criteria being clearly explained.

The focus group's assumptions about the students' preference for verbal direction was shown to be well founded, as only 73.6% of the students were content with the written explanations, whereas 80.6% were satisfied with the explanations given in class, and 84% thought that the one-on-one discussions were very helpful. The advantages of the small size of the university and close verbal contact with the faculty seemed to be appreciated, but it was noted that no question earned the possible 100% approval.

Conclusion

Over the last three years, the process of this project has gradually changed in response to the research activity; these changes should be considered in summing up the experience of gathering data from the second small liberal arts university. The original project emphasized the objective accumulation of data useful to professionals in writing studies for a Canada-wide project. The actual process revealed the importance of the project to the individual college and the professors and emphasized the value of the interaction of quantitative and qualitative data.

At the beginning of their discussion of Departmental profiling, Anson and Dannels (2009) state that "assessment methods can ... be shaped to ... [a] department's culture and students' career trajectories," and this dictum can be applied to the assessment of an entire college. Of their own activities, they say: "We do not enter a ... [college] armed with a fixed protocol for gathering data or presenting results... rather, we adapt our methods to each ... [college's] culture and needs." The interactions of researchers, administrators, faculty, and students drawn into the research process at College B demonstrated the value of this attitude. In the coming months, the departmental data from College B will be offered to all departments who agreed to contribute to the research. It is anticipated that their reactions will be very like those in the focus group. Statistics will be assessed and the implications for the departments will be considered.

Analysis of the data from College B revealed that the interaction of collegial and departmental administrations, individual professors, and interested students is necessary in the evolution of a syllabus that supports the students' writing activity. Reports by Theresa Hyland to CASDW in 2012 indicated that the data-gathering project at College A also initiated, in Anson's terms, "a series of more modest ongoing inquiries involving the participation of faculty and administration." College B is also launched in that direction.

References

Anson, C. A., & Dannels, D. (2009). Profiling programs: Formative uses of departmental consultations in the assessment of communication across the curriculum [Special issue on Writing Across the Curriculum and Assessment]. *Writing Across the Disciplines, 6.* Retrieved from http://wac.colostate.edu/atd/assessment/anson_dannels.cfm

Bean, J. C. (2001). *Engaging ideas: The professor's guide to integrating writing, critical thinking, and active learning in the classroom.* Jossey-Bass: San Francisco.

Dias, P., & Paré, A. (Eds.). (2000). *Transitions: Writing in academic and workplace settings.* New Jersey: Hampton Press.

Graves, R., Hyland, T., & Samuels, B. M. (2010). Undergraduate assignments: An analysis of syllabi at one Canadian college. *Written Communication, 27*(3), 293-317. doi:10.1177/0741088310371635

Hyland, T., McDougall, A., & Howell, G. (2017). Upstairs/downstairs: Conversations from the attic about the classroom below. In R. Graves & T. Hyland (Eds.), *Writing assignments across university disciplines* (pp. 180-217). Winnipeg, MB: Inkshed Publications.

Kellogg, R. T. (1994). *The psychology of writing.* New York: Oxford University Press.

Light, R. J. (2001). *Making the most of college: Students speak their minds.* Cambridge, MA: Harvard University Press.

Melzer, D. (2003). Assignments across the curriculum: A survey of college writing. *Language and Learning Across the Disciplines, 6*(1). Retrieved from http://wac.colostate.edu/atd/archives.cfm

Melzer, D. (2009). Writing assignments across the curriculum: A national study of college writing. *College Composition and Communication, 61,* 240-261.

Appendix A: Students' Exit Survey

Exit Questionnaire (Approval Rates Inserted)

Student Reaction to Pedagogical Direction and Prompts

Underline one option per statement:

1. The types of writing that were asked of me (e.g. annotated bibliography, argumentative essay, briefing note, memo) were clearly explained and described.

80.6%   Strongly agree   Agree   Neutral   Disagree   Strongly disagree

2. The length of each assignment (either word count or number of pages) was clearly defined.

80.6%   Strongly agree   Agree   Neutral   Disagree   Strongly disagree

3. The learning objectives in each assignment were clearly communicated.

69.1%   Strongly agree   Agree   Neutral   Disagree   Strongly disagree

4. The intended audience of each assignment was generally clearly identified and described.

61.4%   Strongly agree   Agree   Neutral   Disagree   Strongly disagree

5. The length of each assignment was generally suitable to the type of the assignment.

75%   Strongly agree   Agree   Neutral   Disagree   Strongly disagree

6. The number of assignments per course was fair.

81.9%   Strongly agree   Agree   Neutral   Disagree   Strongly disagree

7. The marking criteria were clearly explained.

66.7%   Strongly   Agree   Neutral   Disagree   Strongly
             agree   disagree

8. The written explanations in the syllabus and the assignment sheets were very helpful.

73.6%   Strongly   Agree   Neutral   Disagree   Strongly
             agree   disagree

9. The explanations given in class were very helpful.

80.6%   Strongly   Agree   Neutral   Disagree   Strongly
             agree   disagree

10. The one-on-one discussions with the professor were very helpful.

84%   Strongly   Agree   Neutral   Disagree   Strongly
             agree   disagree

Chapter 3

Undergraduate Writing Assignments in Mechanical Engineering: Targeting Communication Skills, Attribute 7 (A7)

Anne Parker
University of Manitoba

Introduction: Defining the Context

In this chapter, I will report on the written assignments our undergraduate students in Mechanical Engineering are being asked to do and on the development of faculty-wide rubrics to help us in the assessment of these assignments. This paper has grown out of two initiatives, one at my institution, and one undertaken independently as part of a national study. For the faculty-wide initiative, we prepared rubrics that can be used throughout the faculty as guidelines for attribute assessment in undergraduate Engineering courses. However, we have little information on communication skills, Attribute 7 (A7). Which courses in Engineering, for example, target A7 in their course syllabi? What kinds of assignments are students being asked to complete? More broadly, how is A7 assessed? Interestingly, it is the independent national study that will help us determine both which Engineering courses instantiate A7 in their syllabi as well as the kinds of assignments students are being asked to write.

For the national study, we first collected course outlines from all the Engineering departments, determined which courses targeted communication skills (A7), and then analyzed the written course assignments according to 20 identifiable variables, such as length, genre, and grading criteria. The national study can inform not only the rubrics developed for A7, but also what they have been designed to measure. In both cases, the goal is to help all the stakeholders—faculty, students, and industry—to recognize, develop, and improve literacy levels.

Finally, although linking attributes to learning objectives and determining the levels of communicative competence can be very challenging, researchers in engineering education (like Paretti and McNair) stress the need to integrate communication and engineering in ways that will mirror engineering practice. This paper shows how these two initiatives help to make the task less daunting and more manageable for all the stakeholders in the education of our Engineering students.

As a professional faculty, Engineering is required to be accredited by a national governing body, the Canadian Engineering Accreditation Board (CEAB). For the board, we must map learning outcomes and expected competency levels on our course syllabi as well as the 12 graduate attributes that the CEAB has adopted. Every Engineering student must demonstrate proficiency in each of these attribute areas once they enter the professional world. Below is a sample taken from a senior (capstone) design course (MECH 4860) that shows what our course syllabi must now include:

Learning Outcomes

1. Apply and evaluate engineering knowledge, investigation, and design skills to solve open-ended "real" design projects.
2. Learn and apply the steps and associated tools in the engineering design process.
3. Analyze designs from technical, practical, cost, social, and environmental perspectives.
4. Build on teamwork skills using tools in project and team management and prepare for teamwork in industry.
5. Maintain appropriate design records such as logbooks and meeting minutes.

6. Enhance technical communication skills with clients, users, and others both orally and in writing.
7. Instill a sense of professionalism.

Table 1

Expected competency level **

Learning Outcome	Attribute*											
	A1	A2	A3	A4	A5	A6	A7	A8	A9	A10	A11	A12
1	3	6										
2				4	4							
3									4			
4						6	3	3		3	3	
5							3	3		3		
6							6					3
7								3				

Attributes:

A1 A knowledge base for engineering

A2 Problem analysis

A3 Investigation

A4 Design

A5 Use of engineering tools

A6 Individual and team work

A7 Communication skills

A8 Professionalism

A9 Impact of engineering on society/ environment

A10 Ethics and equity

A11 Economics and project management

A12 Life-long learning

**Competency Levels:*

1 - Knowledge (Able to recall information)

2 - Comprehension (Able to rephrase information)

3 - Application (Able to apply knowledge in a new situation)

4 - Analysis (Able to break problem into its components and establish relationships)

5 - Synthesis (Able to combine separate elements into whole)

6 - Evaluation (Able to judge of the worth of something)

Dr. P. Labossiere, P.Eng. (Used with permission)

The Canadian Engineering Accreditation Board (CEAB) introduced attributes and outcomes as standards to be met, not merely to standardize the curricula of the various Engineering schools, but also to encourage these schools to take a step back and reflect on the quality of the students we were graduating. In other words, did our program impact what our students know and what they can do with that knowledge? Were these new graduates able to transition successfully to the world of the professional engineer, where the work can be multifaceted and complex, and where the concomitant communication demands on the engineer can be equally challenging? These are questions that others have also been asking over the years (such as Knecht et al., 2000; Broadhead, 1999; Donnell et al., 2011). Our industry partners would often answer "no"—which was disappointing, to be sure—but the discussion would be anecdotal. Consequently, our Engineering school was one of many who decided that we needed some way to gauge just how design-ready our graduates were; we *thought* they were, but we lacked the evidence. Nor did we have any idea as to how proficient our graduates were in the *communication* of that engineering work. Determining communication proficiency, however, has proven to be difficult. For example, just how many courses in Engineering do, in fact, develop communication skills?

As Marjorie Davis (2010) has already noted, these "professional skills" (or "soft skills" as they have sometimes been called) are difficult to define and their success—or failure—is even harder to measure. Coupled with this difficulty is the engineering penchant for measuring everything, including communicative competence. Relying on templates as a way to (somehow) measure competency is just one instance of how some engineering professors continue to think that a technical genre is "a static recipe" rather than a flexible way to adapt to various rhetorical circumstances (Broadhead, 1999, p. 24). The result, as Broadhead notes, is often a reduction of "technical writing" to "sterile notions of traditional grammar" (p. 25), something that can be quantified, and a set of mechanical skills that are somehow separate from disciplinary knowledge, even though writing specialists acknowledge that "skill in writing is clearly relevant to a student's preparation for the workplace activities of an engineer, which in most cases involves the production of discourse" (p. 21). Artemeva (2011), for example, has noted that students must acquire content knowledge as well as genre knowledge if they are to recognize the connection between these and the practice of engineering (p. 344). Perhaps the "relatively unsophisticated notions about rhetoric, language, and writing" account for what Broadhead

(1999) calls the "paucity of requirements for writing instruction" (p. 22) within an engineering context.

Furthermore, as Cargile Cook (2002) points out, our students now need to demonstrate multiple literacies that will encompass the various ways that "people use language in producing information, solving problems, and critiquing practice" (pp. 5-6). In the final analysis, technical communication in an Engineering school must be seen to be more than a remediation of writing deficiencies; it must be acknowledged as a means to develop our students' communicative competence as well as their disciplinary knowledge, and this should include knowledge of the discipline-specific genres.

One way to do that is by integrating communication skills into engineering education, something that Davis (2010) has recently argued for. However, integrating communication into courses and into a program implies that it has the "same weight and attention" as any other outcome. Contrary to the "add-on" model—where, for example, instructors from "English" are parachuted in as communication instructors—this integrated, practice-based model ensures a stronger performance (pp. 42-43); students must solve problems, to be sure, but they must also communicate solutions (Ramey & Hudgins, 1999; Orr, 2010). Just as important, "students perceive that professional communication is woven into their jobs and their employers' expectations" (Davis, 2010, p. 43); they come to appreciate that communication is "equally important to engineering practice" (Orr, 2010, p. 1). Nevertheless, while such observations may all be true, the possibility still exists, as Ford and Riley (2003) caution, that students continue to view the technical work as the "real" work (p. 80) and forget to notice that they need to be able to shape their documents and oral presentations in ways that will "best support the engineering work" (Paretti, 2008, p. 493). So, integrating communication skills into engineering courses may help to ameliorate that tendency to believe the "real" work is purely technical while, at the same time, strengthening the perceived importance of the communication work. Perhaps then we can indeed, as Davis (2010) urges, acknowledge the very real importance of communication to engineering success.

Similarly, in her study of successful engineering schools, Reave (2004) notes that a "well-designed" program will include a solid foundation in communication skills, something that a technical communication course can do, provided that it is directed by communication specialists who work to "provide high quality instruction," direction, and feedback (p. 482). As Reave said, it is important to note that our students still have to learn how to be *good* writers, on one level, and *successful* writers, on another. In Reave's words, "different disciplines also create writing genres that have specific rhetorical demands" (p. 468)—demands that all students need to master if they are going to be successful at what they do.

Our Faculty of Engineering at the University of Manitoba has long recognized the importance of communication skills to the discipline, something the profession has likewise endorsed. In a series of industry forums, we have been told—repeatedly—that communication skills are some of the most critically important attributes (Ferens et al., 2014). Recently, both the faculty and the profession have pushed this recognition into action and now actively promote communication skills. All of this activity began after our 2012 accreditation visit, at which time the Faculty set out to discover what the proficiency levels of our graduates might be and tried to determine what they should be. This initial drive for that information prompted us to develop a plan whereby we could continue to gather the data and successfully integrate these 12 CEAB attributes into the fabric of our Engineering education. At the same time, we wanted feedback from two important stakeholders: industry, as to how "ready" our graduates were; and the students themselves. The industry forums (six so far) are helping us to gauge the first (Ferens et al., 2014), while the faculty-wide initiative is helping us to determine the second (Seniuk Cicek et al., 2014).

Similar to the initiative begun by the Association of American Colleges and Universities, which drew on existing rubrics and the expertise of faculty in developing a tool that would articulate learning outcomes and performance descriptors, this faculty-wide initiative involves developing rubrics that will help us to fulfill our pedagogical and professional goals; to define our expectations; to help us think about our performance in meeting these expectations; and to help us think about the performance levels of our students. Ultimately, these rubrics will be the tools that we can use to communicate with all of our stakeholders, including students, alumni, and industry partners. Thus, in the long term, we are trying to use these rubrics as "benchmark[s] for institutional improvement," to be sure—but only in part (Anson et al., 2012, p. 1). The rubrics are also intended to be useful tools that will inform our pedagogy by encouraging faculty to adapt them to their needs within a discipline-specific course.

Therefore, we must be cautious in applying them as standards that are not situated within the context of a particular discipline or even a particular course; otherwise, their usefulness may be compromised since departments can emphasize writing quite differently (Anson et al., 2012; Graves, Hyland, & Samuels, 2010). Each rubric must be flexible enough for individual instructors to use effectively; in other words, to adapt it to the context in which it is to be used. That context will include the outcomes and attributes and expected competency levels envisioned by that individual instructor within a particular department. In this important way, then, these initial iterations are like building blocks that departments can use to develop future assessment tools that each of us can adapt to our needs while working toward a common vocabulary (Ferens et al., 2014).

To that end, the findings from another initiative, a national study that is investigating the kinds of written assignments our undergraduate students are being asked to write in a variety of contexts—including engineering ones—offer insight into what we need to be targeting in our communication rubrics. In our study of over 4,000 written assignments from 36 departments in 11 institutions, these assignments were classified according to 20 variables, including length, feedback provided, genre, and grading criteria. In the case of our Faculty of Engineering at the University of Manitoba, we have also tabulated how many courses target A7 and have collated that information with the kinds of assignments these students write and the kinds of feedback they receive. One measure of a student's communicative competence, for example, will be reflected in the expected competency level for a particular written assignment, and this level can then be matched with the competency level defined in the rubric by both professors and industry representatives.

In this important way, based on what each of these initiatives has to tell us about communication skills, communicative competence and assessment, we may then begin to see what kinds of things we should be teaching and assessing if we target A7 in our outlines, including those for the undergraduate communication courses.

The Faculty-Wide Initiative

One initiative that has helped to create a culture of engagement in engineering education and in how we deliver our programs is the faculty-wide development of rubrics. The Faculty of Engineering at the University of Manitoba opted to create rubrics for all the attributes so that, among other things, every instructor could use them as measures of student performance in a course and as indicators of content mastery. To that end, the Faculty appointed an expert in engineering education, one who was familiar with the engineering attributes and rubrics, as well as the Associate Dean for Undergraduate Studies or his delegate. Professors with expertise in certain attributes (such as the Engineering Communication Professor, who has experience with communication skills, professionalism, and teamwork) were then invited to participate in the meetings where we would discuss the attributes to be considered and develop the rubrics, based on the input from the industry forums and the rubrics other institutions have used.

The Rubrics

For each attribute, the benchmark—the level that we expect our students to achieve—is "competent;" according to what we learned at the series of industry forums that we held, industry's expectations are similar (Ferens et al., 2014). Each focus area, however, also includes a series of indicators that can then be assessed according to whether the trait is "strong," "competent," "developing," or "needing work," each of which is defined within the rubric. For example, for the focus area of "main idea or thesis," a "competent" designation indicates that the writer's statement of the central message is "understandable, and is used as a central organizing focus." Alternatively, in a "needs work" scenario, the main idea is very difficult to understand and is not used to focus the work. In this way, the rubrics are primarily descriptive, but they can also be used more analytically to assess performance in one assignment or even over time, as Knecht et al. (2000) suggested. The rubrics offer a common ground for assessing these traits as they apply to a variety of scenarios.

Indeed, we have found that the value of these rubrics can be far-reaching. Through the development of common indicators, we have found that rubrics help us to define each attribute more clearly and concisely. Using the rubrics, we are better able to outline the performance levels exhibited by students as well as demarcate more precisely what the expected competency level is; in this way, we try to make explicit what the criteria for success are within the context of the assignment. For the students, as Saunders et al. (2003) pointed out, rubrics are thereby designed to help them evaluate their learning.

Another important benefit is the development of a comprehensive assessment tool that everyone can use and adapt; in doing so, we have begun to develop a common language that will serve us well as we build a foundation of shared understanding and common goals between all the stakeholders, as Seniuk Cicek et al. (2014) suggested. And, of course, this kind of discussion also helps us as educators to deliberate on the competencies an engineering graduate must possess, including communicative competence. Doing so means we better prepare our students to receive the necessary academic qualifications to begin their journey toward becoming professional engineers in Canada (http://www.engineerscanada.ca/accreditation-resources).

For the instructor, as Boettger (2010) noted, the rubric counters the commonly held notion that students need only provide what the instructor subjectively likes or wants in their student papers; the rubrics clearly outline exactly what the expectations are and, at the same time, "educate students on how to meet those expectations" (p. 4). As well, the various levels can be translated into numerical equivalents, a practice we follow in the technical communication rubrics as a way to silence the plaintive cries of "subjective" marking (Parker & Topping, 2013). Indeed, this practice may be even more important in a communication course because numerical equivalents ensure that students see the "mark" for a trait, something they will ask for regardless. In this way, students can measure their progress in a course, but they also receive valuable qualitative feedback that is useful for improving that particular characteristic (Boettger, 2010, pp. 4-5).

However, this initiative goes far beyond an exercise that tries to define competence. It has forced us to consider all the things we as educators expect our students to be able to do, both as undergraduates and as future engineers. As well, we have had to consider our roles as educators, both in what we teach and how we teach it. As Anson and Dannels (2009) have suggested, it is this kind of reflective thinking, done within the context of our programs, that helps us learn and move forward. In essence, the rubrics demand that we know exactly which topics should be covered in a course and, secondly, exactly what topic traits we intend to measure.

In the rubric for A7, for example, we first outlined what we meant by "communication skills." These encompass reading, writing, speaking, and listening skills; all skills that competent engineers should be able to use when they must communicate complex concepts both to members of the profession and to the general public. Writing effective reports and effectively responding to instructions are also part of what we mean by "communication skills." After defining which skills we were targeting, we then separated communication into written, oral, and graphic communication before establishing the indicators that would help us to define what each of these entailed. For oral reports, for example, we (of course) included delivery, where we would measure such things as a speaker's tone, diction, volume, pacing, and enunciation. But delivery also includes a "nonverbal" element; namely, the evidence of preparation shown by a speaker's reliance on prompts like slides or note cards; the control of posture and gestures; the speaker's body positioning in relation to the audience; the use of "stall" words like "um;" and the level of sustained eye contact that the speaker demonstrates as he or she gains a rapport with the audience.

As we determined the various levels, we first focused on what we would consider the "competent" level; that is, the level we expected our students to attain as they progress through the program and prepare for entry into the profession. For the "non-verbal delivery" indicator, for example, a "competent" speaker would do the following:

- Make eye contact
- Be easily heard
- Speak comfortably with some prompts (like note cards or slides)
- Move far enough away from the screen so that slides could be seen easily
- Appear comfortable

Alternatively, a "developing" speaker would have minor difficulties with the non-verbal delivery of a speech, while a presentation that "needed work" would have major difficulties with such things. Clearly, a "strong" non-verbal delivery of a talk would include sustained eye contact and show real polish.

In the case of written communication, one of the indicators is "genre and disciplinary conventions," an indicator that ties in with one of the variables being studied in the writing assignment initiative. In the rubric, we define this indicator as "familiarity with, understanding of, and use of the conventions," such as organization, formatting, or even style choices that are inherent within engineering genres and disciplines. Engineering genres would include proposals, progress reports, formal and informal reports, and lab reports. As shown in Table 2, to be "competent," the student will demonstrate this kind of understanding, while a developing writer would only show "some" of this familiarity. In both these cases, the students would at least use—or attempt to use—these conventions. Alternatively, a report that "needed work" would show little or no understanding of this indicator while the "strong" writer shows a "sophisticated" understanding of issues related to genre and disciplinary conventions.

While students are now in the process of providing feedback, industry has already provided significant testing and input over the course of six industry forums. Some changes will undoubtedly be called for over time, especially as we become more adept at using the rubrics to assess our students' proficiency.

Table 2

Sample of "Genre and Disciplinary Conventions"

Focus Area	Indicator	Level 4	Level 3	Level 2	Level 1
		Strong	*Competent*	*Developing*	*Needs Work*
Written/Oral Communication Skills	*Genre & Disciplinary Conventions: Familiarity with, understanding of, and use of the conventions ... inherent within a variety of engineering genres and contexts/ disciplines...*	Demonstrates thorough/ sophisticated understanding of and skillful use of the conventions within the engineering genre and context/ discipline.	Demonstrates familiarity with, understanding of, and use of the conventions within the engineering genre and context/ discipline.	Demonstrates some familiarity and understanding of, and attempts to use, the conventions within the engineering genre and context/ discipline.	Demonstrates little or no familiarity with, understanding of, or effort to use the conventions within the engineering genre and context/ discipline.

Nevertheless, there is now the *possibility* of measuring the degree of competency a student achieves in terms of such things as purpose definition, awareness of an audience, formulating the purpose, gathering and presenting the evidence to support the claim, organizing the information, and the accurate use of language. Ultimately, the writing assignment initiative may well be the means to help us in this endeavour.

The Writing Assignment Initiative

This initiative is based in a larger, national study that so far includes 11 universities and 36 academic departments. This is a nationally funded study of the written assignments that undergraduates in a variety of disciplines are being asked to do. For the study, we have defined "written assignment" as course assignments that require extended prose, i.e., a sustained piece of writing that functions as a self-contained unit of discourse. Such written assignments exclude written tests, but include reports written during class time as well as reports that receive a separate grade. By examining criteria such as assignment length, time to complete the assignment, the type of assignment (genre), feedback provisions within the assignment, and the frequency of assignments according to program year (Graves, Hyland, & Samuels, 2010; Graves & Chaudoir, 2011; Graves, Parker, & Marcynuk, 2012), the study has found great variability across the disciplines and even between departments within the same discipline. Thus, its findings can help to initiate discussion within departments and faculties about the way writing is taught and supported.

The Faculty of Engineering at the University of Manitoba has been involved in this national study since 2012 and has so far collected data from all the Engineering departments (Civil, Electrical and Computer, Mechanical, Biosystems and Design Engineering), although this paper focuses specifically on the results from the department of Mechanical Engineering. Our objective as a research group was to promote discussion at all levels so that our Engineering school could continue to fulfill our ongoing commitment to develop and improve our faculty's curriculum. On the one hand, this study may help the faculty to tailor assignments to help students learn how best to shape their writing so that it does indeed support the engineering work (Paretti, 2008, p. 493). On the other hand, this kind of analysis may help us in our ongoing drive to meet the demands of the profession.

To date, we have analyzed the syllabi of 37 courses in the Department of Mechanical Engineering that include A7 as a specific goal and have identified 105 assignments from them. Interestingly, most syllabi did not specify the requirements for each assignment. Indeed, many of the assignments have been coded as "unclear" simply because no description of the assignment was included on the course syllabi, though this is a fairly common practice according to Anson et al. (2012, p. 3). In those cases where "assignment" was listed without any further information, the assignments were coded as a written assignment *only* if the instructor identified Attribute 7 under learning outcomes.

While course length was mostly given as 13 weeks, no information as to how long students had to complete assignments was given; the completion dates for the written assignments were rarely, if ever, specified. Syllabi were likewise often unclear regarding the required length of an assignment, the content to be included and evaluated, and the formatting requirements. Few specified which citation style (such as IEEE) was to be followed. Nor was there much information about the genre of writing that students were being asked to produce, since almost half of the assignments listed in the syllabi were simply labeled as "assignments" (47/105 or 45%). Table 3 (below) shows the types of assignments indicated in the course outlines that were collected in Mechanical Engineering.

Table 3

Types of writing assignments

Number	Genre
47	"Assignment"
25	Research, project, progress, or draft report
	Laboratory
11	Design project, problem, or work
3	Mini project
1	Meeting minutes
1	Poster
1	Oral Presentation
105	TOTAL

Of those that were listed, most (as indicated) were simply labeled "assignments." Otherwise, the most frequent genre in Mechanical Engineering was the "report" (25/105 or 24%), which included "research, project, progress, or draft" reports, and, finally, the ubiquitous "lab reports" (16/105 or 15%). Taken together, these various reports represent over half of all assignments. Interestingly, most written work is done in the form of "projects," and projects make up a significant portion of the grades in Mechanical Engineering.

It's also worth noting that, in the Department of Mechanical Engineering, students must write, on average, three writing assignments per course throughout their undergraduate degree. In 3rd year, however, students average fewer than three assignments per course, a significant change from what we see in 2nd and 4th years, when students write at least four assignments, as shown in Table 4 below:

Table 4

Average number of written assignments in each program year: Mechanical Engineering

	Total	Year 4	Year 3	Year 2
No. Courses	27	17	6	4
Total # of written assignments	105	71	18	16
Average written assignments /course	3.9	4.2	3	4

These numbers compare well with the averages in various disciplines. As shown below, where only the service learning and nursing departments write more (on average), especially in the final 4th year of a program, students in Mechanical Engineering often write more (on average) than Political Science and Geography, and even the Liberal Arts.

Table 5

Average number of written assignments in each program year: Disciplinary results

	Liberal Arts	Political Science	Service-Learning	Geography	Nursing
Year 1	34/**1.5**	7/**1.4**	42/**10**	15/**3.8**	17/**3.4**
Year 2	225/**2.5**	39/**2.3**	12/**4**	40/**2.2**	33/**5.5**
Year 3	189/**4.1**	40/**2.4**	35/**6**	24/**1.85**	50/**4.2**
Year 4	56/**3.0**	112/**4.2**	74/**6.7**	107/**3.5**	57/**4.4**

However, some of these assignments may not compare that well in terms of the relative weight assigned to the written components. As shown in Figure 1, projects with a written component in Mechanical Engineering are worth at least 25% in 14 classes and 50% of the final grade in 6.

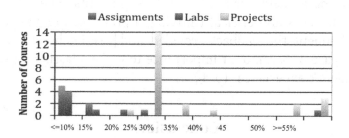

Figure 1. Percentage of total marks in course.

Furthermore, most assignments required a competency level of 3, the "ability to apply knowledge in a new situation." Asking students to apply their knowledge, and to do so in writing, demands more of them than just the mere recall of information (level 1) or simply being able to rephrase information (level 2). They will have moved to a deeper understanding of the material.

Both the amount and the type of written work vary in each year of the Mechanical Engineering program. While the CEAB attributes and the course outcomes were clearly included on each course syllabus, assignment-specific detail was notably missing. Indeed, apart from attributes and outcomes, any additional information was difficult to find because so few details were given in the course syllabi. For example, we could not determine the relative length of any of the written assignments, nor was the audience specified—with the notable exception of one assignment that specified that the audience was not the instructor or students in the class. Only lab reports mentioned how feedback would be provided. Finally, only one course syllabus indicated the criteria that would be used to evaluate the assignment.

Nevertheless, the paucity of detail in these course syllabi seems to be a common trait according to Anson et al. (2012, p. 3). Of course, the details of some of the assignments will undoubtedly be given verbally in class, or written on the lecture slides or on the course website. Regardless of where students have to go to find the information, however, the rubrics can offer useful guidelines as to how the assignments are evaluated by showing what the descriptors are, what each of the descriptors means, and how each will be assessed. As Schor et al. (2011) found in their Electrical and Computer Engineering Student Forum, "even if assignments appear to foster design elements and critical thinking, a professor's explanation of the assignment, the feedback provided, and [its] timely return to the students are of paramount importance to make a lasting impact on the student's experience" (p. 3).

Conclusion

Almost 50 years ago, W. Earl Britton (1965) noted that in too many instances an undergraduate would write "the wrong thing, for the wrong reason, to the wrong person, who evaluates it on the wrong basis" (p. 116). Even today, we risk a similar outcome, especially if our expectations are unclear and our methods of evaluation equally so.

These findings from the national study suggest a real need for faculty to clarify the course requirements for assignments on the syllabi as to the genre of assignments and how they will be evaluated. We have found, for example, that genre identification is critical to student performance. If there is a lack of genre identification or even a misidentification of genre, then student writing performance can be negatively impacted; the lack of clarity can confuse the student writer and slow down the effort to respond to the writing prompt (Graves, Hyland, & Samuels, 2010; Graves & Chaudoir, 2011). Indeed, it is in the course syllabi where we map the course outcomes, competency levels, and attributes, so assignments should do likewise. As Schor et al. (2011) found with student forums in Electrical and Computer Engineering, students value the explanation as well as the feedback on the assignments (p. 3).

Providing feedback was the overarching goal of the faculty-wide rubrics. We wanted to move beyond merely checking for things like correct formats or good grammar; rather, these rubrics are meant to exemplify what we want to achieve on a variety of levels. At the faculty level, these rubrics indicate what exactly is being measured. At the accreditation level, they are designed to give us an insight into whether—and how well—our students have mastered the material. At the professorial level, they help us to gauge a student's progress and, ultimately, competency in the subject area. At a pedagogical level, however, this faculty-wide initiative is even more significant. Implicit in this kind of activity, where we designed common rubrics for faculty to use, is the need for us to consider what constitutes a "good engineer," on one level, and, on another level, to define several skills associated with being a "good" or "competent" engineer, communicative competence among them.

Attribute 7 can be an especially difficult attribute to define and measure, even within technical communications. At the University of Manitoba, our Advisory Board for the program, which is comprised of young engineers and established professionals in industry, has helped us to determine those elements that need more emphasis, especially as to the genres we need to include, such as the briefing note. In the course, we can then explicitly teach these genres, not just by emphasizing the conventions and the formats, but also by demonstrating a particular genre's adaptability to a particular context. As Paretti pointed out, we need to provide meaningful contexts for communicating (2005, p. 3).

Nevertheless, as the national study of undergraduate writing assignments has illustrated, for our faculty-wide rubrics to work effectively, our course outlines could well be more explicit. These outlines need to clarify our pedagogical goals, outline our expectations, and define the length of our assignments, feedback provided, and genre type (Graves, Hyland, & Samuels, 2010; Graves, 2013; Graves, 2014a; Graves, 2014b). We need to emphasize the disciplinary knowledge gained through written assignments in our engineering courses where the "generation of a document [will create] meaning by mediating between the author's wishes, the reader's expectations, the user's needs, and the task's constraints" (Broadhead, 1999, p. 24).

Based on what each of these initiatives has to tell us about communicative competence and assessment, we may better see what kinds of things we should be teaching and assessing in our courses. In an Engineering school, this insight assumes even more importance since we are now expected to base our assessments on defined and measurable outcomes. Likewise, if we target Attribute 7 in our outlines (including those for the undergraduate communication courses), we need to ensure that what we are asking students to write is equally defined and measurable. Together, the writing assignment project and the rubrics initiative demonstrate the need to think deeply about what we teach, how we teach it, and how we assess it. As we move forward, we can use the rubrics as guides to tailor our course assignments and syllabi. In this way, we can then begin to create a new paradigm for success.

Acknowledgements

The national study of undergraduate written assignments has been made possible by a grant from the Social Sciences and Humanities Research Council of Canada. The Faculty of Engineering's study of faculty-wide rubrics has been made possible by the funding provided by the NSERC Chair in Design Engineering, Dr. Douglas Ruth, NSERC Design Chair. The author would also like to thank Kathryn Marcynuk (Vanier Scholar, University of Manitoba) and Roger Graves (Professor, University of Alberta) for their hard work on the course syllabi project as well as J. Seniuk Cicek, Nariman Sepehri, J.P. Burak, and Paul Labossiere for their valuable work on the rubrics, and Ken Ferens for his facilitation of the Industry Forums.

[1]This is an updated version of a paper presented at the CEEA (Canadian Engineering Education Association) conference held in Canmore, Alberta in June, 2014, and posted on the Association's website.

References

Anson, C. A., & Dannels, D. (2009). Profiling programs: Formative uses of departmental consultations in the assessment of communication across the curriculum. *Across the Disciplines: A Journal of Language, Learning and Academic Writing* [Special Issue on Writing Across the Curriculum and Assessment], *6*, 1-16. Retrieved from http://wac.colostate.edu/atd/assessment/anson_dannels.cfm

Anson, C. M., Dannels, D. P., Flash, P., & Housley Gaffney, A. L. (2012). Big rubrics and weird genres: The futility of using generic assessment tools across diverse instructional contexts. *Journal of Writing Assessment, 5*(1), 1-17.

Artemeva, N. (2011). "An engrained part of my career": The formation of a knowledge worker in the dual space of engineering knowledge and rhetorical process. In D. Starke-Meyerring, A. Paré, N. Artemeva, M. Horne, & L. Yousoubova (Eds.), *Writing in Knowledge Societies* (pp. 321-350). Fort Collins, CO: The WAC Clearinghouse.

Boettger, R. K. (2010). Rubric use in technical communication: Exploring the process of creating valid and reliable assessment tools. *IEEE Transactions on Professional Communication* [Special Section on Assessment in Professional Communication], *53*(4), 4-17.

Britton, W. E. (1965). What is technical writing? *College Composition and Communication, 16*(2), 113-116.

Broadhead, G. J. (1999). Addressing multiple goals for engineering writing: The role of course-specific websites. *Language and Learning Across the Disciplines* [Special Issue on Communication across the Engineering Curriculum], *3*(2), 19-43.

Cargile Cook, K. (2002). Layered literacies: A theoretical frame for technical communication pedagogy. *Technical Communication Quarterly, 11*(1), 5-29.

Cargile Cook, K. (2003). How much is enough: The assessment of student work in technical communication courses. *Technical Communication Quarterly, 12*(1), 47-65.

Davis, M. T. (2010). Assessing technical communication within engineering contexts tutorial. *IEEE Transactions on Professional*

Communication [Special Section on Assessment in Professional Communication], *53*(4), 33-45.

Donnell, M., Aller, M., Alley, M., & Kedrowicz, A. A. (2011). Why industry says that Engineering graduates have poor communication skills: What the literature says. In *ASEE Conference Proceedings* [DVD]. (Vancouver, B.C; 26-29 June 2011), AC2011-1503, 13.

Engineers Canada. (2014). *Accreditation Resources.* Retrieved from http://www.engineerscanada.ca/accreditation-resources

Ferens, K., Seniuk Cicek, J., Sepehri, N., Kinsner, W., Burak, J. P., Parker, A., McNeill, D., Ruth, D., Jeffrey, I., Godavari, N., & Ingram, S. (2014). Industry forum III: Towards a common language. In S. Maw & M. Eggermont (Eds.), *Proc. CEEA Canadian Engineering Education Conference: Paper 35* (Canmore, AB; 8-11 June 2014).

Ford, J. D., & Riley, L. A. (2003). Integrating communication and engineering education: A look at curricula, courses, and support systems. *Journal of Engineering Education, 92*, 325-328.

Graves, R. (2013). Why students struggle with writing: What to do about it. *University Affairs, 54*(8), 37.

Graves, R. (2014a). Five strategies to improve writing in your courses. *University Affairs.* Retrieved from http://www.universityaffairs.ca/career-advice/career-advice-article/five-strategies-to-improve-writing-in-your-courses/

Graves, R. (2014b). Genre by numbers: A data-driven description of academic discourse. In *Conference on College Composition and Communication.* Retrieved from http://prezi.com/sao9lcamvqg6/genre-by-numbers/

Graves, R., & Chaudoir, S. (2011). Writing assignments in the community service learning program at the University of Alberta. Retrieved from https://www.artsrn.ualberta.ca/WAC/ResearchReports/CSLWritingAssignmentsReportFeb2011.pdf

Graves, R., Hyland, T., & Samuels, B. M. (2010). Undergraduate writing assignments: An analysis of syllabi at one Canadian college. *Written Communication, 27*(3), 293-317.

Graves, R., Parker, A., & Marcynuk, K. (2012). Undergraduate writing assignments in Engineering: Some preliminary findings. In *CEAA Conference Proceedings* [DVD]: Paper 50 (Winnipeg, MB; June 2012).

Knecht, R., Moskal, B., & Pavelich, M. (2000). The design report rubric: Measuring and tracking growth through success. In *ASEE Conference Proceedings*, Section 2330 (St. Louis, MO; 18-21 July, 2000), 5.618.1-5.618.10.

Mallapragada, S., Griffin, M., Huba, M., Shanks, J., Saunders, L., & Glatz, C. (2003). Using rubrics to facilitate students' development of problem solving skills. In *ASEE Annual Conference Proceedings, 2003* (Nashville, TN), 8.1256.1-8.1256.22.

Orr, T. (2010). Assessment in professional communication: Editorial. *IEEE Transactions on Professional Communication* [Special Section on Assessment in Professional Communication], 53(4), 1-3.

Paretti, M. C. (2005). Communication as professional practice: Designing assignments to develop Engineering professionals. In *ASEE Southeast Section Conference, 2005* (The University of Chattanooga, TN; 3-5 April, 2005).

Paretti, M. C. (2008). Teaching communication in Capstone Design: The role of the instructor in situated learning. *Journal of Engineering Education, 97*(4), 491-503.

Paretti, M. C., & McNair, L. (2008). Introduction. *IEEE Transactions on Professional Communication* [Special Issue on Communication in Engineering Curricula: Mapping the Landscape], *51*(3), 238-241.

Parker, A., & Topping, A. (2013). Designing rubrics for communication courses in Engineering: A work in progress. *Proc. CEEA Canadian Engineering Education Conference:* Paper 143 (Montreal, QC; 17-20 June 2013).

Ramey, D., & Hudgins, J. (1999). The evolution of integrating writing into Engineering: Tracing iterations of writing instruction in a sophomore Engineering course. In *Proceedings, Frontiers in Education Conference* (10-13 Nov.1999), v.3, 12b5-1 - 12b5-5.

Reave, L. (2004). Technical communication instruction in Engineering schools: A survey of top-ranked U.S. and Canadian programs. *Journal of Business and Technical Communication, 18*(4), 452-490.

Schor, D., Marcynuk, K., Sebastian, M., Kinsner, W., Ferens, K., Shafai, C., & Sepehri, N. (2011). Curriculum enhancement and evaluation of graduate attributes and outcomes through student-run forums. In *Proc. of the 2nd Annual Canadian Engineering Education Conference* (Memorial University, St. John's, Newfoundland, June 2011).

Seniuk Cicek, J., Ingram, S., Sepehri, N., Burak, J. P., Labossiere, P., Mann, D., Ruth, D., Parker, A., Ferens, K., Godavari, N., & Oleszkiewicz, J. (2014). Rubrics as a vehicle to define the 12 CEAB graduate attributes, determine graduate competencies, and develop a common language for Engineering stakeholders. In S. Maw & M. Eggermont (Eds.), *Proc. CEEA Canadian Engineering Education Conference:* Paper 31 (Canmore, AB; 8-11 June 2014).

Shwom, B., & Hirsch, P. (1999). Re-envisioning the writing requirement: An interdisciplinary approach. *Business Communication Quarterly, 62*(1), 104-107.

The Canadian Engineering Accreditation Board. (2008). *Accreditation criteria and procedures.*

Chapter 4

Writing Assignments in a Life Sciences Department: More Opportunity than Motive?

Andrea L. Williams
University of Toronto

"Rhetoric . . . is both a discipline and a perspective from which disciplines can be viewed."
   Alan G. Gross, *The rhetoric of science*

"writing produces biology"
   Greg Myers, *Writing biology: Texts in the social construction of scientific knowledge*

Introduction

Scholars of rhetoric, along with those working in the history and sociology of science, have, since the 1980s, challenged the view that science writing involves merely recording natural facts. Rather than scientific writing merely reporting knowledge, Bazerman (1988), Gross (1990), and Myers (1990) have instead argued that writing produces and reproduces knowledge and the authority of that knowledge. For Bazerman, acknowledging the rhetorical nature of scientific texts and understanding how such writing works (1988) is essential to helping people write better. In *Writing biology: Texts in the social construction of scientific knowledge* (1990), Myers examined the common texts that biologists write during the research cycle—from grant proposal to article to expert reception to writing for the public. Myers saw his project "not as revealing what is hidden in biology, but as making explicit what its practitioners know, and perhaps take for granted" (xiii). This chapter extends Myers' project by exploring the writing tasks that novice biologists are asked to do in undergraduate courses. If, as Bazerman (1988) has argued of all texts, including scientific ones, "words arise of out of the activity, procedures, and relationships within the community," (p. 47) then analyzing undergraduate writing assignment prompts can tell us something about the values, beliefs, and expectations with respect to the writing of a particular departmental community, one which is connected to those of the larger disciplinary community.

Like many scholarly fields, rather than being a clearly defined and stable discipline, the life sciences comprise an evolving group of sub-disciplines; however, the field can best be described as the study of living organisms: animals (including humans), plants, and microorganisms. Yet, despite the amorphous nature of the field, there is widespread agreement on the importance of writing for life science undergraduates, whether it is seen as a "skill" (Grant & Piirto, 1994),essential for disseminating scientific knowledge (Morgan, Fraga, & Macauley, 2011), or as a means of creating knowledge, as rhetoricians have argued. Much of the literature on teaching writing in the life sciences describes local classroom practices rather than presenting systematic inquiry into how writing is taught and learned. The literature can be classified according to five main areas of focus, the first of which examines stand-alone writing-intensive or composition courses aimed at science students (Labianca & Reeves, 1989) and first year and capstone composition courses linked with a biology course (Bayer, Curto, & Kriley, 2006; Grant & Piirto, 1994; Moskovitz & Kellog, 2005; Wilkinson, 1985). A second focus of the literature concerns writing to learn in both secondary (Hohenshell, Hand, & Staker, 2004; Klein & Aller, 1998; Moore, 2006) and post-secondary contexts (Balgopal & Wallace, 2013; Kisinksi-Collins & Gordon-Messer, 2010; Langsam & Yancey, 1997). Teaching specific genres of life science writing such as lab notebooks, lab reports (Morgan, Fraga, & Macauley, 2011), abstracts, species accounts (Yahnke, Dewey, & Myers, 2013), grant writing (Blair, Klein & Bowen, 2007), and case writing (Kendler & Grove, 2004) comprises a third focus of the literature, while a fourth area of scholarly inquiry concerns how writing can serve as a vehicle to teach related skills such as critical thinking (Quitadamo & Kurtz, 2007; TePaske, 1982), reading (Janick-Buckner, 1997), and research and information literacy (Freeman & Lynd-Balta 2010; Yahnke, Dewey, & Myers, 2013). Lastly, and most relevant to this chapter, is the literature on holistic approaches to writing instruction whereby writing is fully integrated into science courses (Holyoak, 1998; Taylor & Sobota, 1998) rather than taught in stand-alone or linked writing courses. Although the literature outlined above explores writing instruction (including assignments), it does so in a piecemeal way. Scholars such as Holyoak have instead argued that writing should be taught throughout the biology curriculum and by all department members (p. 187), challenging the traditional writing across the curriculum (WAC) model in the US whereby students have only sporadic opportunities to write: initially in first year composition, followed by a couple of general education courses with writing components, and culminating with a writing-intensive course in their major in third or fourth year. Advocating an integrated approach to writing instruction in the biology curriculum, Holyoak likens students producing good writing to "committing a crime—it requires motive and opportunity" (p. 190). Motive and opportunity are two of three key concepts used in criminal law to determine guilt, and the third is means. These provide useful lenses through which to view the writing assignments students are asked to do, although it is the second concept, opportunity, which is the focus of this study. Winterman and Malacinski (2015) have argued that the strengths of traditional biology curricula include providing a strong foundation for knowledge building and problem solving, and helping students to develop skills sets such as the design of experiments, data analysis, dealing with complexity, understanding networks, acknowledging mechanisms of change, engaging in field studies, and predicting animal behaviour (p. 426). However, they have decried the lack of instruction in information literacy and the emphasis on writing as information transfer rather than as a way of learning disciplinary content (pp. 426-427). Instead, Winterman and Malacinski have argued for a more "authentic" approach to writing instruction that would be more meaningful for students by requiring them "to translate and synthesize their own thoughts and those of others into an original product that is both significant and interesting" (p. 427).

In examining the writing assigned to undergraduate students in one particular disciplinary and departmental setting, this study creates what Anson and Dannels (2009) call a "program profile." Program or department profiles can be useful tools for assessing whether a particular unit is living up to its stated objectives for student learning and implementing practices that will help students achieve the desired learning outcomes. To determine this we asked four basic questions: (1) How often (and how much) are students writing? (2) When in the four years of their programs are they writing and where (in what types of courses)? (3) What kind of assignments are they writing? (4) What information and guidance are students given in writing assignments about audience, structure, length, time to complete, how to cite sources, how not to plagiarize, how they will be evaluated, and where they can get help? Beyond its local use value to the department, this chapter contributes to our understanding of writing demands placed on novice life scientists and, together with the work of scholars like Myers (1990) and Bazerman (1988), we can begin to see the extent to which undergraduate life sciences education prepares students for the writing they will do after graduation.

The Local Context: The Department of Life Sciences at a Central Canadian University

Writing assignments, like all texts, are neither created nor disseminated in a vacuum; rather, they are informed by both local institutional culture and circumstances and broader disciplinary beliefs and exigencies. The Department of Life Sciences (DLS) at Central Canadian University (CCU), a major research-intensive university in southern Ontario, is one of the largest departments of its kind in North America with strong graduate and undergraduate programs and internationally renowned faculty. DLS enrols about 2000 undergraduate students and offers courses in topics such as molecular evolution, population and quantitative genetics, genomics, animal behaviour, population, community, evolutionary and ecological theory, biodiversity, conservation biology, and systematics. In the mid-2000s, DLS, along with other departments, was involved in a faculty-wide curriculum renewal project, which resulted in a document articulating communication goals for undergraduate students in the Faculty of Arts & Science. Notably, these goals are generic rather than discipline-specific, which as I will suggest, makes them less effective for both instructors and students in terms of creating and completing writing assignments that are relevant to the life sciences. These generic faculty-wide communication goals require that students be able to (1) organize ideas into coherent arguments supported by appropriate evidence; (2) communicate effectively to various audiences and in various contexts; (3) produce effective writing; and (4) effectively communicate orally and visually according to the appropriate conventions of the area of study. In addition to the Arts & Science writing goals, the department's participation since 2010 in a faculty-wide WAC initiative forms part of the context for student writing in DLS. So far the department has focused WAC resources on its large enrolment first year gateway course. The course has a three-stage scaffolded assignment, on which students receive formative feedback from TAs who receive WAC training, and through which students learn information literacy skills, concepts key to evolutionary biology, and scientific writing skills. The department's decision to focus resources on its first year course was likely influenced by the fact that CCU, like most universities in Canada and those outside of the US, does not have a required first year writing course. However, this study has acted as a catalyst to expand the department's WAC efforts beyond first year to the undergraduate curriculum as a whole. One of the initial sparks for change was the report submitted to the department in the spring of 2016, which summarized the findings presented here. As explained in the concluding section of this chapter, this study and the related report have also prompted a wider ongoing departmental writing inventory involving participation from faculty, alumni, and students.

Data Collection, Study Procedure, and Analysis

Syllabi are one of the key ways instructors communicate to students about writing and other assignments. Although the amount of detail in syllabi varies considerably across different courses and instructors, it is a consistent feature of most university courses and at CCU (as at many other institutions) is considered a contract between the instructors and students with respect to course requirements, expectations, and grading, including writing assignments. Of course, many instructors supplement the information in the syllabi with handouts and other materials and discuss writing assignment expectations with students in class and during office hours. However, for this study, we limited our analysis to information in course syllabi and handouts provided by the instructor on the assumption that syllabi analysis provides reasonably accurate data about assignment characteristics and frequency (Graves, Hyland, & Samuels, 2010), although it certainly does not capture all writing instruction that occurs in courses, which is a limitation of our study.

Electronic copies of course syllabi were provided to the researchers (who also included three graduate research assistants (RAs) from the department who were all advanced Ph.D. students) by the department. If the syllabus did not provide assignment details, but mentioned that additional information was available elsewhere, then one of the research assistants contacted the course instructor or TAs to obtain that information. If no additional information was mentioned then we relied solely on the syllabus or course website for assignment information. During data collection, we learned that a couple of the independent research project courses (where students work on faculty research projects) do not follow the assignment guidelines posted online. For example, although some of the independent research projects mention writing assignments, we were told that the writing component is sometimes dropped from the course. As this varies from year to year and by instructor, it was not possible to adjust for this in our analysis. Although the current study focused exclusively on the writing assignments mentioned in syllabi and online course guidelines, identifying how often there are discrepancies between syllabi or guidelines and actual practice would be a useful future project.

One of the RAs read through syllabi separately and coded them for frequency, genre, and instructional characteristics using a coding scheme accessible online through the central research project's database. The RA and I were in regular contact with the project's principal investigator (who oversaw the larger multi-institutional project) to ensure that our coding interpretations were consistent with studies conducted at other institutions. After data crosschecking was completed, we created a spreadsheet in Microsoft Excel to input the data from the coding sheets. We checked each line item against the coding sheet and crosschecked the spreadsheet for consistency. Once crosschecking was complete, the data were analyzed using R software (v. 2.10.1). I re-coded approximately 10% of the data to check for reliability and a member of the principal investigator's team from the University of Alberta also reviewed the coding. For the frequency and number of assignments, both the mean value and interquartile range are presented: the mean because it is a standard measure of central tendency, and the median and quartiles because the data is non-normally distributed and the median is not as influenced by non-normality as means are. Therefore, together, these values provide a good representation of the distribution of the data.

Results

Frequency and Type of Assignments

Of the 59 courses offered by the Department of Life Sciences in 2011-2012, electronic course syllabi were obtained from 50 courses, and we used posted guidelines for the remaining 9 independent research project courses, which did not have syllabi. From the 59 course syllabi and online guidelines we identified 195 writing assignments. DLS students are therefore writing often: as shown in Table 1, the majority (80%) of courses assign writing, with a particularly high percentage in first and fourth year courses. All three first year courses and almost all (16 of 17 courses or 94%) fourth year courses have at least one writing assignment. After a drop from first to second year where students are asked to write in 64% of courses, the percentage of courses where students are assigned writing increases to 76% in third year. Most (96%) DLS writing assignments are concentrated in years two through four, with first year courses comprising only 4% of the department's writing assignments. However, the smaller number of assignments in first year can be attributed to the fact that although all first year courses assign writing, there are only three courses. More meaningful than the percentage of total writing assignments by year is the average or mean number of writing assignments (Table 1). The mean is 2.51 (SD = 2.28) and it varies little across all four years. The median across years was similar to the mean (median = 2), but it varied more across years, with a median of four assignments per course in fourth year, and a median of two in first and third year.

Table 1

DLS courses with writing, total writing assignments, and mean writing assignments per course by year

	Year 1	Year 2	Year 3	Year 4	Total
Total courses	3	14	25	17	59
Courses with writing	3 (100%)	9 (64%)	19 (76%)	16 (94%)	47 (80%)
Total writing assignments	8 (6%)	77 (39%)	63 (32%)	47 (24%)	195 (100%)
Writing assignments per course (mean ± SD	2.67 ± 2.08	2.14 ± 2.309	2.52 ± 2.62	2.67 ± 1.86	2.51 ± 2.28
Writing assignments per course (Q1, median, Q3)	(Q1: 1, median: 2, Q3: 5)	(Q1: 1, median: 3, Q3: 5.75)	(Q1: 2, median: 2, Q3: 4)	(Q1: 1.5, median: 4, Q3: 5)	(Q1: 1, median: 2, Q3: 5)

Note: Q1 refers to the first quartile (the value that represents the first quarter in the ranked dataset) and Q3 refers to the third quartile (the third quarter point)

Number of Writing Assignments by Course Type

As the department offers a variety of different course types, we were also interested in determining if the number of assignments varied by type. After consulting with key faculty members in the department (including the undergraduate coordinator), we classified the courses according to the following seven types: (1) Lecture only; (2) Lecture and lab; (3) Lecture with tutorials led by TAs; (4) Seminars; (5) Field courses held at various off-campus sites (2-week courses held in the summer, although the writing portion takes longer); (6) Independent research involving students in faculty projects; and (7) Breadth courses (for non-science students). As Table 2 and Figure 1 show, students tend to write more assignments per course in seminars (mean: 3.5 (SD = 2.65); median: 3), and research courses (mean: 3.08 (SD = 1.23); median: 3), and fewer in field courses (mean: 1.33 (SD = 0.58); median: 1), breadth courses (mean= 1.33 (SD = 1.53; median: 1), and courses with TA-led tutorials (mean: 1.00 (SD = 0.82); median: 1.5). Research and seminar courses often have smaller enrolment numbers (data not shown) and are highly selective: students who apply must submit their transcripts and describe any research experience. This means that often the same students work on more than one research project, so a small minority of the strongest students do substantially more writing than the typical student in this department. Although course categories vary in the average number of assignments, there is considerable variation within categories in the number of assignments (Figure 1); for example, for courses that include both lecture and lab components, in some courses, students do only one assignment during the term, while in others, students complete up to 10 assignments. This variation in assignment number prompted us to focus on some additional qualitative aspects of assignments, which will be described in the next section. To sum up, students in CCU's Life Sciences program write in most courses and write regularly throughout their four years; however, the number of assignments varies more by course type than by year, with more writing assignments in smaller enrolment seminar and highly selective research courses.

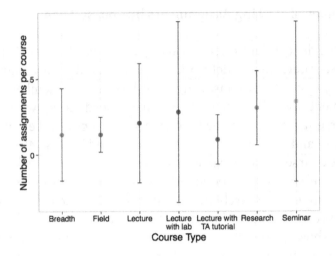

Figure 1. Average number of writing assignments by course type. Points are the mean number of assignments and error bars indicate standard deviation.

Table 2

DLS courses with writing, total writing assignments, and mean writing assignments per course, by course type

Course type	Lecture	Lecture + Lab	Lecture + TA Tutorial	Seminar	Field	Research	Breadth	Total
Total courses	11	22	4	4	3	12	3	59
Courses with writing	8 (73%)	15 (68%)	3 (75%)	4 (100%)	3 (100%)	12 (100%)	2 (67%)	47 (80%)
Total assignments	26	59	4	13	4	85	4	195
Average no. of writing assignments per course (± SD)	2.09 ± 1.97	2.82 ± 2.99	1.00 ± 0.82	3.5 ± 2.65	1.33 ± 0.58	3.08 ± 1.23	1.33 ± 1.53	2.51 ± 2.28
Median no. of writing assignments per course (Q1, median, Q3)	(Q1: 0, median: 1, Q3: 3)	(Q1: 0, median:2, Q3: 5.25)	(Q1: 0.25, median: 1.5, Q3: 5)	(Q1: 1.25, median: 3, Q3: 6.25)	(Q1: 1, median: 1, Q3: 2)	(Q1: 2.25, median: 3, Q3: 4)	(Q1: 0, median: 1, Q3: 3)	(Q1: 1, median: 2, Q3: 4)

Note: Q1 refers to the first quartile (the value that represents the first quarter in the ranked dataset) and Q3 refers to the third quartile (the third quarter point).

The preceding data set tells us when (year of study) and where (course type) DLS students are writing the most, but what are they writing? What information do syllabi and assignment instructions tell students about instructor expectations and what guidance do they provide for writing tasks? Moreover, how much of the writing students are asked to do gives them practice with writing tasks common to workplaces both within and beyond university? Table 4 shows the assignment features for which we coded, which can be grouped according to features that (1) communicate instructor expectations to students, (2) help students with the writing task, and (3) give students practice with writing tasks common to workplaces both within and beyond university.

Assignment Features that Communicate Instructor Expectations

This section presents our findings related to those assignment features that communicate instructor expectations such as assignment name, length, value, description, time to complete, rubrics (scoring guides or evaluation criteria of any kind), examples or models of completed assignments, resources, a specific style manual for referencing sources, and a plagiarism warning.

Naming assignments. As Shaver (2007) has argued, assignment names can provide important information to students: how writing assignments are named gives students their first clue as to what their instructor wants them to do and produce. All 195 assignments were coded first with the generic label instructors used in their syllabi to identify the task. Of the 86 genres assigned, 47 were assigned just once (data not shown). The diversity of genres suggests that instructors are giving the same or similar assignments different names as in the case of "poster," "project poster," and "research fair poster," a practice that is potentially confusing to students. The top five most frequently occurring genres (according to instructors' labels and shown in Table 3) were final report, lab report, proposal, assignment, and paper critique. After analyzing the names instructors gave their assignments, we categorized these genres into broader component types. Our own classification system identified about a third of assignments as some form of "report" (for example, a summary of results, often from students' own data collection and analysis was labelled a report), although the specific type of report varied. After reports, the most common assignment types were posters, critiques (such as critiques of published or peer work), proposals (for example, where students explain their rationale for an experiment or project), presentations (we included this type of assignment because, although oral, it almost always has a written component), and journals (such as a summary of the literature or field observations). Analyzing the distribution of assignment types and genres across years (data not shown) revealed no particular pattern by either year or course type.

Table 3

Top ten genres (instructor's name for assignment)

Genre	Number of assignments
Final report	14
Lab report	12
Proposal	8
Assignment	8
Paper critique	7
Written assignment	6
Discussion	6
Lab assignment	6
Scientific proposal	5
Short lab report	5

Length of assignments. In addition to assignment names, we analyzed assignment features that communicate instructor expectations and found considerable variation on assignment instructions, depending on the feature. Whereas the percent mark value and the time to complete were usually specified (in 92% and 73% of assignments, respectively), the length of the assignment and the use of references were specified less often (in 34% and 22% of assignments, respectively). In terms of how much students were asked to write, in first and second year, most assignments were 1500 words or less and students were not asked to write more than 2500 words, as shown in Figure 2. However, in third and fourth year, students were asked to write some much longer assignments (over 6500 words) without much build-up in the intervening years.

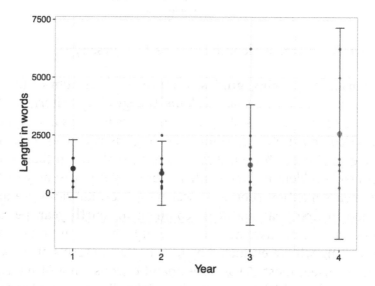

Figure 2. Assignment length in words, by year.

Analyzing assignment length by course type rather than year, as shown in Figure 3, we found that research and seminar courses had the widest variation in the length of assignments and that courses with TA-led tutorials and lecture-only courses had the least variation, perhaps because these tend to be large enrollment courses and marking writing is perceived as time-consuming.

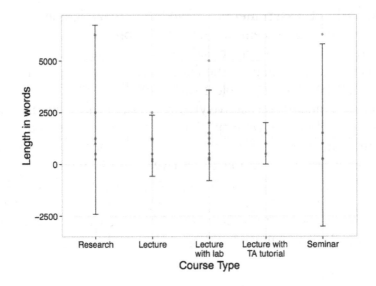

Figure 3. Assignment length in words, by course type.

Rubrics or scoring guides. Features such as rubrics (or any kind of scoring guide that explains the grading criteria of the assignment) and samples of assignment types (such as a lab report) are particularly useful for communicating instructor expectations to students (Stevens & Levi, 2005). However, as shown in Table 4, DLS assignments seldom included either rubrics or samples: only 11% of assignments mention rubrics or scoring guides. Rubrics were most common in first year and least common in fourth year, perhaps because instructors assume students will be able to anticipate how their writing will be evaluated by fourth year. In terms of the kind of rubrics used, most (59%) were analytic (consisting of multiple, separate scales, which were usually weighted), whereas nine (41%) were holistic (data not shown). Even less common than rubrics were samples of writing assignments: only 14 (7%) of assignments had associated examples, which like rubrics, were most common in first year where they were used in 38% of assignments, after which their use decreased.

Plagiarism warnings and guidelines on using sources. Using and citing sources is a key part of most academic writing across the disciplines, yet many students to struggle to move from "patchwriting" (Moore Howard, 1996; Moore Howard, Rodrigue, &

Serviss, 2010) to using sources effectively and ethically. Plagiarism and academic integrity have become vexing issues for universities, yet Soto, Anand, and McGee (2004) found that plagiarism could be decreased with explicit instructions in referencing along with other teaching strategies. So what kind of guidance are students given in DLS courses on finding and integrating secondary sources into their writing and on academic integrity and plagiarism? As Table 4 shows, of the 195 assignments, 42 (21%) required references, but only 28 assignments (14%) mentioned a specific style manual that students should use. However, students were warned about plagiarism (or "academic integrity" as it is often referred to on syllabi) on over half (52%) of all assignments. In other words, students were more often warned on syllabi and assignments not to plagiarize than they were given written guidelines about how to cite. As in the case of rubrics and sample assignments, required or suggested sources and style manuals occurred most often in first year where half of all assignments have these features, after which these features were far less common. First year assignments, as shown in Table 4, generally included more features that communicate instructions to students, but there were no meaningful differences in these features across the various course types, as shown in Table 5. It is possible that so many of these assignment features occurred in first year because DLS's large gateway course has participated in a WAC program since 2010, and the writing assignments have benefitted from an instructor committed to integrating writing instruction in a meaningful way along with input from graduate writing fellows, writing centre instructors, and WAC faculty.

Table 4

Assignment features that communicate instructor expectations, by year

	Year 1	Year 2	Year 3	Year 4	Total
Number of courses	8	77	63	47	195
Percent mark value specified	8 (100%)	64 (83%)	61 (97%)	47 (100%)	180 (92%)
Length specified	5 (63%)	18 (23%)	22 (35%)	22 (47%)	67 (34%)
Time to complete specified	5 (63%)	60 (78%)	45 (71%)	33 (70%)	143 (73%)
Rubric/scoring guide	3 (38%)	6 (8%)	11 (17%)	2 (4%)	22 (11%)
Example	2 (38%)	1 (8%)	5 (17%)	6 (4%)	14 (7%)
References required or specified	4 (50%)	8 (10%)	17 (27%)	13 (28%)	42 (22%)
Style manual	4 (50%)	2 (3%)	14 (22%)	8 (17%)	28 (14%)
Plagiarism warning	6 (75%)	20 (26%)	41 (65%)	35 (74%)	102 (53%)

Table 5

Assignment features that communicate instructor expectations, by course type

Course type	Lecture	Lecture + Lab	Lecture + TA Tutorial	Seminar	Field	Research	Breadth	Total
Total courses	11	22	4	4	3	12	3	59
Courses with writing	8 (73%)	15 (68%)	3 (75%)	4 (100%)	3 (100%)	12 (100%)	2 (67%)	47 (80%)
Total assignments	26	59	4	13	4	85	4	195
Average no. of writing assignments per course (± SD)	2.09 ± 1.97	2.82 ± 2.99	1.00 ± 0.82	3.5 ± 2.65	1.33 ± 0.58	3.08 ± 1.23	1.33 ± 1.53	2.51 ± 2.28
Median no. of writing assignments per course (Q1, median, Q3)	(Q1: 0, median: 1, Q3: 3)	(Q1: 0, median:2, Q3: 5.25)	(Q1: 0.25, median: 1.5, Q3: 5)	(Q1: 1.25, median: 3, Q3: 6.25)	(Q1: 1, median: 1, Q3: 2)	(Q1: 2.25, median: 3, Q3: 4)	(Q1: 0, median: 1, Q3: 3)	(Q1: 1, median: 2, Q3: 4)

Assignment features that help students with the writing task

In addition to coding for assignment features that communicate instructor expectations to students, we collected and analyzed data on features that can help students with the writing task such as learning goals, nested assignments, formative feedback, and mentions of resources such as writing centres.

Learning goals. Learning goals, which are explicit statements about the learning objective(s) of the assignment, were included in 42% of assignments, as shown in Table 6. For example, a first year assignment includes the following learning objectives:

> After completing this exercise you should be able to: 1. Find, evaluate, and synthesize primary literature; 2. Synthesize your ideas with information you obtain from the literature; 3. Develop a hypothesis; 4. Design and describe an experiment to test your hypothesis; 5. Communicate your ideas concisely, and 6. Incorporate TA feedback into your writing.

Learning goals are stated most in first and fourth year courses (63% and 62%, respectively) and less often in second and third year assignments (23% and 48%, respectively). In terms of course types, learning goals are stated most in breadth (75%), seminar (54%), and lecture courses (54%), and less in field (25%) and research (33%) courses.

Nested or staged assignments. Because smaller tasks are usually easier to complete than larger ones, it is often helpful for students to have writing tasks broken into parts and submitted separately over the term (e.g., an outline, proposal draft, and revised proposal—all staged or nested in one topic). We analyzed how often assignments are "nested" within each other. Some of these nested assignments may receive separate grades while others do not. Overall, DLS assignments are often nested, providing students with opportunities to build on their writing skills throughout the term. We found that 63% of all assignments are nested, with the remaining 37% as isolated assignments. Nested assignments occur most in independent research courses (96% of assignments), as shown in Table 7.

Formative feedback. In addition to nested assignments, in-process or formative feedback is helpful for guiding students through writing assignments. Research shows that student writing improves with feedback (Bean, 2001; Nicola & Macfarlane-Dick, 2006), which can take different forms such as peer review, written comments on a draft, or a meeting with the instructor or TA. Few assignments (7%) in DLS include this kind of feedback (Table 6). Students receive the most formative feedback in first year (25% of assignments) and fourth year (15% of assignments). If we analyze the data according to course type (as shown in Table 7), we find that lecture with TA-led tutorial courses and research courses provide the most formative feedback (25% and 11%, respectively), perhaps because more TAs and graduate students are available to provide such feedback in these courses.

Suggested writing resources. So, if students in DLS are rarely getting formative feedback on their writing assignments from course instructors and TAs, are they at least being directed to places such as writing or academic skills centres where they can get help? Resources are suggested in only 37% of assignments and most often in first year where resources are included 88% of the time; 66% of fourth year assignments suggest resources, but only 9% and 43% of second and third year courses, respectively, do this. Of course, instructors and TAs may be announcing these resources in lecture, labs, and tutorials, but we weren't able to capture this data.

Table 6

Assignment features that help students with writing tasks, by year

	Year 1	Year 2	Year 3	Year 4	Total
Total assignments	8	77	63	47	195
Learning goals stated	5 (63%)	18 (23%)	30 (48%)	29 (62%)	82 (42%)
Formative feedback	2 (25%)	3 (4%)	1 (2%)	7 (15%)	13 (7%)
Nested assignments	5 (62%)	60 (78%)	33 (52%)	25 (53%)	123 (63%)
Suggested resources	7 (88%)	7 (9%)	27 (43%)	31 (66%)	72 (37%)
Topic choice	1 (13%)	10 (13%)	14 (22%)	13 (28%)	38 (19%)

Table 7

Assignment features that help students with writing tasks, by course type

Course type	Lecture	Lecture + Lab	Lecture+ TA Tutorial	Seminar	Field	Research	Breadth	Total
Assignment Feature	26	59	4	13	4	85	4	95
Formative feedback	0	2 (3%)	1 (25%)	1 (8%)	0	9 (11%)	0	3 (7%)
Nested assignments	9 (35%)	23 (40%)	0 (0%)	7 (54%)	(0%)	82 (96%)	2 (50%)	23 (63%)
Suggested resources	16 (62%)	31 (53%)	3 (75%)	11 (85%)	(50%)	9 (11%)	0	2 (37%)
Learning goals stated	14 (54%)	27 (46%)	2 (50%)	7 (54%)	(25%)	28 (33%)	3 (75%)	2 (42%)
Topic choice	4 (15%)	6 (10%)	2 (50%)	0	(75%)	20 (24%)	3 (75%)	8 (19%)

So far this chapter has examined DLS syllabi for how often, how much, and what kind of writing students are asked to do, as well as what information about instructor expectations and help on writing tasks is available to students. The third and final category of assignment features that we coded includes those that give students practice with two common writing tasks: writing for general or non-scientific audiences and group or collaborative writing.

Assignment features that give students practice with workplace writing tasks. To return to Holyoak's (1998) two requirements for producing good writing (i.e. motive and opportunity), we have so far focused on the latter, analyzing when and what DLS students are asked to write across their four years. But what about the former, motive? As we saw in the preceding section, relatively few assignments provided an explicit learning outcome related to writing, so there is an opportunity to give students a much stronger motive to write, particularly given the central role that writing plays in disciplinary knowledge. We can also discover the degree to which students are motivated to write by analyzing the purposes and audiences for whom students are asked to write. In terms of audience, are students writing merely to display their knowledge to an expert audience for evaluation (i.e. for instructors and TAs)? Or are they writing to effect action from an audience (real or hypothetical) who may know less than they do? Given the many controversial and politically charged issues pertaining to the life sciences, such as climate change, species extinction, and evolutionary theory (which is still contested in some parts of the United States), the fact that students in this department are doing very little writing for non-scientific or public audiences is surprising. Because most DLS graduates will need to write many different kinds of texts for a variety of audiences, assignments that give students practice communicating specialized knowledge and concepts to lay audiences will help them develop an important and useful skill. However, as no specific audience was given for most writing assignments in the department, students presumably wrote mostly for their instructor and/or TA, as shown in Table 8. Only four out of 195 assignments asked students to write for a specific audience: one assignment had students writing for a local non-profit organization and three assignments asked students to write for the "general public" or a "general audience."

Table 8

Assignment features that help students transition to the workplace, by year

	Year 1	Year 2	Year 3	Year 4	Total
Total assignments	8	77	63	47	195
Academic target audience					
(TA/Instructor/Peers)	8 (100%)	74 (96%)	63 (100%)	46 (98%)	191 (98%)
Other target audience (General					
Public, General Audience, Other)	0	3 (4%)	0	1 (2%)	4 (2%)
Group work					
(optional or required)	0 (0%)	5 (6%)	10 (16%)	1 (2%)	16 (8%)

Discussion

We know the importance of practice for students learning to write, and DLS undergraduates fortunately have many opportunities to do so. They write in most (80%) of their courses and do so regularly (2.51 assignments on average per course). Although students write regularly throughout their four years, the small minority of students who take research project courses and seminars write far more assignments than most DLS students, a disparity that is likely in part because this subset of students is highly motivated. However, the department may nonetheless wish to address this disparity to ensure that as many of their graduates as possible have all the practice they need to become strong writers in their discipline. Although the department does not necessarily need to increase the amount of writing students do to improve its curriculum, DLS should consider which courses have the most writing to ensure that all its graduates get the practice they need to develop their writing abilities. Moreover, minor changes to better communicate disciplinary and instructor expectations, support student skill development, and diversify writing assignments to better reflect the broad range of writing students will do after graduation would also likely improve writing instruction in DLS as much as additional resources aimed at giving students more formative feedback.

Students in this department write a wide array of assignment genres: proposals, reports, critiques, and discussions. However, many very similar assignments are given different names by instructors. Such idiosyncratic naming of assignments is a potential barrier to helping students integrate and transfer their learning across courses (Shaver, 2007), particularly given subtle genre and disciplinary differences which can cause confusion for students, as McCarthy (1987) found. Therefore, instructors would do well to consider how they name assignments and try to label them more consistently across their own courses as well as those throughout their department. Student confusion could be decreased and unnecessary repetition avoided by improving departmental communication about assignments so instructors know what kinds of writing their colleagues are assigning in different courses and years. In short, more faculty conversations about writing assignments would likely result in better and more coordinated assignments throughout the department.

Although DLS students write frequently, they receive minimal written guidelines on course syllabi and in assignment descriptions about how to write effectively and what their instructors expect from student writing. Although this study can't speak to whether or not expectations for writing are discussed at length in class, given the pressure on instructors to cover disciplinary content, it is unlikely that detailed and regular discussions about writing occur in all or even most courses. While some assignment characteristics are specified most of the time (for example, mark value is specified in 92% of assignments and time to complete in 73% of assignments), other features that communicate instructor expectations are often omitted (such as suggested length and use of references, which are specified only 34% and 22% of the time, respectively). Specifying due dates and the length of assignments on syllabi could help students better manage their time and other course work. There is a big jump in the length of individual assignments from the first two years where most assignments are 1500 words or less and no assignment is more than 2500 words, to third and fourth year where some assignments are over 6500 words. Students either need help preparing to write these much longer (and likely more complex) assignments, or the longer assignments could be eliminated. Rubrics or scoring guides, writing samples, and style guides that tell students how to cite evidence are seldom included. Rubrics are mentioned in 11% of assignments, samples in 7% of assignments, style manuals in 14% of assignments, and suggestions for resources students can use to complete the assignment appear in 37% of assignments. On the other hand, generic plagiarism or academic integrity warnings are mentioned in over half (53%) of all assignments. The higher frequency of plagiarism warnings compared to other features that communicate instructor expectations about appropriate source use reflects the tendency of universities to focus more on punishing plagiarists rather than teaching students how to work with sources. A proactive approach focused on deterrence rather than mere detection is far more effective in addressing plagiarism (Moore Howard, 2001). Incorporating instruction on source use in tutorials where students could practice summarizing and paraphrasing activities would ensure that more students learn the intricacies of what they often view as an opaque and arcane practice.

As for features that help students with the writing task, the majority of DLS (63%) assignments are nested, which gives students the opportunity to develop their writing skills over the course of the semester. However, the small minority of students enrolled in research project courses write far more nested assignments (96% of assignments in research courses are nested), which gives these students a distinct advantage. Students rarely (only 7% of the time) receive formative feedback on their writing, which research has shown is important for helping students learn to write (Wingate, 2010). If we return to Holyoak's (1998) claim that producing good writing requires both motive and opportunity, DLS certainly provides students with plenty of opportunities to write. However, whether the department provides students with sufficient motive to write is less certain. The department would benefit from articulating discipline-specific goals that faculty could agree on and from which they could draw when developing their course syllabi. At the time of writing, fewer than half (42%) of assignments indicate the types of writing and critical-thinking skills instructors want students to learn. Including learning goals, or at least some kind of explanation of why students are being asked to write, within the assignment descriptions could help motivate students to take these assignments more seriously, particularly if instructors explain, whether in class or in the assignment itself, the importance of writing to the discipline. Connecting writing assignments to disciplinary knowledge and the day-to-day work of scientists might make students willing to invest more of their limited time and energy in completing writing assignments.

Another assignment feature directly related to motive is audience. As discussed at the beginning of this chapter, one of the communication goals for students in the faculty where DLS is housed is that they learn to communicate to different audiences. However, very few of the department's assignments specify an audience, and only one specifically gives students a non-academic audience. Therefore, although students write a wide range of assignments, they write almost exclusively for academic audiences (i.e., for professors and/or TAs). Instructors could better prepare students for workplace writing by asking them to write for a variety of audiences, whether imagined or real. Another skill useful both within academia and beyond is group or collaborative writing, yet only 8% of assignments mention this, and one of these made group writing optional. Notably, with the exception of providing more formative feedback on writing assignments, all of the strategies discussed so far to improve the writing assignments could be implemented without additional resources by drawing on the support of WAC faculty and graduate writing fellows.

This study has implications beyond DLS. Other departments, regardless of discipline, could improve writing instruction by developing more specific writing goals and basing assignments around these. By increasing communication across courses and instructors so that instructors know the type of writing and communication skills students are learning in other courses (including pre- and co-requisite courses), can help those instructors build on students' skills and prior knowledge. Such inventories are useful for departments seeking to identify both strengths and gaps in teaching and learning, enabling them to adapt their curriculum accordingly. For example, DLS could add assignments that give students experience writing for diverse audiences. New faculty in particular could be encouraged to incorporate assignments that target these skills.

Future Research

Improving Disciplinary Writing Instruction Locally and Globally

Anson and Dannels (2009) touted the value of departmental inventories in providing local formative assessments. Such inventories would be even more valuable if they incorporated enrolment numbers to determine the writing that the average student does, and if the analysis broke down the courses by program stream (for example, this department has a couple of different streams) to see if certain groups of students are exposed to more diverse writing assignments. Despite the limitations of studying syllabi and assignment prompts exclusively, this study suggests useful ways for departments in other institutions to use such research to instigate change at the local level. After the department reviewed our inventory report, I received ethics approval and funding to further investigate writing instruction in the department with a faculty member and graduate student. We surveyed alumni about the writing skills and knowledge they acquired from their undergraduate degrees and began interviewing faculty members about their writing assignments. In the coming year, we plan to explore how students perceive the writing that they are asked to do and any gaps they see between assignment expectations and instruction in order to better support undergraduates' writing development. We have used this data to develop departmental guidelines for writing assignment design and writing workshops for undergraduate students in partnership with two other Life Science departments. In short, we have tried to use this departmental inventory to achieve broader curricular change in the department and realize Holyoak's (1998) vision of a department where writing is integrated into all courses and is the shared responsibility of all faculty members. Such data collection and analysis could be conducted at other institutions to achieve similar aims. Beyond the local, it would be instructive to learn how the writing assigned in this department compares to that of other life science departments and disciplines.

Collaborative research between writing studies faculty and faculty (and, importantly, graduate students) from other disciplines can also prevent writing researchers from becoming self-righteous missionaries by reminding us that workplace genres are sites of struggles within discourse communities (Segal, Paré, Brent, & Vipond, 1998). The next phase of this research, which will involve more disciplinary faculty and undergraduate students, will examine the extent to which syllabi and writing assignments are contested genres and sites of struggle. Possible research questions along these lines might be how do different types of writing assignments reflect different views of the discipline and of disciplinary education? What might the dearth of explicit learning outcomes, collaborative writing assignments, and writing assignments aimed at general audiences tell us about how faculty see the role of writers in writing in the life sciences curriculum? Perhaps most importantly, how can instructors give students not only opportunities, but also the motive and the means to write effectively? The answers to these and other related questions promise to enrich our understanding of the role of writing in the undergraduate life sciences curriculum, and, more broadly, in higher education.

References

Anson, C. A., & Dannels, D. (2009). Profiling programs: Formative uses of departmental consultations in the assessment of communication across the curriculum. *Across the Disciplines, 6*. Retrieved from http://wac.colostate.edu/atd/assessment/anson_dannels.cfm

Balgopal, M., & Wallace, A. (2013). Writing-to-learn, writing-to-communicate, & scientific literacy. *The American Biology Teacher, 75*, 170-175. doi:10.1525/abt.2013.75.3.5

Bayer, T., Curto, K., & Kriley, C. (2006). Acquiring expertise in discipline-specific discourse: An interdisciplinary exercise in learning to speak biology. *Across the Disciplines, 2*. Retrieved from http://wac.colostate.edu/atd/articles/bayer_curto_kriley2005.cfm

Bazerman, C. (1988). *Shaping written knowledge: The genre and activity of the experimental article in science.* Madison, WI: University of Wisconsin Press.

Blair, B. G., Klein, G. R., & Bowen, W. R. (2007). NSF-style peer review for teaching undergraduate grant writing. *The American Biology Teacher, 69*(1), 34-37. doi:10.1662/00027685%282007%2969%5B34%3ANPRFTU%5D2.0.CO%3B2

Freeman, E., & Lynd-Balta, E. (2010). Developing information literacy skills early in an undergraduate curriculum. *College Teaching, 58*, 109-115. doi:10.1080/87567550903521272

Gordon-Messer, S., & Kosinski-Collins, M. (2010). Using scientific purposes to improve student writing and understanding in undergraduate biology project-based laboratories. *American Biology Teacher, 9*, 578-579. doi:10.1525/abt.2010.72.9.11

Grant, M. C., & Piirto, J. (1994). Darwin, dogs and DNA: Freshman writing about biology. *Journal of Science Education and Technology, 3*, 259-262. doi:10.1007/BF01575901

Graves, R., Hyland, T., & Samuels, B. M. (2010). Undergraduate writing assignments: An analysis of syllabi at one Canadian college. *Written Communication, 27*, 293-317. doi:10.1177/0741088310371635

Gross, A. G. (1990). *The rhetoric of science.* Cambridge, MA: Harvard University Press.

Hohenshell, L., Hand, B., & Staker, J. (2004). Promoting conceptual understanding of biotechnology: Writing to a younger audience. *The American Biology Teacher, 66,* 333-338. doi:10.1662/0002-685%282004%29066%5B0333%3APCUOBW%5D2.0.CO%3B2

Holyoak, A. R. (1998). A plan for writing throughout (not just across) the biology curriculum. *The American Biology Teacher, 60,* 186-190. doi:10.2307/4450448

Moore Howard, R. (1995). Plagiarisms, authorships, and the academic death penalty. *College English, 57,* 788. Retrieved from https://eric.ed.gov/?id=EJ515873

Moore Howard, R. (2001). Forget about policing plagiarism: Just teach. *The Chronicle of Higher Education, 16*(12), B24. Retrieved from http://abacus.bates.edu/cbb/events/docs/Howard_ForgeT.pdf

Moore Howard, R., Rodrigue, T. K., & Serviss, T. C. (2010). Writing from sources, writing from sentences. *Writing & Pedagogy, 2,* 177-192. doi:10.1558/wap.v2i2.177

Janick-Buckner, D. (1997). Getting undergraduates to critically read and discuss primary literature: Cultivating students' analytical abilities in an advanced cell biology course. *Journal of College Science Teaching, 27*(1), 29-32. Retrieved from http://static.nsta.org/files/jcst9709_29.pdf

Kendler, B. S., & Grove, P. A. (2009). Problem-based learning in the biology curriculum. *The American Biology Teacher, 66,* 348-354. Retrieved from http://dx.doi.org/10.1662/0002-7685(2004)066[0348:PLITBC]2.0.CO;2

Klein, B., & Aller, B. M. (1998). Writing across the curriculum in chemistry: A practical bibliography. *Language and Learning Across the Disciplines, 2*(35), 25-35. Retrieved from http://wac.colostate.edu/llad/v2n3/klein.pdf

Kosinski-Collins, M., & Gordon-Messer, S. (2010). Using scientific purposes to improve student writing and understanding in undergraduate biology project-based laboratories. *The American Biology Teacher, 72,* 578-579. doi:10.1525/abt.2010.72.9.11

Labianca, D. A., & Reeves, W. J. (1989). Writing across the curriculum: The science segment: A heretical perspective. *Journal of Chemical Education, 62,* 400-402. doi:10.1021/ed062p400

Langsam, D. M., & Yancey, K. B. (1997). E-mailing biology: Facing the biochallenge. In D. Reiss, D. Selfe, & A. Young (Eds.), *Electronic communication across the curriculum* (pp. 231-241). Urbana, IL: National Council of Teachers of English.

McCarthy, L. P. (1987). Stranger in strange lands: A college student writing across the curriculum. *Research in the Teaching of English, 21,* 233-265. Retrieved from http://www.jstor.org/stable/40171114

McGarrell, H., & Verbeem, J. Motivating revision of drafts through formative feedback. *ELT Journal, 61,* 228-236. doi:10.1093/elt/ccm030

Moore, R. (1994). Writing as a tool for learning biology. *Bioscience, 44,* 613-617. Retrieved from https://www.jstor.org/stable/1312461

Morgan, W., Fraga, D., & Macauley, J. Jr. (2011). An integrated approach to improve the scientific writing of introductory biology students. *The American Biology Teacher, 7,* 149-153. doi:10.1525/abt.2011.73.3.6

Moskovitz, C., & Kellog, D. (2005). Primary science communication in the first-year writing course. *College Composition and Communication, 57,* 307-334. Retrieved from https://www.jstor.org/stable/30037917

Myers, G. (1990). *Writing biology: Texts in the social construction of scientific knowledge.* Madison, WI: University of Wisconsin Press.

Nicola, D., & Macfarlane-Dick, D. (2006). Formative assessment and self-regulated learning: A model and seven principles of good feedback practice. *Studies in Higher Education, 31,* 199-218. doi:10.1080/03075070600572090

Quitadamo, I. J., & Kurtz, M. J. (2007). Learning to improve: Using writing to increase critical thinking performance in general education biology. *CBE—Life Sciences Education, 6,* 140-154. doi:10.1187/cbe.06-11-0203

R Development Core Team. (2009). R: A language and environment for statistical computing. *R Foundation for Statistical Computing.* Vienna, Austria.

Segal, J., Paré, A., Brent, D., & Vipond, D. (1998). The researcher as missionary: Problems with rhetoric and reform in the disciplines. *College Composition and Communication, 50*(1), 71-90. Retrieved from http://www.jstor.org/stable/358354

Shaver, L. (2007). Eliminating the shell game: Using writing-assignment names to integrate disciplinary learning.

Journal of Business and Technical Communication, 21, 74-90. doi:10.1177/1050651906293532

Soto, J. G., Anand, S., & McGee, E. (2004). Plagiarism avoidance: An empirical study examining teaching strategies. *Journal of College Science Teaching, 33*(7), 42-48. Retrieved from http://eric.ed.gov/?id=EJ752495

Stevens, D. D., & Levi, A. J. (2005). *Introduction to rubrics: An assessment tool to save grading time, convey effective feedback and promote student learning.* Sterling, VA: Stylus Publishing.

Taylor, K. L., & Sobota, S. J. (1998). Writing in biology: An integration of disciplines. *The American Biology Teacher, 60,* 350-353. doi:10.2307/4450493

TePaske, E. R. (1982). Writing in biology: One way to improve analytical thinking. *The American Biology Teacher, 44,* 98-99. doi:10.2307/4447417

Tessier, J. (2006). Writing assignments in a nonmajor introductory ecology class. *Journal of College Science Teaching, 35*(4), 25-29. Retrieved from http://www.nsta.org

Wilkinson, A. M. (1985). A freshman writing course in parallel with a science course. *College Composition and Communication, 36,* 160-165. doi:10.2307/357436

Wingate, U. (2010). The impact of formative feedback on the development of academic writing. *Assessment & Evaluation in Higher Education, 35,* 519–533. doi:10.1080/02602930903512909

Winterman, B., & Malacinski, G. M. (2015). Teaching evidence-based innovation (EBI) as a trans-disciplinary professional skill in an undergraduate biology writing workshop. *International Journal of Arts & Sciences, 8,* 423-439. Retrieved from http://www.universitypublications.net/ijas/0802/html/S5R157.xml

Yahnke, C. J., Dewey, T., & Myers, P. (2013). Animal diversity as a teaching and learning tool to improve research & writing skills in college biology courses. *The American biology teacher, 75,* 494-498. doi:10.1525/abt.2013.75.7.9

Appendix A: Master Table of Assignments and Assignment Features, by Year

	Year 1	Year 2	Year 3	Year 4	Total
Total courses	3	14	25	17	59
Courses with writing	3 (100%)	9 (64%)	19 (76%)	16 (94%)	47 (80%)
Total assignments	8	77	63	47	195
Writing assignments per course (mean ± SD)	2.67 ± 2.08	2.14 ± 2.309	2.52 ± 2.62	2.67 ± 1.86	2.51 ± 2.28
Academic target audience (TA/Instructor)	8	74	63	46	191
Other target audience (e.g. General Public)	0	3	0	1	4
References required	4 (50%)	8 (10%)	17 (27%)	13 (28%)	42 (22%)
Nested assignments	5 (62%)	60 (78%)	33 (52%)	25 (53%)	123 (63%)
Length specified	5 (63%)	18 (23%)	22 (35%)	22 (47%)	67 (34%)
Percent mark value specified	8 (100%)	64 (83%)	61 (97%)	47 (100%)	180 (92%)
Time to complete specified	5 (63%)	60 (78%)	45 (71%)	33 (70%)	143 (73%)
Suggested resources	7 (88%)	7 (9%)	27 (43%)	31 (66%)	72 (37%)
Topic choice	1 (13%)	10 (13%)	14 (22%)	13 (28%)	38 (19%)
Style manual	4 (50%)	2 (3%)	14 (22%)	8 (17%)	28 (14%)
Rubric/scoring guide	3 (38%)	6 (8%)	11 (17%)	2 (4%)	22 (11%)
Group work (optional or required)	0 (0%)	5 (6%)	10 (16%)	1 (2%)	16 (8%)
Example	2 (38%)	1 (8%)	5 (17%)	6 (4%)	14 (7%)
Formative feedback	2 (25%)	3 (4%)	1 (2%)	7 (15%)	13 (7%)

Appendix B: Master Table of Assignments and Assignment Features, by Course Type

Assignment Feature	Course type							Total
	Lecture	Lecture + Lab	Lecture+ TA Tutorial	Seminar	Field	Research	Breadth	
Total courses	11	22	4	4	3	12	3	59
Courses with writing	8 (73%)	15 (68%)	3 (75%)	4 (100%)	3 (100%)	12 (100%)	2 (67%)	47 (80%)
Total assignments	26	59	4	13	4	85	4	95

Writing assignments per course (mean ± SD)	2.09 ± 1.97	2.82 ± 2.99	1.00 ± 0.82	3.5 ± 2.65	1.33 ± 0.58	3.08 ± 1.23	1.33 ± 1.53	2.51 ± 2.28
Academic target audience (TA/ Instructor/ Peers)	25 (96%)	59 (100%)	4 (100%)	13 (100%)	4 (100%)	84 (99%)	2 (50%)	191 (98%)
Other target audience (General Public, General Audience, Other)	1 (4%)	0	0	0	0	1 (1%)	2 (50%)	4 (2%)
References required	7 (27%)	19 (32%)	2 (50%)	3 (23%)	1 (25%)	9 (11%)	1 (25%)	42 (22%)
Nested assignments	9 (35%)	23 (40%)	0 (0%)	7 (54%)	0 (0%)	82 (96%)	2 (50%)	23 (63%)
Length specified	9 (35%)	25 (42%)	3 (75%)	7 (54%)	0 (0%)	23 (27%)	0 (0%)	7 (34%)
Percent mark value specified	24 (92%)	59 (100%)	4 (100%)	13 (100%)	4 (100%)	72 (85%)	4 (100%)	80 (92%)
Time to complete specified	22 (%)	51 (%)	3 (%)	12 (%)	2 (%)	49 (%)	4 (100%)	43 (73%)
Suggested resources	16 (62%)	31 (53%)	3 (75%)	11 (85%)	2 (50%)	9 (11%)	0	2 (37%)
Topic choice	4 (15%)	6 (10%)	2 (50%)	0	3 (75%)	20 (24%)	3 (75%)	8 (19%)
Style manual	6 (23%)	15 (25%)	0	2 (15%)	1 (25%)	4 (5%)	0	8 (14%)
Rubric	1 (4%)	16 (27%)	2 (50%)	0	0	2 (2%)	1 (25%)	2 (11%)
Group work (optional or required)	1 (4%)	12 (20%)	0	0	0	1 (1%)	2 (50%)	6 (8%)
Example	0	9 (15%)	0	4 (31%)	1 (25%)	0	0	4 (7%)
Formative feedback	0	2 (3%)	1 (25%)	1 (8%)	0	9 (11%)	0	13 (7%)

Chapter 5

Helping Engineering Students to Communicate Effectively: How One University Applied What It Learned from an Environmental Scan

Judi Jewinski and Andrew Trivett
University of Waterloo

Introduction

In October 2012, the final report of the Task Force on Support for English Language Competency Development at the University of Waterloo called for a major overhaul of practices for assessing and enhancing writing skills at the University of Waterloo. Around the same time, a SSHRC-funded Canada-wide research project (Writing Assignments Across the Undergraduate Curriculum) provided the framework for an extensive environmental scan of assignments across Waterloo's six faculties and a national comparison. Results from the survey of Waterloo engineering courses paralleled those of other institutions: while there was a surprising amount of writing required, there was little formal instruction in writing and even fewer assignments that required revision as part of the writing task. Moreover, initial assessments of how writing and writing instruction might be viewed by students suggested that considerable work would be needed to integrate oral and written communication skills into the program. One part of the problem was the lack of attention to teaching writing skills; the other part was the readiness of students to deal with such a requirement.

Teaching writing is a task that most engineering educators agree is important, and one that is mandated in engineering accreditation policy (Canadian Engineering Accreditation Board, 2008), but one that engineers feel inadequately prepared for. The protagonist in Terry Fallis' novel, *The Best Laid Plans*, expressed it well:

> I'm only teaching one class this term – first-year English for Engineers. It's a little like force-feeding ballroom dancing to Sumo wrestlers. They don't understand it. They're not very good at it. They don't like it. And it's not pretty.

Waterloo's Task Force on Support for English Competency recommended developing pilot studies to identify best practices, including scaffolded assignments with regular formative feedback and peer review. The new approach needed to integrate skills and attitudes, it needed to blend aptitudes and expectations, and it needed to offer students the opportunity to be involved and engaged (individually and in groups) so that they could recognize the importance and value of honing their communication skills in activities relevant to students in engineering. As Table 1 shows, the data collected from the Environmental Survey of Mechanical Engineering at Waterloo confirmed the curricular emphasis on several genres of writing. It also revealed a dependence on lab report writing in the early years: writing that received no feedback that might inform later assignments. While apprenticeship genres like lab reports contribute to what Carter et al. (2007) call "socialization of undergraduates into disciplinary communities" (p. 295), the seeming lack of attention to rubrics and formative feedback was a missed opportunity.

Table 1

Types of writing assignments (Environmental Survey of Mechanical Engineering Students)

Syllabus defined classification	Percentage (total of 77 over 16 months)
Report	13
Lab report	45.4
Design Report	1.3
Proposal	3.9
Paper	9.1
Essay	1.3
Presentation	2.6
Other	23.4
Total	100

This chapter presents an approach to teaching communication skills in Mechanical Engineering at Waterloo, which was developed, modified, and refined from 2014 to 2016. It has largely been informed by departmental response to environmental scan results from within the Faculty and in engineering schools across Canada, as well as curricular conversations with the University's Centre for Teaching Excellence. The survey of writing in Mechanical Engineering showed that, while students were required to write more than 75 assignments throughout the program, little instruction in strategies for writing and revising effectively was provided. Another discovery was that students had no opportunity to interact, in writing, with their peers. The aim of the 2014-2015 pilot was to correct both perceived weaknesses in a context that students would accept as authentic.

For those unfamiliar with the structure of Waterloo Engineering, it helps to know that the purpose of the first year course, *ME100: Introduction to Mechanical Engineering,* is to initiate students to performing writing tasks in the engineering profession and to communicating in both graphics and writing. Before 2014, the course was heavily weighted to graphics rather than communications practice. Students would deliver a brief technical talk once in the semester and write two technical memos graded by the teaching team, but the level of class/peer interaction was minimal. While the content had evolved over several years to address a variety of worthwhile topics, no teamwork skills were taught, and there was no opportunity for revision which might have helped students improve their communication skills.

A series of focus groups within the department in the Winter 2014 term revealed persistent issues within the program that could be addressed in the first year course. Several key objectives came out of the meetings. The highest priorities were to improve three areas:

- the employability of students
- their understanding and modelling of professionalism
- the collegiality of the cohort (building a strong class community)

The question was how to revise the existing course to deliver on these outcomes while addressing the need for formative feedback on activities emphasizing communication.

ME100 is divided into two components that run in parallel and are taught separately by two instructors. On the one hand, there is "Engineering Graphics and Design" (EGaD), which consists of 10 weekly workshops on sketching, mechanical drawing, and Computer-Aided Design. The EGaD portion of *ME100* is delivered to other engineering programs besides Mechanical Engineering, and its format cannot be modified. The other component "Design Communication and Professionalism" (DCaP) is delivered in three weekly one-hour lectures, with a weekly tutorial and a weekly two-hour active lab. Because it is unique to Mechanical Engineering, it was possible to redevelop DCaP to meet the desired outcomes. The underlying philosophy of the revision would follow an approach

Zinsser (1988) describes as "writing to learn" rather than "learning to write."

Assignments were developed in a way that might be accepted, or at least tolerated, by first year Mechanical Engineering students. The following sections explain each of the above desired outcomes and demonstrate how they relate to the redesign of *ME100* into a core course for communications in engineering.

Writing to Improve Employability

When asked "Why Waterloo Engineering?" students predominantly reply "co-op." To graduate from Waterloo, every engineering student completes mandatory work terms, needing at least four successful placements over as many as six co-op terms. Employment income helps them pay tuition. Co-op is so integrated with Waterloo Engineering that it fully informs student perception, course progression, and formal accreditation of the program. The program is highly regarded for producing graduates who enter the workforce with significant and relevant professional experience. This essential career experience is intended to motivate them in their academics.

Waterloo's Mechanical Engineering program receives around seven applications for each seat in the first year class. The highly competitive applicants are proficient communicators with exceptional high school grades. Since employment is an essential expectation, applications are vetted for not just academic excellence, but also employment potential. Each applicant receives an "employability score," an assessment of pre-admission work experience and extracurricular activities that students report in their own writing on an Admission Information Form (AIF). Students may be ranked higher or lower according to the effectiveness of their communication skills and their potential employability as projected from the AIF.

The employability of students is critical to the success of a co-op program. Acceptance into the program is merely a first step, especially in relation to assessment of communication skills. Admitted students may have very high academic grades but still be ineffectual writers or presenters. While this may not hinder their academic success, it does decrease their likelihood of securing co-op employment. Waterloo's Mechanical Engineering program brings in high-performing candidates from all over the world. Most students have written a résumé before, and many think that the résumé they created in high school is good enough: "I've done this already..." is a common response. This self-assurance means that many first year students are unprepared for the increase in competition and the expectations of real co-op employers. Waterloo's Centre for Career Action (2016) reports that students with weaker résumés and weaker communication skills tend to suffer lower rates of employment. It is such a crucial issue that the Centre for Co-operative Education and Career Action (CECA) has created lectures to help students see that communication skills are essential to successful co-op placements. The series is intended to guide students in creating successful résumés and cover letters as well as managing their first interviews. Delivered by CECA staff, sessions are embedded within all first year engineering classes equivalent to *ME100* at Waterloo.

The key to success for students, as well as the program itself, is for each student to embark upon an outstanding sequence of co-op internships. The licensing body for engineering programs, the Canadian Engineering Accreditation Board (CEAB), has created, based upon research from other countries, a list of twelve "Graduate Attributes" (2008), which identify skills required by employers of engineers. Because co-op employment is a core component of Waterloo Engineering, it is key to the development of the CEAB attributes relating to communication, professionalism, and the practice of engineering.

Thus, both the acquisition of the skills and the accreditation expectation of how those skills are acquired depend upon the students' co-op experiences. The first co-op position is often the most difficult for students to find, and they need considerable help to have the best chance to get it. The ability to communicate complex technical and professional information to a broad audience is a fundamental skill that is repeatedly requested—and is crucial to an engineer's success in finding excellent job opportunities. Résumés need to showcase the individual. Revamping of the "old reliable" high school résumé is a first step on the road to new standards. Therefore, a new peer-review process for resumes was introduced to augment the CECA lectures in *ME100* and to help students learn about their colleagues, both as collaborators on teams and as competitors for jobs. *ME100* incorporates a practical approach to enhance communication skills by having students read, discuss, evaluate, revise, and re-read the résumés of their classmates. The collegial interactivity of the class has measurably improved their skills and, therefore, potentially, their employability. Comparing their résumés with their peers' made many students realize that their original résumés were inadequate. One of the successful outcomes of the activity has been an increased number of students seeking help with their résumés from the CECA counsellors.

Writing to Model Professionalism in the Workplace

The incoming engineering students have impressive scores in high school writing, though they typically are not enthusiastic writers, especially when it comes to the detailed, exacting type of professional writing required by engineering. Engineers rarely write free flowing personal or creative compositions; rather they write to and for their supervisors and co-workers." It's an exacting form, and one that is adapted to the discipline.

There is a genuine engineering culture that students are expected to reflect in their writing. Engineers must be clear, accurate, and specific in a design proposal; they must explain, and often justify, the evidence to the non-professionals seeking their expertise. Engineering reports and proposals must make recommendations according to a rigorous and well-researched set of arguments. Technical communication is typically factual, impersonal, and objective. Graphics are integrated with explanatory text, and the balance between visual illustration and written exposition is often the mark of a successful engineering document. The expectations can be daunting to incoming students. The writing needs to be particularly clear and impartial when an engineer must criticize (or even wholly reject) prior analyses, alternatives, or past reports. Effective criticism is central to the role of writing in engineering. The *ME100* course was redesigned around the fundamental concept that writing criticism is a skill that must be taught, then practised by designers.

To enhance their chance of success in the workplace (and in co-op placement), students need practice writing in a way that suits their engineering work. They need to recognize features unique to engineering writing, one of which is the utter absence of the personal focus. The engineering code of conduct bars unprofessional criticism or personal assessments. Criticism is to be confined to technical decisions, without "making it personal." Article 77 of the Engineering Act for the Province of Ontario, the professional code of conduct, states the engineer's responsibility for "extending the public knowledge thereof and discouraging untrue, unfair, or exaggerated statements with respect to professional engineering." This obligation is complicated by the provision later in the same code to "co-operate in working with other professionals engaged on a project" and, more specifically, to "not maliciously injure the reputation or business of another practitioner." This is a subtle, yet vital distinction. However complex these provisions are, the engineers' professional code makes it essential to teach students the difference between inappropriate personal criticisms of colleagues and necessary professional criticism of engineering decisions based upon science and experience.

Trying to teach such concepts in a lecture would have met with significant resistance from the students. How does an instructor effectively get students who are interested in design, science, and technology to attend to writing style, sentence structure, and clarity? The *ME100* solution was to focus on the engineering tasks which engaged the students while helping them realize that they must attend to their writing in order to be understood by their colleagues.

To that end, the pilot project for teaching engineering writing in *ME100* assigned each student to a studio team of colleagues with whom they were assigned a realistic team design project. Without exception, the process of developing solutions as a team leads students to disagree about the best methods or proposals; then, they begin to appreciate the need to negotiate ideas based upon facts, while not destroying personal relationships and making further teamwork impossible. The team projects help students learn to present engineering proposals clearly and objectively—in writing— while learning to "criticize" the proposals forwarded by fellow team members. Students must also learn to put disputes behind them while they move forward as a team. The course structure described in the following section takes advantage of this difficult balance, extending it within each tutorial section of approximately 30 students and, beyond, to the cohort of 120. Thus, class community is built upon mutual criticism in a class studio setting, and everyone learns to structure criticism fundamentally in their writing while being careful to maintain collegial interpersonal relationships.

Writing to Develop Class Community

First year students generally come to university having excelled in a high school environment in classes of 25 to 35 students. At Waterloo, Engineering is fundamentally a cohort-based system where, on average, each student is assigned to a class of 70-120 students, which is more than twice the size of a typical high school class. In Mechanical Engineering, the 2014-2016 cohort sizes were 100-120 students. While there are always small adjustments, the number of students in the first year cohort remains consistent at the University of Waterloo: upwards of 97% of the students in a cohort remain to the end of first year. A sense of group unity usually develops, though sometimes personality conflicts result, leading to dysfunctional social interactions and poor learning.

Merely assigning students to a cohort and letting culture develop on its own can prove to be inadequate. Observations of Waterloo Mechanical Engineering students in class, augmented by focus group interviews with each class cohort in Winter 2014, revealed some surprises. Repeatedly, upper-year students reported knowing fewer than five to ten of their classmates. Indeed, some students, at the end of four years in their cohort, had barely met other students at all. In-class observation revealed that their only opportunity for interaction was sitting in lectures, where they might meet the few students sitting near them. Most lectures were held in the same room, with professors changing each hour, so students never even changed seats as the class instructor changed. There was little teamwork in most courses, and the teams were always the same three or four students who had known each other from the first year.

Since 2014, the pilot project has set out to redeploy the cohort structure by creating smaller sections. In *ME100*, each of the two cohort classes now comprises four tutorial sections. Thus, we have simply divided the incoming class of 240 into eight small sections of 30, each of which meets together during the weekly active class sessions in a one-hour tutorial and a two-hour active lab. Tutorial sections are given unique names and are assigned their own undergrad TA, who is employed full-time for the full semester. The TA is introduced as the students' main point of contact, and students develop a strong bond with this senior student. In this new social structure, students have overwhelmingly commended their TAs, confirmed by the number of students who have recommended their TA for teaching awards compared to students from other engineering programs each year.

The tutorial sections each involved the same 30 students for three hours a week in dynamic, active classes led by student TAs. Based on their activities in class, writing was assigned for students to submit online in a forum that all thirty—but only those thirty—could see. By exchanging ideas and experiences in writing with their colleagues, every student communicated regularly while getting to know the others and building a tutorial culture guided by the positive example of a senior TA. In writing, as well as in the active tutorials and lab activities, ideas were exchanged, evaluated, criticized, revised, and finally approved by the group, a process that called for open communication by all. In the process, students were practising the skill of communicating as engineers with colleagues who were their equals. Students got to know each other as engineers, and they received coaching from the instructional team through tutorial activities and feedback on their writing. The class community was built around the individual writing and the necessity to read each other's writing for each activity.

Class Activities

Given the broad goals governing the redevelopment of *ME100*, we describe here some of the unique activities created to achieve the desired outcomes. The *ME100* course carries the weight of 1.5 standard courses, both in terms of contact hours and as a contributor to the student's academic term average. Figure 1 shows the major activities in the DCaP (Design and Professional Communication) portion of the course and their timing. Here is where all the writing is done.

Weekly writing activities. Four major DCaP activities for students are assigned over the 12-week term: (1) an introductory team-forming project, (2) a design project for students to build a prototype, (3) a second project to propose a design solution for a problem, and finally (4) a "design-it-yourself" project for independent development. The course embeds weekly hands-on tasks to provide students with concrete graphics and design skills. Students are not explicitly told that these are supporting skills; rather, they are placed in team discussion situations where the experiences from both the EGaD (Engineering Graphics and Design) classes as well as the team-oriented hands-on activities naturally become topics of conversation and debate.

	Design Communication and Professionalism (60%)				Engineering Graphics and Design (40%)
	Major Topic	Solowriting	Team Discussion	Hands-On Tasks	Major Topic
Week 1	Resumes and team-forming	Create resume draft	Sharing draft resumes	Coffee-maker discussion	Introduction to Graphics, Freehand and Instrument Drawings, Lateral Thinking
Week 2		Resume final submission	Skills discussion	In-class interviews	Orthographic Projection, Fasteners, Introduction to AutoCAD
Week 3	Project 1: Assistive Technology RC Car	Describe individual skills and interests for team	Team goals discussion, develop Team Charter	Dissect RC Cars	Common AutoCAD Commands/Tricks
Week 4		Initial design Concepts	Debate alternative design concepts	Laser-cut and build prototype	Isometric Views, Chamfers & Fillets, more AutoCAD Commands
Week 5		Detailed design concepts	Discussion of designs and fabrication	Test prototype	Accurate Proportioning in freehands, Technical Drawing in AutoCAD, Dimensioning
Week 6	Study Break	Reflection, what to do differently next time	Reflection on team work and design		Study Break
Week 7	Midterm Exams: All first-year classes cancelled for the week				
Week 8	Project 2: Open Innovation Challenge	Design Concepts	Deciding which problem to solve	Hardware Café	Drawing Helices, Section Views, Using Calipers, Layers & Blocks in AutoCAD
Week 9		Design Report section(s)	Report writing collaboration	Hardware Café	Introduction to Solid modeling CAD using SolidWorks
Week 10	Project 3: Design Yourself	Career options and drafting final report	Critical Design self-evaluation	Engine Dissection	Thinking Artistically, more SolidWorks
Week 11		Draft Report	Reflection on life goals	Engine Dissection	Assemblies and Orthographic Drawings in SolidWorks
Week 12		Report	Formal conference presentation	Conference	Geometric Dimensioning and Tolerancing

Figure 1. A summary of the major content and timing for the activities throughout *ME100*.

As follow-up surveys indicate, of the activities required to complete the central task each week, the least enjoyable for the students is the writing. However, because their attention is kept on the experiential learning tasks in both the EGaD and hands-on activities, they are encouraged to accept that writing is simply a necessary and inevitable part of an engineering career. As Figure 1 shows, they post weekly "solo" pieces to an online discussion forum, after which they are required to discuss, comment on, and revise each others' work through feedback and comments in a "team discussion" which takes place online in a threaded discussion forum. In this way, the students produce from 14,000 to 19,000 individual posts over a semester (an average of 70-77 individual posts per student, the majority of which are longer than one paragraph, many incorporating graphics). The students may not be enthusiastic about the writing component, but their dedication to it shows that they have grasped its importance for conveying ideas to teammates.

Rubrics are a key feature of the writing activities of *ME100* in that they are visible and open to the student colleagues and the instructional team. Writing is never presented as an interaction between student and professor, something which the environmental scan had identified as typical of almost all (98.7%) mechanical engineering writing assignments in 2013. The writing assignments of the new *ME100* have been designed to foster and encourage interaction between students, encouraging development of professional conduct and responsibility for their actions.

Draft Resume	100%	67%	33%	0%
	complete, helpful and thorough first draft of a resume having sections on educational background, work history, interests and skills	good basic draft having helpful sections but missing or weak in one of the key sections of a typical resume	rough draft that generally helpful but is missing or incomplete in more than one major component	extremely weak, unhelpful, or missing

Discussion Comments	100%	67%	33%	0%
Helpful	Very helpful to the recipient by giving useful criticism of the draft and sufficiently detailed comments so that a better product can be made based upon the advice	Somewhat helpful and encouraging, offering not just criticism, but ways to improve	Present, but not very helpful, such as "looks great," or "great job"	Not helpful, or not encouraging, "sucks"
Clear	Writing is clear, specific examples are given of things that can be improved in the text, sentences all make sense, no spelling errors or grammar problems.	Feedback is good, but not written completely correctly, may contain errors.	Some good ideas, but written in a way that is not directing the author to specific issues, or advice that is not possible to act upon.	No significant feedback comments
Respectful and honest	Comments show that you have read and thought carefully about the author's draft, and you have presented criticism in a way that is respectful and clear without being harsh or hurtful.	You have given encouraging helpful comments but a bit brusque or harsh.	You have offered comments that are either not directed to clearly help the author, or have been too shy about giving the honest truth.	No comments, or comments that are harsh, or discouraging, or overly smiley and useless to the author
Detail and volume	Thoughtful comments on many more than 5 or other resumes, engaged in discussion with our students in the forum on the subject writing.	Gave thoughtful comments on at least 5 other resumes	Gave comments on fewer than 5 other resumes	No comments

Figure 2. Grading rubric for resume drafting activity with a focus on peer-comments and professionalism in an online discussion forum.

As Figure 2 indicates, the grading criteria for the weekly postings represent the essentials of professionalism as it pertains to working with colleagues. These are: helpful, clear, respectful, and honest. "Helpful" is key to developing a collaborative reputation with colleagues, one essential to building a solid professional attitude.

"Clear" is crucial in ensuring that others can understand what the engineer has written (clarity is essential for a high-performing engineer). "Respectful and honest" relate to the professional code of conduct: telling the truth protects society from engineering mistakes, though the truth must be presented in a fashion that avoids aggressiveness, enmity, or emotion.

As a human quality, "sincerity" is hard to measure and, thus, difficult to grade. Too much rides upon the intent of the writer rather than on an objective assessment of the writing. The rubric equates this term with "helpful." While not a synonym, it is more appropriate for evaluating writing which responds to another student's writing. Phrases like "useful criticism" or "sufficiently helpful" appear in the rubric to assess whether the student has made a "sincere" (i.e. helpful) effort to assist. In course evaluations, students often remarked that responses seemed sugar-coated and insincere. "Helpful" in the rubric emphasizes the need for more precision.

"Respectful and honest" are easier to evaluate when viewing student comments in context, given that members of a team who disagree about a design detail may have strong opinions. Some may interpret the requirement to be "respectful" as calling for euphemisms and evasive responses. Pairing it with "seen as helpful," however, emphasizes that the graders expect authors to say what they actually believe—in addition to what is appropriate—and not just what the reader wants to see. Students learn to recognize the demands of facing a double audience: the reader and the evaluator. In this way, they are forced to balance genuine criticism and tact when dealing with close colleagues as well as those in a position of power.

The criteria and their definitions are introduced early in the semester, with students adopting them as guiding principles in the ongoing discussion forums with their colleagues. Then, halfway through the term, students attend a traditional lecture introducing the concept of professionalism along with the engineering code of ethics, all of which are illustrated in the tutorials by current discipline cases from the bulletin of the Professional Engineers of Ontario. Students argue these cases and then post in their weekly discussion logs a summary of how the cases were handled. Thus, students are reminded that many of the detailed aspects of the

Engineering Act and the Code of Ethics can be traced to the same simple guiding principles they apply in the weekly writing.

Résumé and skills-development via design team selections. Waterloo's Centre for Co-operative Education and Career Action requires students to attend several lectures and take a short course on the co-op process in the first three weeks of their first semester, culminating in their submission of a résumé that is graded. That grade has always formed part of their course grade for *ME100* as well. To animate the co-op experience and introduce students to their new classmates, the pilot *ME100* course linked the process of revising the résumé with the activity of forming class teams. The goal of the process is to have students reflect upon their responses to someone else's résumé.

Students post a first draft of their résumé in a discussion forum that can be seen by approximately 30 of their classmates, who have all been assigned to the same tutorial section for the term. Once they have posted their draft résumés, they are asked to review each other's on line and post suggestions. The peer assessment is augmented by an in-class activity, which pairs students to revise the résumé with and for each other. By the end of the first week of classes, students will have read, reviewed, and critiqued résumés of up to 30 students in their section. They will also have revised their own résumé and re-posted it on the tutorial discussion forum.

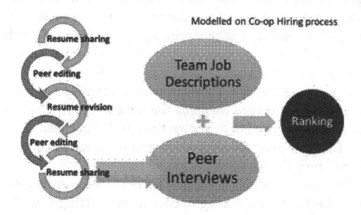

Figure 3. An illustration of the peer-review and revision model for résumé creation and team-forming in *ME100*.

Figure 3 presents a graphic depiction of this first résumé activity. Students are asked to give feedback to their classmates a second time in an online discussion forum open to all students in each tutorial section. The comments are to help peers revise and submit an improved résumé. At the end of the second round of comments, students meet in a 2-hour lab session for a series of 4-minute interviews of each other for a place on "My Design Team." The set of job descriptions given each student is shown in Appendix A, and students provide a ranked assessment of their classmates for each job based upon the résumé and the brief interview. After all the students submit their rankings, the teaching team assigns individuals to teams on basis of the best matches. The approach is modelled upon the Waterloo method for matching students to co-op employers, where both employee and employer must rank the other highly for a match to occur.

In each of the major design activities throughout the semester, students are expected to work with the same team. Over three years of *ME100*, there have been a total of 139 teams. Of all those teams (which are expected to last all term), only four teams (<3%) have had to be restructured by re-assigning particular members. Other teams have required intervention in the form of meeting with the TA and professor to discuss interpersonal problems. The issues, for practical purposes, were resolved.

Design projects and discussion forums. Students entering a Mechanical Engineering program discover the profession as one in which "design" is central. It is generally agreed in engineering that the "design cycle" is one that continually repeats, regardless of what is being designed (Dym & Little, 2008). Evidence is found everywhere in technology. If design were not fundamentally a continuous cycle of improvement, the latest Ford would be the same as the first Model T on the road. Students need to be shown the parallel between design, something they are typically engaged in and passionate about, and writing, something they are often resistant to.

Typically, junior writers, including first year engineering students, write high school assignments in one sitting, and then submit them as "complete." Even if they were to have taken an English course which emphasised revision, the practice would not translate from their narrow view of "English" to their equally narrow and separate view of "engineering." Thus, we introduced the professional practice of engineering to them with writing as a key skill done in small, recurring iterations akin to the accepted, iterative notion of engineering design (Dym and Little, 2008).

In *ME100*, we assign four core design tasks relevant to Mechanical Engineering:

- a team charter for their design team
- design and prototyping of a model "assistive technology" device
- solution to an external design challenge
- a plan for "my career"

These tasks include major writing assignments formulated and documented from their weekly written discussion forum postings.

In addition to these four major written assignments submitted as a single document by each team of 4-6 students, a number of separate hands-on activities prompt many of the ideas for the writing. Rather than require students to do a literature search and write papers, a task that most first year engineering students are reluctant to take seriously, Bean (2011) recommends that the assignments be structured to allow students to use hands-on activities. Accordingly, students dissect various pieces—a simple coffee maker, a piece of consumer hardware, a small radio-controlled car, and a single-cylinder engine—and record their components. Later in the term they build a prototype carrier for the radio-controlled car as well as a prototype proof-of-concept model for an open-innovation challenge. The hands-on activities, which we refer to as the "hardware café," are popular with students, so it is easy to have them engage fully with the tasks.

The instructions that students receive for one of the above "hardware café" activities can be seen in Appendix B. The instructions are a step-by-step explanation that helps students carry out the activity, as well as manage the reporting afterwards. The instructions confirm that hands-on or applied activities require sharing of ideas in a team environment before, during, and after the activity. In this case, the hands-on activity is offered as "research" in support of solving real engineering challenges and is the subject of several written posts in the online forum. For all of the activities, reflections and opinions are shared with the other members of each design team within a tutorial section. The activities themselves are not graded, but the reporting is. The weekly writing tasks as assessed following a rubric similar to that used in the earlier résumé critique activity (see Figure 2).

There is a sample of student discussion in the forum in Appendix C. This discussion took place after the team had begun to consider the solutions they might develop for a comprehensive design-build-test activity which would take three weeks to complete. The discussion occurred midway through the design process, after the students had spent a week understanding the challenge and had steadily begun to assess solutions. Without much coaching, they developed a factual and pragmatic writing style. One student in a team (Student A in the example) typically takes the lead in starting a team conversation after everyone has met or worked together once. The most engaged students on a team post ideas frequently and in increasing detail as the work evolves. In Figure 6, the grammar and sentence structure, while not flawless, are generally clear enough to be understood. For two of the students, English was not the first language, yet they communicated key design ideas successfully enough to make sense to other team members and be integrated into follow-up discussions.

The example also reveals that the students understood that they could not simply give negative criticism or attempt to make it palatable with a few vague positives. Student B criticizes Student A's ideas in a way that is constructive, essentially starting with accurate positive encouragement and then developing clear and practical suggestions.

ME100 lectures focus on how to be "helpful" to a design team. The comment by Student C represents a typically unhelpful comment, one which provides insufficient detail for others to understand the message. Although Student C's suggestion was vague and unclear, Student B picked up on the key concept of "safety" from both Student A and Student C, contributing useful ideas without specifically calling out the teammate for a confusing comment. The conversation continued throughout the week, and the team began to add technical sketches as well as timing and tasks. By the end, the team had created a very positive and professional work environment, where they all felt they had contributed.

In the forum, the peers naturally gave feedback to Student C in two forms: (1) the other members of the team did not understand what Student C was trying to communicate. Student B carried on with the next comment to respond to Student A's comment about safety without specifically pointing to difficulty in understanding the comment by Student C, and perhaps embarrassing Student C. The next time the team met in person during a tutorial, Student C explained what was meant, appreciating that the others had not picked up on the meaning of the original comment. If Student C wanted to contribute significantly to the design, then it was clear that future comments needed to be better written. The team whose comments appear in Figure 6 was typical of the class, and all members contributed to their designs. Student C learned to submit more effective comments to the forum over the next several weeks. (2) Teaching Assistants read and graded the posts on a weekly basis, giving feedback (following the rubric in Figure 2) on the sum of all input by each student. Student C received feedback from the teaching staff when comments were unclear and was given suggestions on what to do to improve, including encouragement to seek help from the university's writing centre.

Reporting of hands-on and design ideas in an online discussion served as an active team log for individual contributions. Teaching Assistants were able to keep an eye on the writing and identify students who were not participating. They would contact students who were seen as inactive in the discussions and remind them that they were falling behind. In most cases, the result was a series of posts and improved participation for the rest of the semester. Thus, for the majority, the design and team discussion forum was a peer-moderated activity in which students learned the value of clear and precise technical communication—and practised it regularly.

Throughout the ME100 course, and particularly during the hands-on activities, students are reminded that "engineering" is not the same as working in the technical trades. Skill in hands-on tasks is helpful but not key to success. Rather, engineering is more about understanding the science, being familiar with the technology, and applying this knowledge to plan what and how to implement technological solutions. Practising engineers do not normally build a project; they usually—either orally or in writing—instruct others on how and what to do. Such a role demands excellent communication skills. The activities in *ME100* are delivered with this expectation in mind. In the Figure 6 example, the students coached themselves to offer useful, helpful, and encouraging communication. They developed their own positive style through primarily indirect, but carefully focused coaching from the instructor and teaching assistants. As the term evolved, the level of writing in this and other teams improved measurably.

Results

The process of résumé creation, followed by peer review and revision, has had a significant impact upon student hiring rates. Table 2 shows the comparison of the 2013 and 2014 Mechanical Engineering "4-stream" students (i.e. those who are going on their first work term after only one semester on campus). In Oct 2014, hiring rates rose significantly, from 12% of the class in 2013 (14 students) to 24% in 2014 (23 students), although the overall hiring rate for the class was unchanged by the end of the semester. As usual, more than 97% found co-op positions eventually as most of the hiring activity happens only a few weeks before the co-op work term starts. What is most significant to this study of enhanced communication skills is that while the same number of students in the two classes were interviewed during the main round (47), 42 of the students interviewed in 2014 were "ranked" by the employer, compared to only 34 in 2013. This difference is significant since an employer chooses to rank ONLY those applicants it would be willing to hire if its top candidate were not available.

Table 2

Outcomes from resume-building activities in First Year Mechanical Engineering (xFY ME) compared with faculty-wide averages

	2013		2014	
	FY ME	Other Engn	FY ME	Other Engn
# of applicants	112	2255	96	2513
Employed	12%	29%	24%	31%
Interviewed	42%	63%	49%	64%
Ranked	72%	80%	89%	82%

The results of the employer hiring statistics are presented in Table 2. The only different influencing factor between the cohorts in Fall 2013 and those in Fall 2014 was the delivery of the new ME100 model. The difference in outcomes for employer interviews, high ranking of candidates, and eventual hiring of the students in 2013 compared with those of 2014 rested on two factors: (1) the degree to which their vetted and revised résumés impressed employers, and (2) their increased communication skills in interviews. Comparators in other engineering disciplines within Waterloo Engineering showed no significant changes in these statistics from 2013 to 2014, and there was nothing to indicate that there was a sudden industry demand for first year mechanical engineering students.

Despite the statistical success of employer evaluation of students, the survey of student opinion carried out at the end of each semester, using a variety of question templates, was disappointing. In general, students hated the writing component of ME100. They thought that much of the writing, despite all efforts to encourage "respect, truth, and honesty," seemed insincere "fluff." The course evaluations that were carried out near the end of the course in each of 2014, 2015, and 2016 were generally very low overall, though the spread of the scores on most questions was wide. When surveyed about each of the specific activities in which all students of ME100 from 2014-2016 had participated, 122 students responded. Figure 4 shows the response to statements regarding each of the activities where each activity was presented with a positive or negative statement in a multiple-choice question. Students responded overwhelmingly positively for the usefulness and value of all of the hands-on activities, and of the design projects. Likewise, when asked in the same survey whether "design projects were ... important," respondents chose 4 or 5 on scale of 0-5 for the usefulness of design projects in first year. The scale was shown as 5 equating to "Yes, that was really valuable for me."

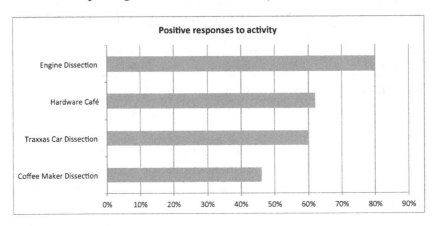

Figure 4. Positive responses to activity.

For the purpose of this study of writing skills and ME100, it must be reported that most of the free comments in the survey, as well as in the numeric course evaluations, were negative, even hostile, about the writing component. The more mature students acknowledged that the writing and communication instruction helped them in co-op jobs, but in comparison to the reaction to "hands-on activities," the student comments were unquestionably negative. Does this mean that we should stop requiring the first year students to write? Does this mean that we should continue with the practical activities while simplifying or reducing the volume of reporting done through writing? Clearly students would support that recommendation. However, our study of the advancement of communication through writing and résumé revision shows that employers showed an increased confidence in student skills (24 rather than 12 students received rankings).

A second intention behind the class structure in ME100 was to help encourage general communication skills by placing students in a cohort where they would discuss, debate, and criticize ideas and proposals professionally. In 2015, in two different third year mechanical engineering cohorts, students were asked to respond, by a show of hands, to the question of recognizing their peers: i.e. if they knew the names of more than five students in their class, more than ten, and more than 25. These students would have been in first year together in 2012, the year before the environmental scan that led to our overhaul of *ME100*. Most who were present could say that they knew the names of more than five, but very few knew the names of ten, and not a single student was willing to say that they knew the names of more than 25 students in the class. This after five semesters of attending all their classes together! By 2016, at the same time in the academic term, the first year class which had gone through the team-oriented discussions of *ME100* and had partially completed the follow-up second semester course *ME101* (also a team design course) was polled. This time, every member of the class knew the names of more than ten other students, and the majority were willing to say they knew the names of 25 or more. A substantial number of the class claimed to know the names of 50 or more of their classmates.

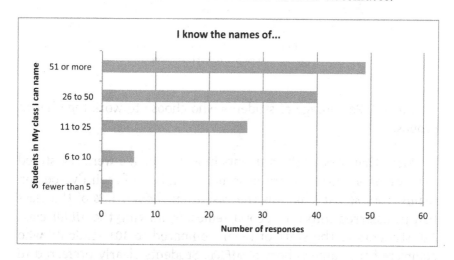

Figure 5. Number of classmates each student knows by name.

A survey of students from the classes in *ME100* from 2014 to 2016 showed that more than 73% of the students who responded claimed to know the names of more than 25 of their classmates. An impressive 40% of the respondents claimed to know the names of over 50 of their colleagues (see Figure 5). Compared to results in the informal senior classes, this number is remarkable.

The extensive teamwork in the *ME100* course seems to have a lasting effect on the collaboration and collegiality of students in the class. In the 2014 cohort, self-selected teams who completed a team-based design project course in their second semester were compared with team memberships in the first semester *ME100* course. Figure 6 shows the breakdown of students who were formed into a team which had members from their earlier teams.

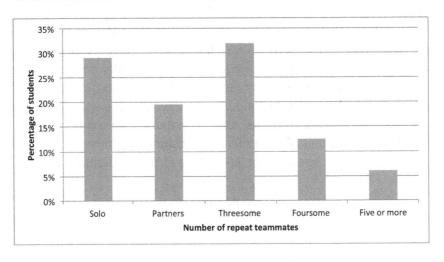

Figure 6. Percentage of students who choose to work together in groups.

More than 45% of the students in a class of 120 were registered in new teams containing three or more members of their five-person teams from *ME100*. This was the case even though 15% of the class had transferred into the second semester, making the *ME101* class 120 students at the start of term, compared to 101 students who completed the same cohort of *ME100*. Students clearly preferred to work with their previous teams.

Conclusion

The *ME100* project created an interactive communications skills program that has demonstrably helped students receive co-op placements. Employers have shown increased confidence in our students, and they ranked them at higher levels in 2015 than in former years. Students, however, individually unaware of the overall success of the program in the workplace, continue to bristle at increased writing and communication skills requirements in the classroom. They assume that a design "speaks for itself," when, in fact, it is mute until the engineering expert clarifies its multiple facets to the everyday person who—because of the lack of expertise—consults the engineer. Communication really is an essential skill in professional engineering.

Regrettably, increasing the workload of an already difficult engineering course like *ME100* will not be seen positively by students, no matter how beneficial the communications workload may be in the future. Perhaps blending communication skills instruction with *ME100* engineering is an awkward marriage—but regardless of how much the students disliked being required to write, they produced a substantial volume of quality writing. They did this in a professional manner which was tied both to the activities that were core "mechanical engineering" and in a forum that paralleled the requirements of their professional life to come.

The methods employed in *ME100*—writing, rewriting, résumé submission, evaluation and revision, web post commentaries, and evaluations—have shown immediate and practical results in terms of clear evidence of enhanced communications skills by the students involved. Only the historical problem of "Hey, like, I know this stuff..." has not been entirely overcome. The increased complexity of advanced engineering design demands advanced communication skills in our students, and if we are to do service to them, we will keep exploring and refining methods of integrating writing projects and hands-on designs for the engineering students of the University of Waterloo.

References

Ager, S., D'Alessio, S., Olson, A., Stubley, G., & Walker, B. (2012). *University of Waterloo task force on support for English language competency: Final report.* Retrieved from_https:// uwaterloo.ca/provost/sites/ca.provost/files/uploads/files/ EnglishLanguageCompetencyDevelopment_FinalReport_0.pdf

Bean, J. C. (2011). *Engaging ideas: The professor's guide to integrating writing, critical thinking, and active learning in the classroom* (2nd ed.). San Francisco, CA: Jossey-Bass.

Canadian Engineering Accreditation Board. (2008). *Accreditation criteria and procedures.* Engineers Canada.

Carter, M., Ferzli, M., & Wiebe, E. (2007). Writing to learn by learning to write in the disciplines. *Journal of Business and Technical Communication, 21*(3), 278-302.

Council of Writing Program Administrators. (2011). *Framework for success in postsecondary writing.* Retrieved from_http://wpacouncil.org/ framework

Dym, C., & Little, P. (2008). *Engineering design: A project based introduction* (4th ed.). Hoboken, New Jersey: John Wiley & Sons.

Engineers Canada. (2015). *Engineering labour market in Canada.* Engineers Canada.

Rhodes, T. (Ed.). (2010). *Assessing outcomes and improving achievement: Tips and tools for using rubrics.* Washington, DC: Association of American Colleges and Universities. Retrieved from_http://www.aacu.org/ value/rubrics/index_p.cfm?CFID=42165298&CFTOKEN=87036689

Slomp, D. L. (2012). Challenges in assessing the development of writing ability: Theories, constructs and methods. *Assessing Writing, 17*(2), 81–91. doi:10.1016/j.asw.2012.02.001

Trivett, A., & Champion, S. (2012). Using online open-innovation challenges to introduce design in first-year engineering courses. *ASEE Annual Conference.* San Antonio, TX.

Trivett, A., Lambert, S., & Baleshta, J. (2016). A workshop on criticism in engineering design. *Canadian Engineering Education Association Annual Conference.* Halifax, Nova Scotia, Canada.

Waterloo Centre for Career Action. (2016). *Self-marketing: Resume writing e-guide.* Waterloo, ON: University of Waterloo.

Zinsser, W. (1988). *Writing to learn.* Harper.

Appendix A: Job Descriptions for "My Design Team" Résumé Activity

ME100: DESIGN TEAM MEMBERS

Each team will have 5 roles with different personalities–a tracker, a communicator, a theorist, a builder, and a scout. As with any small startup enterprise, nobody can exclusively fill just one role, but it is best to find teammates where these positions are covered. Likewise, there can be two people occupying a role, so long as all roles are covered. Many of the duties required of members in a small team overlap, and the best teams work to everyone's natural strengths. Each team member is expected to contribute equally to every assignment, and to every area of work.

Tracker: A tracker is someone who finds the way through a forest. This person needs to be good at coordinating duties related to the project, and must be able to keep all team members fully engaged, and working towards a common goal. This person will be respectful, encouraging, personable, and able to demonstrate a number of ways to keep the team on track. This is the member to smooth out any personality conflicts, arguments, and keep everyone working on the same goal. They are the sort of person who can make you laugh and get things done, but doesn't waste your time.

- Self-motivated, and be capable of motivating others
- Flexible to opinions, and open to ideas
- Attention to detail in all areas of work
- Organized with good time management skills

Communicator: A communicator is comfortable sharing ideas with others verbally and in writing. This is the sort of person who listens to what others have to say, then is quickly able to distill that into a clear explanation or story. A communicator will be happy ensuring the team ideas are clear, and can provide support to other team members with their individual written, verbal, and graphical communications.

- Excellent communication skills, both verbal and written
- Confident, comfortable talking in front of a group
- Can write easily and efficiently as required
- Great Listener

Theorist: A theorist excels when analyzing a situation from a mathematical, or scientific perspective. They can easily relate real life situations to scientific principles. Data analysis is a breeze. They do not struggle with theories and they like to see them applied to real-world problems.

- Familiar with many tools, materials, and manufacturing techniques
- Interested in computer aided design (CAD) and sketching
- Experience with many mechanical and electrical components
- Good at explaining things to others

Scout: A scout loves to be out there on the horizon looking for new things. They don't specialize in any of the areas listed so far, but they have many of the characteristics listed above... but they naturally want to think about the ideas nobody else has brought up. They are always questioning, "why should we do it that way?" They'll argue their point, and make everything the team does stand up to scrutiny.

- A general understanding of all the areas listed above
- A fast learner, and can move quickly from one task to another
- Always sees the bigger picture of a project
- Great sense of humor, and a thick skin

Appendix B: Instructions for "Hardware Cafe" Activity

ME100: HARDWARE CAFE

Your design team has been given the task to come up with a solution to a real design challenge. Your solution ideas need to be based upon some solid foundation of knowledge. In a very real sense, you can't design a solution by "thinking outside the box" until you know what is inside the box. In ME100, you will explore the box by taking it apart...

Before the Activity:

1. Read the challenges before you come to your team's WATiMake appointment.
2. Develop a few simple concepts that you might consider for the challenge before coming to your appointment.
3. For each of your concepts, go through a "what is it like?" exercise... try to come up with as many common items that have similar components, or actions, or features to your concept
4. For each of your design concepts, come up with a "what is it not like" list of common items

During the activity

1. Present your list of "what is it like" to the Clinic staff
2. The staff will walk through the archive of stuff to help you choose items that have features similar to your design concepts, or that are related in some way to your ideas. You need to be open-minded in looking at items. In most cases, almost every item in the Hardware café relates to your design ideas, so be willing to explore.
3. Working in pairs, the team will select one item per pair to dissect.
4. Carefully examine the item on a workbench to assess how it was built, and what it does.
5. Collect the tools that you will need to dissect it. The clinic staff will help you find the right tools.
6. Take it apart... carefully
7. Once the object is apart, lay it out on a large sheet of paper, make annotations on the paper to describe each part, and show how it was assembled.
8. If it can be re-assembled, please try to put it back the way you found it. In some cases, another team may want to use this item too.
9. Go back to the clinic staff and find another item.
10. Each pair of your teammates should take apart at least 2 items... if you have time, feel free to look at more.

After the activity

1. Take a picture of this exploded object and post it to Piazza.
2. In Piazza, explain how this article relates to your design concept, and describe the features which are similar to your idea
3. In Piazza, describe the features of your object that are very different from your design concept
4. Select components that you have examined and reserve them with clinic staff if you are using them in your prototype.

Appendix C: Sample Team Discussion on Design Ideas within the Team Forums

A sample of the team discussion on design ideas within a sample of the team forums. The students were discussing their plans, and research for a design. Contribution of design sketches and further details followed

-
-
-

>>>
Student A:

I think the idea that we presented in class today with the harness is pretty good. We should definitely upload the sketch of the design here as its a good start. The physical prototype that Student C showed us today was quite light and sturdy. It would be a great feature on the design if we could actually manufacture it with the materials with have to work with at the MME clinic.

We may want to consider the overall safety of our design for the passenger as well. It is mentioned in the design challenge document that the passenger remains in a "respectful orientation at all times". A small error in driving may disrupt a set position if we overlook the features and attachment of the seat. The document also mentions about a potential change in weather, which other teams addressed today in class. Overall we're off to a good start so far, but we shouldn't overlook some key factors.
>>>

Student B:

Good Job outlining the basic ideas/concepts that we should be looking at while designing the car. One thing I want to add is that we should experiment with suspension and see whether we need to change the suspension springs; we might be able to bypass this based on how well, we distribute the weight throughout the car. Student C and I have already visited the Ideas Clinic and are familiar with the material(s) that we will be working with. We should visit to the clinic as a team, so we are on the same page.
>>>

Student C:

Hi guys the ideas present by Student A are pretty good. But I need changing the spring the increase suspension is of no good because the strings are pretty good to hold the weight of the book. We should consider the safety and how our team thinks of about platforms and all.
>>>

Student B:
My ideas for safety are as follows:
1. Attaching a belt to secure the passenger.
2. Designing a platform in ideas clinic to hold the weight of the book.
3. Designing a transparent plastic semicircular platform which we will attach in front of the seat.
>>>

-
-
-

Chapter 6

Writing in Teacher Education: From Genre Analysis to Program Redesign

David Slomp, Robin Bright, Sharon Pelech, and Marlo Steed
Faculty of Education, University of Lethbridge

The study reported in this chapter, like the others in this book, began with a review of assignments contained in course outlines. Unlike other studies in this book, we did not limit our focus to writing assignments (though most assignments did have written components to them). Instead, we mapped and analyzed the full range of tasks required of students in the Bachelor of Education program at the University of Lethbridge. This study became a catalyst for reimagining our Bachelor of Education program.

This chapter describes the way in which the genre analysis led to the redesign process. We begin with a description of our program, with an emphasis on the first professional semester (PS I). This description is important for providing a clear understanding of the context in which this work was completed. We then describe the genre assignment analysis which had three goals: (1) to understand the demands placed on our students in each of the professional semesters in our program, (2) to determine the breadth of expectations, and (3) to review the consistency of those expectations across semesters and cohorts of students. We discuss the findings and implications from this analysis which motivated our program redesign. We discuss the theoretical framework that positioned this redesign process. Finally, we describe the redesign process, its timeline, and implementation. We close with a discussion of challenges, successes, and future directions.

Background

The Faculty of Education at the University of Lethbridge offers a suite of Bachelor of Education degrees that are designed to foster the next generation of excellent teachers who understand the importance of being research-focused reflective practitioners who are committed to lifelong learning. Our programs are designed to foster independent thinkers who value collaboration and ongoing professional growth. We offer several degree options at the Bachelor's level. These include a five-year combined degree (BA/BEd; BSc/BEd; BFA/BEd) and a four-semester after degree program.

The Faculty of Education admits 236 students to the undergraduate program each fall. Entry into the Faculty of Education is competitive. The Faculty uses both cumulative grade point average (a minimum GPA of 2.5—though frequently higher in many subject areas) and ratings from Education 2500 to rank qualified applicants. Applicants are also expected to have completed a minimum of 60 credit hours, a designated number of courses in a teachable subject, and a writing proficiency requirement.

The program values practicum experiences. Students acquire 27 weeks of classroom experience during the program. This is almost double the number of practicum hours required for interim certification in Alberta. Graduates of this program are eligible to apply for teacher certification for Kindergarten to Grade 12 in the Province of Alberta.

Students are required to complete a preliminary practicum experience prior to applying for the Bachelor of Education program. Orientation to Teaching (Education 2500) is designed to open applicant's eyes to the realities of teaching by assigning them to a school classroom for 60 hours. During this time, they function in a role similar to a teacher assistant. The goal of this practicum is to help students determine if teaching is the career for them by experiencing what it is like to be in a classroom.

The core of this BEd program is built around three professional semesters. Each of these semesters includes a suite of courses designed to prepare students for a practicum placement which they also complete as part of this semester. Students are enrolled in cohorts for each of these three professional terms. In the first professional term (PS I), cohorts are based on the location of students' practicum placements. In the second (PS II) and third (PS III) professional terms, cohorts are based on students' majors.

Professional Semesters

After students have been admitted to the Faculty of Education (either on the basis of a previously completed degree, or on the basis of their completed work in the first two years of a concurrent degree), they enter Professional Semester One (PS I). PS I involves a blend of 6 on-campus courses that students complete on a tightened timeline of eight weeks. These courses are followed by a five-week practicum. In the PS I practicum they are assigned full-time to a classroom for approximately 125 hours (5 weeks). They tend to be placed in classrooms at a grade level from 1-7. Students gradually assume increased responsibilities for lessons with the overall aim of teaching one third of the time, assisting one third of the time, and observing or preparing one third of the time.

While in their practicum, they are paired with a Teacher Associate who will mentor them through the process. The student teachers are also assigned a Faculty Consultant who does at least three formal observations and liaises with the Teacher Associate to provide feedback through a formative-assessment form. This is done periodically to document and support student progress and reflective practice. At the end of the practicum, the University Consultant and Teacher Associate meet to discuss and assess the student's overall performance based on expectations for this stage of teacher development using a summative report form.

The course component of PS I is structured as a generic semester where the focus is on basic teaching skills across all subject areas. In this semester, students are placed in cohorts of 36–40 students who take the same 6 courses together regardless of major. These courses include: Curriculum and Instruction (EDUC 3501), Educational Psychology (EDUC 3502), Language and Education (EDUC 3503),

Evaluation of Learning (EDUC 3504), Teaching Seminar (EDU 3505), and Communications Technology and Education (EDUC 3508).

These courses are designed so that students are in a better position to meet the challenges and issues they face as teachers in the field. They are taught by full-time faculty members, term instructors, master teachers, and seconded educators from the schools. While secondments, master teachers, and term instructors bring relevant recent experience and perspectives from the field into our program, a challenge we face in depending on them for program delivery is ensuring they are connected to current research on quality teacher education and ensuring they are familiar with the program and module outcomes and with program changes. In fact, for all instructors, ensuring program coherence is an ongoing challenge.

To ensure both program coherence and equity with respect to students' experience, the Faculty runs a week of planning days each August, a single planning day in December, and a two-day Faculty retreat in May. These planning days enable instructors in their horizontal groups (all instructors in the same cohort) and vertical groups (all instructors of the same course) to collaboratively plan their courses.

After completing PS I, students may enter their second professional semester (PS II) immediately, or they may choose to take more courses toward their major and minors before opting to continue with practicum. PS II begins with 4 on-campus courses. These courses are entitled: Principles of Curriculum and Instruction for Majors (EDUC 3601), Educational Psychology of Exceptional Learners (EDUC 3602), Social Context of Schooling (EDUC 3602), and Evaluation of Student Learning (EDUC 3602). Following the on-campus component, student teachers are assigned full-time to a classroom for approximately 150 hours (6 weeks). Student teachers assume approximately one half of the Teacher Associate's teaching load during the first week, moving to approximately two thirds of a teaching load for most of the remainder of the practicum. At a certain point, a student teacher will teach full-time for a shorter period (3–5 days), if appropriate. When not teaching, student teachers actively assist and observe their teacher associates.

The final practicum students complete in this program is Professional Semester III (PS III). This experience is a 15-week teaching internship. PS III consists of an internship, group seminars, professional inquiry project, and preparation of a showcase portfolio. Intern Teachers are assigned to schools for the semester, during which time they assume responsibility for approximately one half of a teacher mentor's work assignment. This experience not only prepares them as a teacher, it helps them nurture professional relationships that will benefit them, their career, and the students they teach. This experience is designed to act as a transition to their first year of teaching.

The Bachelor of Education program enjoys a reputation for developing excellent teachers. This reputation is largely based on feedback from superintendents and principals who hire our graduates. An institutional program of research designed to monitor the program has been maintained by the Faculty. Each year data is collected in terms of formative assessment, professional semester questionnaires, and course evaluations. That data is analyzed and interpreted by the instructors, PS I, II, and III coordinators, associate deans, and the dean. Those results are discussed in the Undergraduate Program Development Committee where potential changes and tweaks to the program are examined. The results of this research, however, have not been published. A less coherent, published body of research has been conducted by faculty members. This work focuses on the development of instructor's assessment capacity, the efficacy of mentorship programs for First Nations students, and the use of digital portfolios for evaluating students in both on and off campus environments (Roscoe, 2013; Walker, 1990; Winsor, 1998; Steed & Vigrass, 2011; Beaudin, 2013).

The current iteration of the program's design was first introduced in 1994; it has been 22 years since we have undertaken a full-scale critical review of the program. The Quality Assurance Review of the program conducted in 2012/13 produced no recommendations regarding the structure, delivery, or content of our professional semesters. The study that initiated the program design work reported in this chapter was designed to provide a picture of the assignment load students in the program were required to complete in each of their professional semesters. It was hoped that this overview of the range, frequency, and distribution of assignments would help initiate a critical review of the program.

Data Collection

In Chapter 1 of this book, Roger Graves describes the data entry and coding process developed for this research. We will not recreate that description here; instead, we will focus on the details specific to our analysis.

All course outlines for undergraduate courses taught in the 2012/13 academic year in the Faculty of Education at the University of Lethbridge were collected (n = 130). Each assignment in every course outline was then coded and entered into the database (n= 803). Coded data was then organized according to program year. Year 2 courses were all ED 2500. Year 3 courses included PS I and PS II semester courses as well as educational electives. Year 4 courses included PS III seminars. Courses that included multiple sections were each coded separately, and, in the case of professional semesters, were organized by cohort section. This enabled us to compare assignment profiles for students based on the cohorts they were enrolled in, an important level of analysis for this study. In addition to analyzing assignment profiles, assignments were analyzed for assignment features including outcomes, scoring criteria, audience, function, and genre.

Findings

Within this data set, 77 different assignment genres were identified. The most frequently assigned genres include presentations, lesson plans, reflections, papers, portfolios, and professional growth plans. This range of genres reflects a number of functions associated with the teaching profession. These include enhancing pedagogical expertise, developing a reflective mind-set, communicating with stakeholders, and developing a research-informed practice (Collin, Karsenti, & Komis, 2013; Van Driel & Berry, 2012).

Table 1

Most frequently assigned genres

	Year 2	Year 3	Year 4	Total
Presentation	23	73	32	128
Lesson Plans	6	58	0	64
Reflection	6	49	6	61
Paper	9	35	9	53
Portfolio	10	8	23	41
Professional Growth Plan	0	12	21	33
Report	0	0	30	30
Letter	5	17	1	23
Self-Evaluation	4	13	6	23
Proposal	0	0	18	18
Unit Plan	0	17	1	18
Quiz	0	13	4	17
Statement of Beliefs	0	17	0	17
Journal	10	6	0	16
Response	0	10	4	14

Distribution of genres across program years and professional semesters revealed several trends.

In Education, 2500 students write 10 different genres of assignments. These are a mix of research assignments, reflective assignments, and pedagogical assignments (focused on developing the art of teaching). In Year 3, the number of genres students are assigned increases to 66. Almost half of these genres are related to the pedagogical function with research, reflection, and communication functions being even in number. This emphasis on the pedagogical function seems highly consistent with the focus of the two professional terms that are contained in our third year courses.

Table 2

Assignment genres in Year 3, organized by function

Assignment Genres in Year 3				
Component Type				
Pedagogical (n=29)	Research (n=11)	Reflection (n=10)	Communication (n=10)	Evaluation (n=6)
Artifacts (evidence)	Analysis	Log	Blog	Exam
Assessments (ex. quizzes)	Annotated Bibliography	Logbook	Blog Post	Quiz
Assessments	Case Study	Online posting	Credo	Responses (Exam)
Classroom Management Plan	Concept Map	Professional growth plan	Letter	Test
Descriptions of lesson plans	Forum Postings	Rationale	Pledge	Written Exam
Electronic Presentation	List	Reflection	Promotional document	Written Explanation
Evaluation (performance task)	Mind map	Response	Slideshow	
Handout	Notes	Self-assessment	Statement of beliefs	
Journals	Paper	Video	Website	
Learning Activity (creation of)	Summaries	Webcast	Written autobiography/ visual representation	
Lesson descriptions	Summary and Analysis			
Lesson Overview				
Lesson Plan Analysis				

Lesson Plans				
Lesson summaries				
Long-range plan				
Performance Task				
Portfolio				
Presentation				
Quiz (creation of)				
Resource				
Resource Review				
Table of Specifications				
Teachers' Resource Manual				
Unit Assessment Plan				
Unit Introduction				
Unit Plan				
Unit summary				
Unit template				

Year 4 courses require students to complete 33 different genres of assignments. These are evenly balanced between the pedagogical, communicative, research, and reflective functions. This balance reflects the nature of both the elective courses and the PS III semester in which students are expected to take on the role of practicing teachers responsible for planning, communicating, and reflecting on their teaching. Students in PS III are also expected to complete an original research project associated with their practicum experience.

Table 3

Assignment genres in Year 4, organized by function

Assignment Genres in Year 4				
Component Type				
Pedagogical (n=8)	Research (n=8)	Reflection (n=9)	Communication (n=7)	Evaluation (n=1)
Classroom Management Plan	Critique	Blog Responses	E-mails	Quiz
Electronic Presentation	Forum Posting	E-Portfolio	Form	
Handouts	Outline	Online Postings	Letter	
Lesson Plan	Paper	Portfolio	Poster	
Long-range Plan	Proposal	Posting	Project	
Presentation	Report	Professional Growth Plan	Statement	
Resource	Resource Review	Reflection	Website	
Unit Plans	Self-assessment	Response		
		Visual Reflections (imagery)		

Outcomes and Rubrics

An important ethic in the Bachelor of Education program is that instructors model in our own planning and instruction the very practices we advocate in our teaching. In our assessment courses students are encouraged to base their planning on an Understanding by Design (UBD) framework (Wiggins & McTighe, 2005). Core to a UBD approach to planning is the development of outcomes, which are then linked to assessment tools. In the Faculty of Education, course outcomes are derived from the Quality Teaching Standards. The interim certification our students receive once they graduate from our program is based on our Faculty's commitment to these standards in our instruction and assessment. It is interesting, therefore, to note that while most courses listed outcomes in course syllabi, 61% of assignments in the program are not explicitly linked to learning outcomes. This demonstrates that the faculty is attempting to model the assessment practices it advocates in its own teaching, but it also suggests that there is considerable room for improvement on this front.

The Faculty also advocates for the use of feedback loops linked to formative assessment practices. Feedback loops enhance student learning and performance by providing them with multiple opportunities to receive feedback from instructors and peers. However, with respect to modeling this practice, only 16% of assignments are designed with explicit feedback loops built into them.

The same can be said about the inclusion of rubrics and evaluation criteria on course outlines. While there has been healthy debate regarding the nature and value of rubrics in the evaluation of student work, there is agreement on the importance of clear criteria for fair assessment practices. Only 14% of assignments are explicitly linked to rubrics in the course outline, while an additional 3% of assignments utilize marking systems other than rubrics. The use of clear grading criteria for assignments is likely underrepresented in this analysis; instructors may choose to include this level of information on assignment handouts rather than course outlines.

Frequency of Assignments by Professional Semester

Given the Faculty's emphasis on collaborative planning, a close analysis of the variation and frequency of assignments was important. Inconsistency in assignment types and frequency could mean that students are having dissimilar experiences across cohorts; it could also mean that some students' workloads are much heavier than others depending on which cohort they have been enrolled in. On average, across the entire program, students are required to complete 6 assignments per course. The range, however, is quite large for a number of courses (ED 2500 R= 1-14; ED 3601 R= 4-12; ED 3505 R= 1-10). In PS I, the students in each cohort have a heavy but similar assignment load with most cohorts having between 35 and 39 assignments. One cohort, however, has 51 assignments, a significantly larger number than the other five cohorts. Two courses, ED 3501 and ED 3502, range from 3-10 and 5-12 assignments respectively. Across these six courses and six cohorts, students are expected to write 46 different genres of assignment. Because each professional semester involves a practicum component, coursework is compressed into 10 weeks for PS I courses and 8 weeks for PS II courses. Students in PS I, then, were completing between 3 and 4 assignments per week.

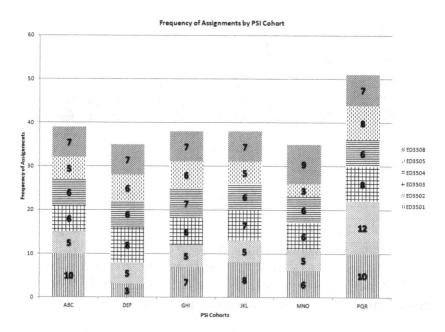

Figure 1. Frequency of assignments, by PS I cohort.

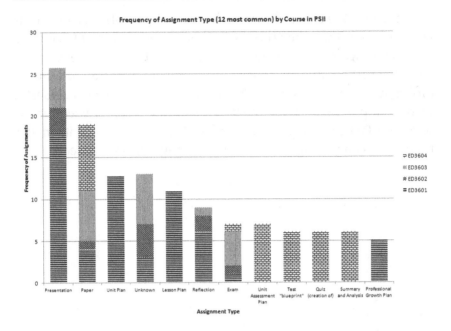

Figure 2. Frequency of assignment type, by course in PS II.

The PS II cohorts tell a similar story with an average of 23 assignments per cohort and a range from 26 to 19. While most courses in PS II have similar number of assignments across cohorts, ED 3601 has a range of 6-13 assignments. Students in PS II were completing between 2 and 3 assignments per week.

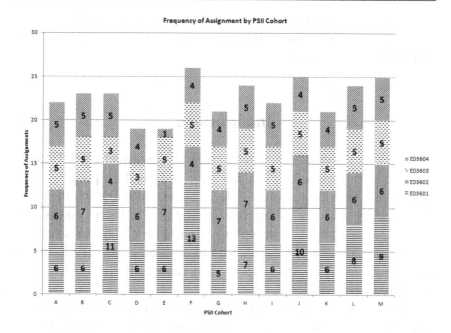

Figure 3. Frequency of assignment, by PS II cohort.

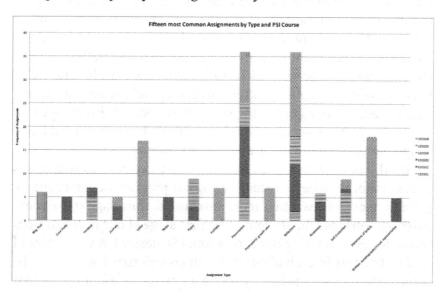

Figure 4. Fifteen most common assignments, by type and PS I course.

Because the PS III semester is not structured around cohorts in the same way that PS I and PII are, a similar analysis for this semester could not be undertaken.

Implications

While not a comprehensive review of assessment practices or workload demands within the Bachelor of Education program, this analysis did provide sufficient data to help faculty understand more clearly what we were asking of our students in their professional semesters. Because of the cohort structure of our professional semesters, this analysis enabled us to develop a clearer picture of assignment loads for students in each cohort and it enabled us to compare workloads across cohorts.

This mapping of assignments raised a number of important questions for our faculty. Chief among these were, "Are we fostering a learning environment that supports deep thinking and exploration, integration of learning across courses and subject areas, and a sense of intellectual well being?" The consensus among faculty members was that the current assignment load was not achieving these outcomes to the extent we wanted but was instead creating a highly stressful environment in which students are constantly scrambling to complete one assignment after the other. Results from exit surveys administered to our graduating students supported this analysis. In particular, exit survey results indicated that students wanted fewer assignments and more integration across courses.

On the basis of this analysis, our faculty determined that it was necessary for us to begin reconsidering our program design to ensure greater depth of learning, more integrated thinking, and a more balanced workload for students. The first stage of our redesign work was to focus on revising our Professional Semester I. A committee of lead instructors in each of our PS I courses was struck and given the mandate to provide the faculty with a vision for redesigning our first professional semester.

Program Redesign: Theoretical Frames

As a committee exploring how the PS I semester may be structured differently, we soon realized that this question demanded that we explore many fundamental assumptions and visions of the program at the University of Lethbridge. In order to make change, understanding the purpose of the teacher education program and what it hopes to achieve became a large part of the process. Russell and Dillon (2015) contend that when education programs begin to explore reforms, often unstated structures of existing programs become exposed, and as a result extensive discussions of the basic program beliefs and vision is essential. Hurley (2013) claims that one of the key elements that often stops proposed action steps is not exploring the strong assumptions embedded within education systems. Similar to the ideas identified by Hurley (2013), two key themes emerged in our work: (1) how to create more authentic and meaningful learning experiences for student teachers, and (2) how to build more responsive learning environments.

Darling-Hammond and Bransford (2005) describe three key aspects of program design in teacher education that are encompassed within either the *what* of the program or the *how* of the program. The *what* focuses on the content of the program, which includes the need to explore the key issues of vision and to develop coherence. The *how*, or the design of a program includes two aspects which are: (1) the process of learning within the program, including how practice is depicted in classrooms; and (2) the learning context in developing practice. Since the redesign was only a part of a larger program, most of the attention of the committee was placed on the content of the program.

Historically, there have been competing views of how best to organize a teacher education program. Phelan, Smits, and Ma (2015) describe that during the 1950s and 1960s, most teacher education research focused on producing a "science of teacher education" (p. 236) that focused on effectiveness training that was competency and process-product based. As a result, practice was to "identify effective interventions so that they could be generalized across a range of program contexts in order to bring about pre-determined outcomes" (p. 236). This framework was based on cognitive psychology that attempted to break down the learning process in the student to discrete units which then could be linked directly to teachers' actions. By the 1980s and 1990s, a recognition of the ineffectiveness of the "technical rational premise" shifted the focus of teacher education research from teacher action to teacher thinking (Garcia & Lewis, 2014; Phelan, Smits, & Ma, 2015). Teacher education programs began to move towards the importance of teachers being able to be reflective and "rational decision makers" (Phelan, Smits, & Ma, 2015, p. 236).

More recently, a review of Initial Teacher Education (ITE) programs throughout Canada show a limited amount of Canadian scholarship that has been done in the design of the teacher education programs (Russell & Dillon, 2015). The authors contend that more attention is needed to explore the "conceptual frameworks of program design and the associated assumptions about learning to teach" (p. 164). Falkenberg (2015) reports that even though scholars (see Russell, 2009; Sheehan & Fullan; 1995) expressed concerns that teacher education reform often happens without exploration of the underlying myths of teaching and learning, large programmatic changes often occur without "open and scholarship-based debate, which is exactly how re-visioning and reforming should *not* happen" (Falkenberg, 2015, p. 8). In fact, Russell and Dillon (2015) argue that many teacher education designs are often developed due to tradition and assumptions that have lingered from a few decades ago, as opposed to more deliberate, pedagogical decisions as to what is best practice. While PS I redesign committee's work did not include large programmatic changes at this time, recognition that the need to explore the research driving the changes that were envisioned is an essential part of the immediate process. More systemic research on the program as a whole may be needed as the implementation of the changes impact other elements of the program.

One of the fundamental tensions that emerged in our work was the issue of the relationship of theory and practice within a program. This issue includes how to best integrate campus-based course work and school-based practicum placements (Russell & Dillon, 2015). Russell and Dillon (2015) found that Canadian Education programs fell into two major categories (as originally described by Schön, 1983). The majority of programs in Canada have been grounded in a technical rational perspective that focuses on a *theory-into-practice* model. The understanding of the relationship of theory and practice within this frame is that theory is taught for students to then apply in practicum placements that often occur in large blocks distinct from on-campus experiences (Russell & Dillon, 2015). The second perspective is described as *practice-and-theory* perspective that is grounded in reflective practice. In this second framework, reflective practices help connect theory and practice where theory is intimately connected with practice to analyze experiences in order to improve it. In this second frame, practicum and coursework often happen simultaneously so that theory is not used as generalities for all situations but seen as a process of theory and practice being an interactive relationship between the two. The second frame structure helps students understand "the complexity of context, the uncertainty of the human condition, and the unpredictability of action [that] characterize the relation between theory and practice" (Phelan, Smits, & Ma, 2015, p. 237).

Schön (1987) described how the two frames are based on fundamentally different views of professional learning and the role of practicum:

> Our view of the work of the practicum and the conditions and processes appropriate to it depends in part on our view of the kinds of knowing essential to professional competence...
>
> If we see professional knowledge in terms of facts, rules, and procedures applied non-problematically to instrumental problems, we will see practicum in its entirety as a form of technical training. It will be the business of the instructor to communicate and demonstrate the application of rules and operations to the facts of practice.... . . If we see professional knowing in terms of "thinking like a"... teacher, students will still learn relevant facts and operations but will also learn the forms of inquiry by which competent practitioners reason their way, in problematic instances, to clear connections between general knowledge and particular cases...
>
> If we see professional knowing in terms of "thinking like a"... teacher, students will still learn relevant facts and operations

but will also learn the forms of inquiry by which competent practitioners reason their way, in problematic instances, to clear connections between general knowledge and particular cases...

If we focus on the kinds of reflection-in-action through which practitioners sometimes make new sense of uncertain, unique or conflicted situations of practice, then we will assume neither that existing professional knowledge fits every case nor that every problem has a right answer. We will see students as having to learn a kind of reflection-in- action that goes beyond stable rules- not only be devising new methods of reasoning, ... but also by constructing and testing new categories of understanding, strategies of action, and ways of framing problems. (Schön, 1987, pp. 38-39, as cited in Russell & Dillon, 2015, p. 160).

One of the problematic elements of theory-into-practice design is that it has a very limiting impact on creating coherence between on campus coursework and practicum experience (Britzman, 1991; Darling-Hammond, 2006; Russell & Dillon, 2015). Research shows that students have difficulty connecting intention to action and as a result much of what they experience in the practicum becomes the leading deciding factor as to their own teaching practice (Britzman, 1991). Huntley (2008) argues that teacher educators need to explicitly help student teachers make the link between theory and practice or else the reflective part of practice becomes a way of strengthening present understandings and practice instead of leading to transformation of their understanding of teaching and learning.

Our PS I redesign work occurred as a shift in education is happening across Canada and the western world as we move from an understanding of learning from a rational/cognitive focus towards recognizing learning as a creative, emergent process. At the school level in Alberta, we see this shift embodied in Alberta Education's Curriculum Redesign project. It calls for a significant rethinking of how education is enacted in the province. The vision has implications for teacher education as well because the redesign envisions new roles for teachers:

> Albertans see the role of teacher changing from that
> of a knowledge authority to an architect of learning –
> one who plans, designs and oversees learning activities.
> The teacher would consider interests, passions, talents,
> and natural curiosities of the learner. He or she would
> inspire, motivate, and plant the seeds for life-long
> learning.... Learners in particular told us that teachers
> need to be innovative, passionate, and positive about
> teaching (Hancock, 2010, p. 7).

In recognition of the research that effective teacher education programs need to have a vision that connects "important values and goals to concrete practices and provide a basis for teachers to develop and assess their teaching and their students' learning" (Darling-Hammond & Baratz-Snowden, 2007, p. 121), much of our discussion included ways to bring the reflective process into the current PS I structure.

Redesign Process

The PS I redesign process began with the assignment analysis discussed in earlier sections of this chapter. These findings captured what many faculty members had discussed informally on many occasions in the past: that students were involved in too many stand-alone assignments in one module. Furthermore, often the work they completed in each of their modules seemed to replicate that in others, causing them to view assignments as less meaningful and repetitive.

Interestingly, the Faculty had discussed initiatives such as this for a number of years, but the research findings provided the impetus to begin the process of collaboration and redesign. Previous instructor surveys had clearly pointed to students' dissatisfaction with the number of assignments and the lack of coordination between instructors. We had received feedback from instructors and students that there was a perception that some of the reflective writing they were asked to do felt like "busy" work and that some course content overlapped with that in several modules. Comments from instructors for the previous two years point to the necessity of addressing the concerns around assignments:

The only recommendation would be to cut down on the number of assignments students are given. My sense is that students are so busy they have a difficult time doing the kind of powerful reflection we hope for.

It seemed for my students that they were so busy just trying to get assignments done, opportunities for deeper reflection was limited. I am wondering how we can do better with fewer.

It would appear, based on my students' comments, that there continue to be redundancies.

We began working together to address this feedback and the findings from the assignment analysis by focusing on: a timeline for the redesign work, assignment redesign that would provide opportunities to integrate knowledge across modules for students, and learning across the course modules, and a method to obtain feedback throughout and at the end of the semester from all groups.

A Timeline for the Redesign Work

The results of the assignment analysis were first discussed with the PS I Coordinator before being shared with the Faculty's Undergraduate Program Development Committee. We suggested a pilot project using one section of PS I which consisted of approximately 40 students and 6 instructors. We discussed the idea of developing an integrated approach to delivering the on-campus components of the semester with fewer but more meaningful assignments. The Dean and other Undergraduate Program Development Committee members indicated that we would need to think about delivering the redesign to all incoming PS I students (approximately 250 students), rather than to only one section. This was suggested because it was felt that if one section was completing far fewer and more integrated assignments, the students in other sections would likely complain about their experiences in comparison.

Having been given this mandate, a new PS I redesign committee was struck. Because envisioned changes would impact each course taught in PS I, it was felt that each aspect of the PS I semester needed to be represented by a lead instructor for that course or program element. The PS I redesign committee consisted of the PS I Coordinator and five instructors, each representing one of the on-campus course modules.

We worked to communicate with and involve faculty in a redesign process that would help our students integrate knowledge, concepts, and skills across the modules and through well-considered assignments that would be planned and implemented collaboratively. Each member of the PS I redesign committee communicated regularly with other instructors of their on-campus modules throughout this process in face-to-face meetings and through email.

The process began in earnest at the Faculty Retreat in May of 2015; the results of the initial research that began the thinking around PS I redesign were shared, and initial thinking was initiated about how we might begin this work together. After presenting our analysis and preliminary thinking to the Faculty, we broke into small group discussions lead by members of the PS I Redesign Committee. Faculty were organized into groups based on which courses best aligned with their area of expertise. Each group was asked to address two questions: (1) What inquiry questions could we orient PS I around?; and (2) What two core inquiry-based questions could we ask students to investigate in each course that would help them to answer the guiding question? Faculty were also invited to provide feedback on the idea of redesigning the PS I semester. This step was important to gauge faculty interest in undertaking a project of this magnitude. Previous to this, it had been at least 20 years since any significant changes to the PS I semester had been entertained. At the Faculty Retreat, we received feedback that indicated there was interest, even enthusiasm, to pursue this initiative.

Results of small group discussions included the following:

Combining assignments is important to make PS I work meaningful and not an act of simply "completion."

We have a "triage" approach by students because of overwhelming number of assignments, "busy work" as opposed to quality.

Looking forward to streamlining course requirements.

PS I needs cross-curricular exploration of different subject areas. What are the foundational purposes of education and how does it influence the approaches adopted?

Orienting questions: what is curriculum? What is learning? How do we engage students in meaningful learning? What is the purpose of education? What are effective instructional strategies?

Need to address: what are the beliefs and values that inform students' understanding of education?

What are the principles of sound assessment and design that support learning?

Overall, the feedback and discussion demonstrated a commitment to working together and with our students in a more meaningful way than had been done in the past. While instructors thought deeply about their assignments, they felt there was room to integrate learning across the modules and to work from one or two overarching questions to guide the work of the entire on-campus component of this professional semester.

Planning the Integrated Assignments

In May and June of 2015, members of the planning group met on a regular basis to undertake the redesign work involved in developing assignments that would meet the goals for integration and reduce the workload for students. Our work together is captured in the following photographs documenting the thinking engaged in during these early meetings.

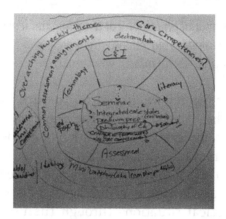

Figure 5. Assignment planning notes.

Our larger goal was to begin to shift the focus of our PS I semester away from a theory-*into*-practice orientation toward a theory-*and*-practice orientation. However, the basic structure of the semester—10 weeks of campus classes followed by 6 weeks of practicum—was not open for change. Program changes of this magnitude have been discussed, but the practical implications of such a change have not been worked through. The greatest barrier to this model is geography: many of our students are placed in rural communities 100 or more kilometers from Lethbridge, making regular travel between the university and their practicum placements very costly. This shift, then, had to be achieved through the redesign of the on campus courses themselves. We decided to reorganize the semester around a critical inquiry focus, one that would have students explore across all of their modules, and their practicum experience a set of guiding questions:

What is your personal philosophy of teaching and learning?
What theories support your philosophy?
How does your philosophy inform your practice?

Our redesign would require that, in each course, students would explore these questions. In the Seminar course, students were expected to integrate the ideas they were developing across each of their courses into a more integrated, coherent statement of philosophy and practice. In this way, the new PS I redesign reclaimed the small seminar classes as a hub to allow students integrate theory into practical situations through the use of case studies and reflection. Students were expected to return multiple times to explore the question of how their current understanding and philosophy of education was being impacted by the work they were experiencing in their other classes. Focusing on opportunities for reflective practice helped bring the theory and practice framework into students' experience. In Russell and Dillon's (2015) comparison of theory-into-practice and practice-and-theory perspectives, they emphasize that practice-and-theory perspectives are strongly grounded in reflection. In this approach, student teachers' pedagogical values are determined from their own understanding of their former teachers and their reflection upon their own "images, emotions, values and experiences" of teaching and learning (p. 161). To support this integrated reflective thinking, we also developed three assignments that would cut across most, if not all, modules. They are described below:

Assignment	Ed. 3501	Ed. 3502	Ed. 3503	Ed. 3504	Ed. 3505	Ed. 3508	Ed. 3500	1	2	3	4	5	6	7	8	9
	Modules							**Weeks**								
1 Mini Unit	✓															
2 Reflective Blog (8)	some	✓	some	✓	✓	✓						F	F	F	S	
3 Digital Portfolio	use/not grade				✓	✓	✓			F		F		F	S	
4 Intro to self (background)					✓						S					
5 Teaching Philosophy					✓							F	S			
6 Professional Goals					✓		✓								S	
7 Curriculum Overview	✓									S						
8 Strategies Catalogue	✓												S			
9 Learning Theories Presentation		✓		some		✓						S				
10 Personal Believes (Bio Poem)		✓								S						
11 Memoir Writing			✓						F							
12 Book Talks (Video)			✓			✓								S		
13 Final Lit Quiz			✓													
14 Digital Citizenship & Concept Map						✓								S		

F = Formative   S = Summative

Figure 6. Assignment planning notes.

(1) The first assignment was called "the mini-unit." It required students to develop a summative performance task and a sequence of three lessons associated with that task. Students were expected to provide a rationale for their unit that explored the inquiry questions it was based on, they had to complete an assessment plan that linked curriculum outcomes to both formative and summative assessments, they had to provide reflections on each lesson that linked their design choices to key questions from each module, and they had to provide a brief defense paper that justified their assessment plan and unit design choices.

(2) A second integrated assignment was called "reflective case study." It involved having students and instructors examine two or three "case study" videos from the video series called "A Public Education." These videos captured real-life scenarios from schools and classrooms around southern Alberta. The case studies were viewed in several course modules. Students were assigned a series of reflective questions that prompted them to apply to these case studies through the lens of their learning in each module:

Drawing on what you have learned in each PS I module this week, answer the following questions:

- How does this video demonstrate meaningful engagement connected to the Programs of Studies?
- What assessment principles would you use to enrich this learning experience? Why?
- How do you use language to facilitate what is happening here?
- What technology could you use to enrich this learning experience? Why?
- How does/could child development theory and/or learning theory inform this learning experience?

Drawing on your answers to the previous four questions, discuss what considerations need to be made for planning and instruction before, during and after this activity,

How do the ideas articulated in your response to this case study challenge and/or expand your theory of teaching and learning?

While students completed these case study reflections in their teaching seminar class, instructors from the other modules read the students' written reflections that were posted through their blog posts.

(3) The third integrated assignment was a digital portfolio. It was decided to return to the PS I model of having Teaching Seminar be the "hub" of the semester by providing time and space for students to reflect on their learning in all of the modules and create a "student website" in order to post blog reflections for all of their instructors to read. However, it would only be the Teaching Seminar instructor who would provide feedback and assess the entries (pass/fail). A website would be created in the Communication Technology module and would house most of the students' assignments, but especially those where multiple instructors were involved in providing feedback and assessing the work. This digital space brought together all the assignments students completed during their on campus portion of the semester, with reflections on their learning, and with exemplars demonstrating how they translated this learning into action during the practicum portion of the semester.

The goal of this series of integrated assignments was for students to recognize the connection between theory and practice. Huntley (2008) asserts that case studies can "provide opportunities for teacher candidates to discuss and reflect on how theory can guide practice" (p. 24). Huntley (2008) describes a research study by Malkani and Allen (2005) that found students who participated in case study discussions along with reflection journal groups were able to demonstrate qualities of deeper reflection practices than those taught in traditional lectures. As a result, the research suggests that this process found that assignments similar to these provided a longer lasting impact on the new teachers' ability to be reflective practitioners. Galea (2012) argues, though, that reflection and reflective practice does not always lead to critical exploration of practice. In fact, often reflection leads to reinforcing current practices (Huntley, 2008). Finding different case studies that showed teaching and learning from multiple perspectives tried to allow a deeper understanding of the complexities of teaching and learning. Feedback to the student reflections was set up to help deepen student understanding by focusing on levels of reflection and students' exploration of the case studies by connecting them to their emerging understanding from their core modules. By Using the case studies and seminar as a place to integrate these ideas together was an attempt to help students reconceptualize learning as a complex system that cannot be understood by being broken down into its "component parts" (Sanford, Kurki, & Starr, 2015, p. 46). Attention to allowing students the space to make connections between their different modules was to help students make the needed connections and recognize the interconnections between all that they were learning (2015).

Rutherford, Whiting, and Smits (2008) argue that teaching can no longer be confined to the "practice of teaching a standardized curriculum to a relatively homogenized group of children" (p. 322), but instead the school itself has become "microcosms of a globalized world" (p. 322), and as a result teacher education needs to support this change through recognizing the complexities of cultural and language diversity in schools, inclusion and demands of students with exceptionalities within the regular classroom, and changes in the structure and nature of communities and family life (Darling-Hammond & Bransford, 2005). Incorporating opportunities in teacher education to explore the changing social systems and external demands and "at the same time nurture hope and possibility for our students in their quests to become teachers" (Smits, Towers, Panayotidis, & Lund, 2008, p. 47) is paramount. This requires attention to creating space for integration of theory and practice through critical reflection.

Dewey (1933) argues that "reflection is a complex, rigorous, intellectual and emotional enterprise that takes time to do well" (cited in Otienoh, 2010, p. 149). As a result, within the limited time frame of course work occurring over eight weeks, much of what the hub of the program focused on was for students to have multiple opportunities to reflect on the learning and the case studies from all of their courses. Schön (1983) expanded on Dewey's definition by stating that reflection occurs in two frames: reflection-in-action, and reflection-on-action. Since the PS I course work is completed before practicum, the case studies were used to bring opportunities for students to use reflection-on-action. Schön's reflection-in-action is described by Liu (2015) as an attempt to make student teachers more aware of "the tacit knowledge and to be critical of the knowledge produced by researchers" (p. 140). Huntley (2008) argues that this is important because student teachers will focus on the mechanized motions of school routines and not recognize the reflective practice that is required for intentional teaching practices. As a result, it is important, Huntley emphasizes, to ensure that reflection is focused on higher levels of analysis and thinking rather than simply focusing on technical issues. In fact, Liu (2015) argues that it is only when student teachers are offered multiple points of view that they are then able to reflect upon their own belief systems and as a result begin to have an open-mindedness that enables them to see multiple ways to address a problem. The key element to this process is critical reflection. Huntley (2008) contends that critical reflection needs to purposefully focus on "unacknowledged conflicts between institutional ideals and the actual contexts of school" (p. 19). One piece that is needed for further study in the PS I redesign is how well the case studies selected lead to this more critical reflection, or whether they reinforce current assumptions of the classroom. Part of the process, Huntley (2008) argues is opportunities to respond to a dilemma that allow for student teachers to identify similar and unique characteristics that are provided in the situation that is presented. As a result, opportunities to frame and reframe the dilemma and consider intended and unintended consequences of different ways of solving the situation could be implemented within the process of reflection.

Although PS I does not focus on critical analysis of the school system in particular, it is hoped that the process of reflection that is experienced in PS I will create the possibilities of more critical reflection as student teachers enter PS II and explore key belief systems in their Social Context course that addresses many underlying assumptions in education. Holloway and Gouthro (2011) argue that it is important for student teachers to become critical educators by exploring what they are asking their students to do. Hufford (2008) agrees, that in recognition of the current educational reality, the role of teacher education is to allow student teachers to ask the challenging questions about the why and who of questions such as "why does [the current] reality exist and who has defined the parameters of what a teacher should know and be able to do?" (p. 85). By providing opportunities to reflect upon their own philosophy of education and revisiting it throughout the PS I program, it is hoped that students begin to explore these complex and important questions.

Implementation

In August, the majority of the Teaching Seminar instructors had received their teaching contracts for the fall, so the PS I Coordinator contacted those individuals who had not yet received any information about the redesign plans and met them for lunch to discuss the process that had begun in January of 2015. These instructors had all instructed in PS I previously, so knew the model from which they were working and were extremely positive and supportive about the changes that were being implemented. There were still a couple of positions that had not been filled, but it was hoped that these new individuals would be in place for the fall planning days later in August, giving these new people time to meet with us face-to-face to discuss how to plan for the new design.

Fall Planning Days in August were held at the end of the month and extended in order to provide extra time for instructors to work together. In the past, PS I instructors were given one day to plan together. This past fall, we were provided with two days so that instructors could plan together, both in their module groups, but also, and more importantly, in their section groups (all instructors who taught the same cohort of students). This would enable them to discuss how the integrated assignments would be organized, described, and evaluated across the modules. Several instructors commented on the importance of these early meetings to the overall success of the redesign process: *I appreciated the early planning days, the focus of the Teaching Seminar and the great support provided throughout the semester,* and *it was excellent to have us all hearing the same messages, planning together, and getting questions addressed together.*

To assist in the implementation process, we decided to hold weekly informal lunch get-togethers on Wednesdays in order to give instructors a venue in which to touch base and discuss questions, concerns, ideas, and challenges in a timely manner. This proved to be a very important and successful initiative. Most Wednesdays, a number of instructors came together to talk together about how the semester was going and to get feedback about topics, issues, and questions. A Culmination Day was held with the students on December 17. This was followed by the final meeting of the PS

I Instructors. Feedback was gathered using an instructor survey. Informal feedback was also gathered from the students.

Challenges and Successes

Overall, faculty and student feedback indicate overwhelmingly that the redesign changes, particularly the integrated assignments, were well-accepted and successful.

Regarding the collaboration efforts and the assignments that cut across most of the on-campus modules, faculty comments were mostly very positive, although in some cases, it was noted that when certain modules were not involved in the integration, that seemed to detract from the overall intent of the redesign. For instance, instructors articulated the elements of PS I they would like to see maintained as follows:

I appreciated attempts to unify the student experience. The degree of collaboration between instructors was useful and needs to remain doable.

The planning days in August were great for coordinating dates and tying together key concepts. It was a great chance for new instructors to become informed and to meet others [education instructors and staff.]

I like the common assignments that cut across the modules. That approach encouraged students to view the integrated nature of teaching and learning.

Being new to the PS I instructional program it was extremely beneficial for me to collaborate with others and get a sense of the other courses in relation to mine.

The integration of assignments and assessments is an excellent model for student learning.

Common assignments shouldn't be optional by some instructors. When instructors opt out of using common assignments it messes with the unified experiences we want for our students.

A more systematic review of the faculty feedback sessions held at the end of the semester and of faculty surveys indicated that instructors felt the major successes of the semester were extensive and appeared in the areas of: (1) better and more meaningful integration across on-campus course modules; (2) more developed student thinking about the theory and practice relationship; (3) evident connections among on-campus course modules noted through their blogs; (4) stronger lesson planning skills, less stress observed in students, stronger level of collaboration among instructors, student websites as the "hub" for student work especially blogs and assignments; and (5) a more focused and shared curriculum in Teaching Seminar through the use of case-study videos and common questions for students. Interestingly, many instructors commented on the way in which these changes affected the student's work in practicum in a positive manner. In other words, we received many comments that the students' work in practicum showed improved curriculum planning, preparedness, and ability to plan for cross-curricula connections. This was an unanticipated but highly desirable result of the redesign work for the on-campus component of the semester. Perhaps most significant has been the feedback from students, instructors, and mentor teachers working with our PS II students this year. A frequent observation across these groups is that this cohort of students better understands the relationship between short-term and longer range planning and assessment than had previous PS II cohorts.

The challenges that were articulated include: (1) coordinating how the instructors present the integrated assignments to students, (2) using the case studies in a more uniform manner, and (3) giving more explicit advice about how to turn the electronic website into a professional portfolio. It appears that while the integrated mini-unit assignment was successful in many ways, there needed to be greater coordination among the instructors who were going to be assessing and evaluating it. While each instructor discussed the assignment at length in his or her on-campus course module, it would have been beneficial for instructors to meet in one of the course modules and discuss the assignment all together with the students. This would allow students and instructors to address questions and perceptions about the assignment expectations, due dates, and evaluation all at once, rather than having students have to wait to hear from each instructor in his or her individual course modules. Furthermore, students' perceptions of the value of working on this assignment throughout the semester, rather than handing it all in at the end, needs to be addressed. It was discovered that a few students in one section were upset that this assignment was eventually worth 40% of their grade in one course module. However, in talking to the instructor, the students were handing in parts of the assignment (worth 10-15%) and receiving extensive feedback every few weeks, with the result that their learning was supported at each stage of putting this assignment together. Nonetheless, some students perceived that the assignment being worth 40% once it was completed was too much. This is one aspect of the redesign initiative that will undoubtedly be changed for next fall.

For most instructors, using three case study videos in Teaching Seminar, as was anticipated before the semester began, proved to be too much content for the instructors to work with given the other aspects of this course module. It was decided in several sections to use only two case studies in order to keep workload for the students and the instructors manageable. In the future, it will be important to suggest using only one of the case studies to examine, discuss, and reflect upon in the students' blogs.

There were a number of issues around using the student websites throughout the on-campus component of the semester. The first concerned privacy and several students asked that their privacy be protected completely. To accommodate these requests, links to these students' websites did not appear in class lists with students' website links; rather, those students sent only their instructors a link to their websites and often they did not use their last names on their websites. Connected to this, many instructors chose to use the portfolio in different ways. Some used them simply as assignment repositories, others left the portfolios entirely for students to use as a space to track their own work requesting students to submit assignments to them directly rather than through the portfolio format.

Another issue that arose was that some of the instructors teaching in the same section had different expectations concerning length and content of blog entries. When students indicated this to their instructors, discussions were held and clearer expectations were communicated to the students. However, next year, it will be important for instructors in each section to discuss and address blog entries, length and content, and perhaps use exemplars from this experience with their students.

Finally, it was anticipated that students, while in practicum, and under the supervision of their university consultants, would turn their websites into professional portfolios. This would be accomplished by adding their goals for the practicum, lesson plans, reflections, and other artifacts to the website and by deleting assignments that they did not want to keep in their professional portfolio. However, this expectation was not fully understood by university consultants, some of whom did not even teach the students at all during the on-campus component. This meant that some students returned to their culmination day activities having not made any changes to their website and, therefore, without their professional portfolio begun. Next year, it has been suggested that students begin their websites with a 'tab' labeled "professional portfolio" as a way to show that the website can be a place to keep artifacts that will eventually become important content for the portfolio. In this way, students will be further along in the development of their professional portfolios than they would otherwise be by the time they finish this semester.

Each of the challenges that were raised by students and instructors appear to be easily addressed for the coming year. It is anticipated that there will be a large turnover in faculty members and sessional instructors for the fall. It will be very important to communicate the findings of this research to the incoming PS I Coordinator, who will be new, and all instructors new to the semester so that the changes implemented as a result of this redesign initiative are fully understood and implemented.

Longer-term challenges were also identified during this redesign process. With shifts in existing programs, unstated structures of existing programs become exposed. Once uncovered, these structures need to be addressed (Russell & Dillon, 2015). This is especially true in our Faculty, where a recent influx of new faculty suggests a revisiting of the purpose and vision of the education program may be needed so that the unstated structures that we have built the program on can be re-examined to determine whether these need to be reinforced or shifted. These complex discussions need to happen in order to understand the focus of the program in its entirety.

Tied to this, we need to examine how the degree to which we want to move our program away from a technical rational perspective that focuses on a theory-into-practice model and more towards a theory-and-practice model. The more significant the shift we imagine, the larger the systemic change to our program is needed. For example, revisiting the distinct separation of on campus and practicum time would be needed if we truly want to move towards a theory-and-practice focus that allows for critical, reflective practitioners. This would help disrupt the very common challenge of the practicum being the real world and thus driving the decisions that students make in their planning and teaching. As Britzman (1991), Darling-Hammond (2006), and Russell and Dillon (2015) argue, the theory-into-practice design has a very limiting impact on creating coherence between on campus coursework and practicum experience. As a result, what the students see and experience in the practicum become the strongest factors impacting how they choose to teach. This is an issue that requires further consideration within the Faculty.

This process demonstrates the power that examining assignment genres offers professional faculties: the process enabled us to develop a clear map of the frequency, range, and distribution of assignments within the program. This mapping made transparent the redundancies, gaps, and possibilities for integration across all assignments. This transparency further enabled a critical examination of the program with respect to how well our assignments supported us in meeting our instructional goals. This enabled us to identify and develop a core set of assignments that better reflected and supported our goal of preparing exceptional teachers who are critical educators.

This process offers a model to other professional faculties who are eager to re-examine their programs. Through our experience, we have learned the value of transparency, open and ongoing communication, and theory driven decision-making to the process of program redesign. This process positions faculty for ongoing critical analysis of their work: our redesign continues. In the semesters subsequent to the initial implementation of our redesigned semester, our planning group has been developing a virtual classroom, populated by videos of real students and their teacher. This virtual classroom will provide a real-world context for future case-study assignments, unit and assessment planning tasks, and critical reflections on contemporary issues in education. The assignment genre analysis enabled us to engage in a thoughtful, critical, and visionary experience that has both transformed our own thinking and that of our students.

References

Beaudin, L. (2013). Transitioning to the ePortfolio: An opportunity to teach digital literacy in pre-service teacher education. *E-Learn: World Conference on E-Learning in Corporate, Government, Healthcare, and Higher Education, 1*, 595-599.

Britzman, D. P. (1991). *Practice makes practice: A critical study of learning to teach.* Albany, NY: State University of New York Press.

Collin, S., Karsenti, T., & Komis, V. (2013) Reflective practice in initial teacher training: Critiques and perspectives. *Reflective Practice, 14*(1), 104-117. doi:10.1080/14623943.2012.732935

Darling-Hammond, L. (2006). *Powerful teacher education: Lessons from exemplary programs.* San Francisco, CA: Jossey-Bass.

Darling-Hammond, L., & Baratz-Snowden, J. (2007). A good teacher in every classroom: Preparing the highly qualified teachers our children deserve. *Educational Horizons, 85*, 111-132.

Darling-Hammond, L., & Bransford, J. (2005). *Preparing teachers for a changing world.* San Francisco, CA: Jossey-Bass.

Falkenberg, T. (2015). Introduction: Canadian research in initial teacher education. In T. Falkenberg (Ed). *Handbook of Canadian Research in Initial Teacher Education* (pp. 1-16). Ottawa, ON: Canadian Association for Teacher Education.

Galea, S. (2012). Reflecting reflective practice. *Educational Philosophy and Theory, 44*(3), 245-258.

Garcia, J. A., & Lewis, T. E. (2014). Getting a grip on the classroom: From psychological to phenomenological curriculum development in teacher education programs. *Curriculum Inquiry, 44*(2), 141-168.

Holloway, S. M., & Gouthro, P. A. (2011). Teaching resistant novice educators to be critically reflective. *Discourse: Studies in the Cultural Politics of Education*, 29-41.

Hufford, D. (2008). Teacher education, transformation, and an education for discontent. *Journal of Philosophy and History of Education, 58*, 83-91.

Huntley, C. (2008). Supporting critical reflection in pre-service teacher education. *Journal of the Scholarship of Teaching and Learning for Christians in Higher Education, 3*(1), 18-28.

Hurley, S. (2013). *What is standing in the way of change in education: Reflections from the Canadian Education Association's Calgary workshop.* Canadian Educational Association. Retrieved from http://reports. cea-ace.ca/calgary 2013 report en

Liu, K. (2015). Critical reflection as a framework for transformative learning in teacher Education. *Educational Review, 67*(2), 135-157.

Malkani, J., & Allen, J. (2005). Cases in teacher education: Beyond reflection into practice. Paper presented at the *Annual Meeting of the American Educational Research Association.* Montreal, QC, Canada.

Otienoh, R. (2010). Feedback on teachers' journal entries: A blessing or a curse? *Reflective Practice, 11*(2), 143-156.

Phelan, A. M., Smits, H., & Ma, Y. (2015). Philosophical issues in initial teacher education. In T. Falkenberg (Ed.), *Handbook of Canadian Research in Initial Teacher Education* (pp. 227-244). Ottawa, ON: Canadian Association for Teacher Education.

Roscoe, K. (2013). Enhancing assessment in teacher education courses. *The Canadian Journal for the Scholarship of Teaching and Learning, 4*(1). doi:http://dx.doi.org/10.5206/cjsotl-rcacea.2013.1.5

Russell, T., & Dillon, D. (2015). The design of Canadian teacher education programs. In T. Falkenberg (Ed.), *Handbook of Canadian Research in Initial Teacher Education* (pp. 151-166). Ottawa, ON: Canadian Association for Teacher Education.

Rutherford, G., Whiting, R., & Smits, H. (2008). Experiences of undergraduate students in an interprofessional course. *The Journal of Educational Thought, 42*(3), 321-337.

Sanford, K., Kurki, S. B., & Starr, L. (2015). Genre issues in initial teacher education in Canada: A research lens. In T. Falkenberg (Ed.), *Handbook of Canadian Research in Initial Teacher Education* (pp. 261-276). Ottawa, ON: Canadian Association for Teacher Education.

Schön, D. A. (1983). *The reflective practitioner: How professionals think in action.* New York, NY: Basic Books.

Schön, D. A. (1987). *Educating the reflective practitioner: Toward a new design for teaching and learning in the professions.* San Francisco, CA: Jossey-Bass.

Smits, H., Towers, J., Panayotidis, E. L., & Lund, D. E. (2008). Provoking and being provoked by embodied qualities of learning: Listening, speaking, seeing and feeling (through) inquiry in teacher education. *Journal of the Canadian Association for Curriculum Studies,* 6(2), 43-81.

Steed, M., & Vigrass, A. (2011). Assessment of web conferencing in teacher preparation field experiences. *Proceedings of Society for Information Technology & Teacher Education International Conference,* 2736-2743.

Van Driel, J. H., & Berry, A. (2012). Teacher professional development focusing on pedagogical content knowledge. *Educational Researcher, 41*(1), 26-28.

Walker, L. (1990). Networks and paradigms in English language arts in Canadian faculties of education. *Canadian Journal of Education/ Revue canadienne de l'education,* 115-131.

Wiggins, G. P., & McTighe, J. (2005). *Understanding by design.* Alexandria, VA: ASCD.

Winsor, P. (1998). *A guide to the development of professional portfolios in the Faculty of Education.* Faculty of Education, Field Experiences Office.

Chapter 7

Upstairs/Downstairs: Conversations in the Attic about the Classrooms Below

Theresa Hyland, Allan MacDougall, and Grace Howell
Huron University College/University of Western Ontario

"Disciplines and cultures are made up of invisible ties
that bind: like some sub-atomic substance that holds
objects in orbit, keeping them in relation to each other and
preventing them from flying off" (Paré, 2008, p. 24).

Introduction

In 2007, a small liberal arts college was the original site for a study which has grown to include departments across Canada (Graves, Hyland, & Samuels, 2010). In this study, all course syllabi throughout the college were mapped for the number and kind of writing assignments that were required, length of assignments, value per assignment, whether or not marking rubrics and explanations of the expectations of the professor were included in the course outline, and whether there was any in-process feedback built into the writing requirements (i.e. peer reviews, discussion with professor, feedback on thesis statement or research proposal, etc.) The purpose of the Graves et al. (2010) study was to try to identify differences and/or similarities in the explanations of professorial expectations of student writing across years within disciplines and across disciplines.

The findings from that study seemed to indicate that the amount of information students were given varied more by professor than by discipline or academic year. One of the limitations of the study was that the course outlines and any supplemental materials provided by professors were the only materials that were analysed to determine how professorial expectations were conveyed to students. Faculty members objected to the results of the study on the grounds that studying the outlines alone would not give the researchers a full picture of how professors convey their expectations with regard to writing assignments. They claimed that offering office hours, engaging in class discussions, and providing supplemental materials were key student mentoring strategies used by faculty, which would be missed out in an evaluation of the course syllabi alone.

The researchers decided that a systematic investigation into the ways in which professors engage with students in talk about their writing would validate these claims and give the researchers a better understanding of how these expectations are conveyed to students. The current study resulted from conversations with faculty, held in the Faculty Attic club, about what went on in their classrooms, which were situated on floors far below the Attic Club.

Catherine Schryer (2011) provided the theoretical rationale for such a study in her discussion of the changing nature of genres within disciplines. She applied Bakhtin's notion of the centripetal and centrifugal forces of society and utterers to genre studies. She claimed that "genres are abstractions or ever-changing sets of socially acceptable strategies that participants can use to improvise their responses to a particular situation" (p. 34). Because genres are subject to continuous negotiation among the readers and writers within the discourse community, "genres are just stabilized enough so that agents can accomplish their social purpose, but [] genres are constantly evolving" (p. 34). What this means is that students need to learn what the stable, unchanging areas of a genre are, and also which specific expectations are built into each genre by each professor for the purposes of fulfilling the needs of a particular course. This opinion seems to be confirmed by a study in 2006 by Thaiss and Zawacki. They examined students' opinions about how they learned about writing through surveys, focus groups, and proficiency essays. They asserted that "students found that teachers were the most important sources of knowledge about disciplinary writing characteristics" (p. 108). In a smaller, but similar study, Hyland, Howell, and Zhang (2010) examined the effectiveness of the Writing Proficiency Assessment and student services, such as the Writing Skills Centre, in developing students' academic writing skills. Hyland et al. found that 59% of the students surveyed felt that the primary influence on the development of their essay writing was not the feedback from the proficiency assessment, nor help that they received from writing services, but the help that they got from their professors. Only 14% attributed improvement to reading and planning; 14% felt that writing courses helped; and 9% felt that the Writing Skills Centre visits helped their writing.

The model used in this study for researching professorial expectations comes from Anson and Dannels (2009). They proposed that a series of program profiles should be created based on surveys, focus groups, individual interviews, course syllabi, and written artifacts that faculty of specific disciplines could provide to the researchers. These profiles would focus on "attention to the subject matter with attention to the genres, audiences, language, presentational modes and other aspects of communication in the field" (p. 2). The resulting profiles would not only help writing services create programs that would help students manage the various disciplinary and genre demands within the academy, but also assist faculty in "creating a profile based on internal, consultative study of a program .... representing the department's current status: how writing and speaking are used, where, to what ends, and in what relationship to broader curricular, pedagogical and career goals" (p. 1).

Profiles, then, will help faculty articulate their goals for students, and also discuss ways in which these goals could be shared and developed between courses and throughout the degree program. Indeed, these two broad principles have been urged by two Canadian writing researchers in two different writing contexts. In his article "Crossing Boundaries: Co-op Students Relearning to Write," Douglas Brent (2012) articulated the need for faculty to make explicit their tacit knowledge of written genres in their disciplines so that students can be introduced to the heuristics that will help them meet the expectations of their mentors. Ann Beaufort argues that faculty have "a very rich, deep, context-specific knowledge, but they also have mental schema, or heuristics, with which to organize knowledge and aid problem-solving and gaining new knowledge in new situations." She says that this deep knowledge must be made explicit so that it can be applied to shaping curriculum. This would enable us as writing instructors to "contextualize writing instruction more fully and have a basis for teaching for transfer [of knowledge from one context to another]" (p. 17). Strachan (2008) organized faculty focus groups at Simon Fraser University in order to stimulate a discussion on the administration of and the principles underpinning new writing–intensive courses that faculty had agreed to pilot. She asked two important questions:

1. What have you done in terms of making students aware of "what they are getting" re: writing intensive that would help them support the initiative?
2. Are we communicating the writing requirement to students?

Given these comments, it seems appropriate to study faculty's tacit and articulated expectations about writing as an adjunct to the Canada-wide mapping project that Graves is engaged in. The researchers decided to propose focus groups comprised of faculty from each of several disciplines which presented interesting or perplexing profiles within the Course Syllabi Project. The timing for such a study was particularly appropriate at this college since a new dean had initiated a series of faculty-wide discussions about the needs of the students and the parameters of a broad-based curriculum review. One of the learning objectives identified by faculty in this review was "to prepare graduates who are effective communicators." We hoped, therefore, that this study would allow professors to critically reflect on how explicitly they are currently tapping this deep knowledge and conveying it to students, and provide input as to further steps that they could take to prepare the students to become effective communicators in writing. The purpose of the research, then, was twofold: (1) to add to our understanding of professorial expectations of students' writing in the disciplines, and (2) to engender the kind of self-reflexive conversations among faculty that would help them better articulate those expectations to students.

Our research questions were developed from our own analysis of disciplinary exigencies in the course syllabi project, from the faculty response to our presentation of that analysis, and from the larger research questions of the national Course Syllabi Project team led by Roger Graves (http://wac.ctl.ualberta.ca/research.aspx). They are:

1. To what extent are writing activities in a department consistent with each other and explicitly stated in the department's learning outcomes with regards to writing?
2. What instructional methods are employed to convey expectations for students' writing?
3. Are the methods employed to convey expectations dictated by individual personalities or by disciplinary demands for writing?

The Participants

In order to entice faculty to participate in our study, we followed the methodology and focusing questions posed by Anson and Dannels (2009): gain entry to a department; identify key players and curricular boundaries; interview volunteers; and finally, assemble and analyse the data (p. 1). After gaining financial support and ethics approval for our project, we began by gaining approval and support from the Teaching and Learning Committee at Huron, who also felt that the project would benefit both the aims of the researchers and the professional development of the faculty. The research team then determined which four departments we would ask to do the focus groups: two departments from Social Sciences and two from Humanities. Two of these departments had been used for a detailed analysis of the results of the earlier Course Syllabi Project. The other two departments were chosen because results from the project posed questions that piqued the curiosity of the researchers, and because the faculty of these departments seemed well-disposed to the work of the writing program, because they often referred students to the writing centre or asked the writing centre personnel to speak to their classes about writing concerns. We did not proceed with setting a date for the focus group until we had secured a verbal agreement to the project (in principle) from at least 3 people in the department.

When a sufficient number of faculty agreed to support the focus group activity, I then asked the chair of that department for support. The rest of the correspondence (setting date and time, reminders of the appointment date, etc.) occurred through email. At about the same time, I invited faculty from the target departments into the Writing Centre to give talks on Writing in the Disciplines for our tutors and for any students who were interested. This measure, I believe, helped the faculty see that we were engaged in a reciprocal learning environment where we valued their expertise and wanted to learn from it.

It was important to the success of the focus groups that our participants were willing collaborators (Anson & Dannels, 2009; Strachan, 2008). While this predisposition may have influenced the tenor of the conversations, and the fact that the conversations took place at all, it didn't affect the aims of the study because the information we gleaned from them had to do with what was being done by the faculty in their classrooms in order to address writing concerns. This meant that these "first adaptors" were willing to give thoughtful responses to our questions and generate a discussion among themselves about these issues. Moreover, all of the faculty members, with one exception, were tenured faculty, with a long history of teaching at the college and of publishing within their own disciplines. Since the college prides itself on the quality of the teaching, all of them perceived themselves to be good teachers, and students' evaluations seemed to bear this fact out. Thus, the conversation was not about whether writing was important, but simply about how writing expectations were conveyed to the students.

Materials

When the chair agreed to the focus group, the research team delivered the Faculty Information Sheets and the Volunteer Agreement Forms to the individual members of the department to ensure that they (a) received them and (b) understood their significance. The Volunteer Forms provided information on the project and the preceding research that motivated this study (see Appendix A). The Faculty Information Sheet (Appendix B) was designed to help faculty begin thinking about their writing assignments and how they strategize these in ways that would help us explore our research questions in the focus groups. The sheets would also allow the researchers to compare this information with the conversations in the focus groups to see whether and how much individual personalities determined the way in which expectations were delivered to the students in each department. Finally, these sheets allowed us to do some quantitative analysis that could enrich the findings from our qualitative analysis.

The focus group discussions were semi-structured in that seven basic questions provided a framework for the discussion (see Appendix C). These questions were designed to directly access supplemental information to what we already knew from the Course Syllabi Project (Graves et al., 2010), and to check to see if there had been any significant changes to the type, length, and purposes of the assignments that faculty are currently asking students to do. This information was supplemented with questions that asked professors to assess the difficulties that students met in writing these assignments and the strategies they employed in the classroom and outside of it in order to help students overcome these difficulties. Finally, we asked questions about departmental administration and how this aided or undermined their attempts to help students meet their writing expectations. Although these were the questions that we felt would help to answer our research questions, other questions were added during the course of the focus group sessions in order to broaden the discussion or compare ideas from one group to others that had been raised in previous groups. Some of the issues that were explored in this way were: (1) the use of and distinction between primary and secondary sources, (2) the kinds of assignments that students were asked to do, and (3) how faculty defined and developed critical thinking and writing in their discipline.

The feedback sheets were given to participants immediately after the focus groups. Some participants filled these out immediately, but others took them away with them. In general, we found that those who filled them out at the time were the only ones to hand in the feedback sheets, so the data collected from these was not complete.

Methods

This mixed methods study combines elements of quantitative survey data and qualitative focus group data. Following Figure 1 from Creswell and Plano Clark (2006), we utilized an embedded mixed methods design.

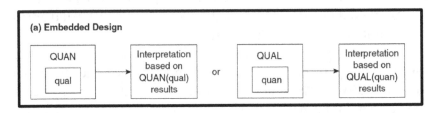

Figure 1. Embedded design (Creswell & Plano Clark, 2006).

An embedded design features a qualitative data set supporting a study based primarily on quantitative data, or vice versa. The qualitative data in our study provides a secondary role supporting our findings from the larger Course Syllabi Project (Graves et al., 2010) in which we examined 485 course outlines for the way in which they conveyed expectations about writing. We felt that some qualitative data collection could add crucial contextual information to our existing data set. Schryer (2011), among others, validates this method as a way of researching for her own research projects in genre studies by including first, a "close reading (objective) of specific texts to describe and critique the strategies evoked within these discursive events and second, interviewing participants and asking them for explanations for their strategies and problem-solving techniques" (p. 39). We selected a grounded theory method aimed at developing a better understanding of what faculty could add to our ongoing exploration of writing pedagogy across the disciplines. Grounded theory is well suited for an embedded design. Unlike some qualitative methodologies, grounded theory permits researchers to approach their questions in light of tacit background assumptions, or sensitizing concepts (Blumer, 1968).

According to Lingard (2008), key features of grounded theory include the intimately related practices of iterative study design (adjusting methods to meet study goals), purposive sampling (gathering data from deliberately selected sources), and constant comparative analysis (recursive data analysis that refines findings while generating them). We will first report early findings from our data analysis of four faculty focus groups. As a research team, we observed all four focus groups and then reviewed the focus group videos at a later date. We further independently coded focus group transcripts using NVivo 9 (QSR, 2010) qualitative data analysis software. After all team meetings, a group memo was created to record analytical insights. For the current report, our data set is formed of 4 study transcripts, 9 researcher notes, 17 group memos, and numerous software data analysis queries (eg, text searches and auto-coding).

Results

Prior to the focus group discussions, participating professors completed a Faculty Information Sheet (Appendix B), consisting of twelve questions which were designed to gather demographic information about professors' discipline, courses taught, status within the department as full-time, part-time, tenured, contract or sessional instructors (questions 1 to 3); types of assignments, supplemental information, and feedback provided to students (questions 4 to 6); length of assignments (questions 7 and 8); and the extent of departmental discussions about developing writing assignments, grading, expectations and communicating expectations (questions 9 to 12). Responses to the questions on the Faculty Information Sheet were tabulated by frequency, totaled by academic department, and also by all respondents across departments.

Demographics

Professors from four different disciplines in the Faculty of Arts and Social Sciences participated. A total of 14 professors completed Faculty Information Sheets; 12 were tenured, one was a contract instructor, and one was teaching part-time. Most of the professors taught a mix of introductory and advanced level courses in their discipline, although about one-third of the group, or four professors, reported teaching only advanced-level courses. One professor taught only introductory-level courses. Table 1 shows the frequency of major assignment types indicated on the Faculty Information Sheet by the participating professors in each discipline.

Table 1

Assignment types

	English n = 5	History n = 2	Pol. Sci. n = 3	Psychology n = 4	All responses n = 14(%)	Rank
Research Essay	5	2	3	3	93	1
Essay proposal	3	2	1	2	57	2
Critique	4		1	2	50	3
Presentation		2	2	3	50	3
Commentary	2		2	1	36	4
Annotated bibliography	2	2			28	5
Reflection		1	2	1	28	5
Thesis 4th year		1		3	28	5
Thesis	3				21	6
Report				3	21	6
First draft	2	1			21	6
Historiography		2			14	7
Book review	1	1			14	7
Outline	1			1	14	7
Summary				2	14	7
Poster				1	7	8

From the information gleaned from the Faculty Information Sheets in our study, the most popular assignment type across all disciplines was the research essay. It was selected as an assignment type by all respondents in English, History, and Political Science, and three of the four professors of Psychology. Conversely, only three professors in Psychology named the report, and only two professors, again in Psychology, named the summary as an important type of assignment that they required the students to write. At least half of the full faculty group chose the essay proposal, the critique, and the presentation as the next most popular assignments, and approximately one-third of the group (36%) chose the commentary as a desirable assignment. Presentations were popular among all disciplines except English. Only one professor from Political Science selected the critique as an assignment. This is rather different from the results reported in the Course Syllabi Project (2010). In that study, the researchers discovered that only 26.9% of all assignments were named "essays," 20.9% were named "papers," and 17.8% were called "reports."

The Information Sheets did not ask the faculty to specify whether these assignments were given to first year or upper year students, or both. On future surveys, we would suggest that professors should indicate what assignments are given to first year or upper year students. There may be different objectives, and therefore, different assignments given to these two groups of students.

Table 2

Supplemental information

	English n=5	History n=2	Pol. Sci. n=3	Psychology n=4	All responses n = 14 (%)	Rank
Out-of-class, written	5	2	2	4	93	1
In-class, oral	5	2	2	3	86	2
In-class, written	4	2	3	2	79	3
Out-of-class, oral	5	2	2	2	79	3
Web-based instructions	3	1	1	3	57	4
Marking grids	2		1	2	36	5

All participants indicated that they provide supplemental information about writing assignments beyond the course syllabus (see Table 2 for this information by discipline). The most popular type of supplemental information provided across all disciplines is the out-of-class written explanation, selected by 93% of all respondents. This selection was followed closely by in-class oral explanations at 86%. The minor variants of both these selections, i.e. in-class written and out-of-class oral explanations, were tied at 79% each. The key finding here is that the traditional oral and written forms of supplemental information are used widely.

Somewhat surprising is the relative lack of the provision of marking rubrics for assignments; in fact, this was apparently the least popular method of providing supplemental information, selected by just 5 professors or 36% of this small group. Neither member of the History Department selected this option. This lack of response could represent a misconception around the term "grid" because this term is used to denote the marking rubric for a specific assignment as well as the allocation of marks for the overall course grade. Additionally, the grid may not be considered supplemental, but rather, a primary form of communication of information about assignment expectations. Certainly, within this faculty group, marking rubrics—as they may be perceived—fare rather poorly as a desirable option for providing supplemental information about assignments. Probing the reasons for this unpopularity in individual follow-up interviews might reveal some rationale for the choices of supplemental information formats

There was no area on the survey for participants to mention any "other" type of supplemental information that they provide. There was a space where they could indicate for which assignments they provide the supplemental material; however, this information was not provided by any of the participants, perhaps because only a single line had been allocated for this response. On future surveys, an assignment-by-information grid might encourage more responses to this query.

Feedback

Participants in all disciplines except Political Science, and only one in Psychology, indicated that they provide a feedback requirement about writing assignments before these are marked. The most popular type of feedback provided is the optional office-hour oral consultations indicated by 50% of all participants, and by 64% of those who reported using this form of interaction with students. Methods of feedback mentioned by the professors and listed by frequency of choice are:

- Voluntary office-hour oral consultations (50%)
- Required office-hour oral consultations (21%)
- Written comments on unmarked first draft (21%)
- Written comments on marked first draft (21%)
- In-class oral peer review (21%)
- In-class written peer review (14%)
- Out-of-class written peer review (7%)

Length of Assignments

The next two questions asked participants about the longest and the shortest pieces of writing that the professors assigned to students, and within these questions, asked in which courses these assignments appear. Some faculty responded by indicating the number of words in an assignment, and others indicated the number of pages in an assignment. In order to yield a consistent and comparable metric, where the number of pages only was provided, the total number of words was estimated to be 250 per page. On average, the longest assignment length was 14.5 pages or approximately 3,637 words, and the shortest assignment length was 3 pages or 750 words.

There was no consistent response in terms of the courses to which the long and short assignments apply; some professors indicated the course by its identification number, while others indicated only the year or type of course to which the assignment applied. The data was re-coded to indicate that the course referred to was either introductory or a first year course, or an upper year, advanced course that usually required students to complete a prerequisite introductory course. Using this distinction, only two of the professors indicated that the longest assignments appear in introductory courses, while seven of the professors, or half of the group, indicated that the shortest assignments occurred in the introductory courses.

Departmental Discussions

The final questions on the Faculty Information Sheet solicited data about the existence of departmental discussions concerning developing writing assignments and each professor's participation in these. The first two questions in this series asked these questions separately concerning developing writing assignments; however, in the questions about grading assignments and increased expectations for student writing from first to fourth year, there was only one opportunity to check "yes" or "no" to the existence of these discussions and whether the professors participated in these. It was decided that the key aspect of these questions was the existence of these discussions, rather than individual participation, and therefore it was assumed that the "yes" or "no" response applied to the first query, i.e. the existence of these discussions. Future versions of this survey might see these questions separated or else reworded to query only the existence of these departmental discussions; participants may be reluctant to disclose non-participation, but would acknowledge the existence of such discussions. Table 3 shows the responses to the questions about departmental discussions.

Table 3

Departmental discussions

	English n=5	History n=2	Pol.Sci. n=3	Psychology n=4	All n = 14 (%)
Developing writing assignments	1	2	0	3	43%
Grading assignments	0	0	0	3	21%
Increased expectations (for student writing from 1st to 4th year)	0	0	0	1	7%

It would appear that neither the English Department nor the Political Science Department conducts discussions at the departmental level about any of the kinds queried. One comment on the survey from a Political Science professor indicated that these discussions may only occur around the introductory level courses. Four of the five English professors checked "no" to Question 9 concerning the existence of discussions about developing writing assignments, and the one person who did indicate that these discussions occur may have been referring to discussions at the course level, as it was indicated by the Political Science professor. This may also have been true for the one Psychology professor who acknowledged that discussions occur in the department around increased expectations; because all the others selected a "no" response to this question, it is quite likely that the professor who responded was referring to course-level discussions.

Generally, there were more discussions concerning the development of writing assignments (43%), fewer about grading assignments (21%), and fewer still concerning the increased expectations for student writing from the first to the fourth year of study (7%). Although the data only indicates whether discussions occur generally, the comment from the Political Science professor would indicate that it might be of value to query the level at which these occur. Future surveys could provide a matrix to reveal the frequency of discussions in first to fourth year courses.

This data appears to corroborate the comments made during the focus groups, where the professors echoed the fact that these discussions largely do not occur. Several participants in the focus groups commented on the value of the discussion generated from the questions posed by the researcher. With this sentiment in mind, and with more detail about the levels at which discussions occur, departments could be provided with a "snapshot" of where these discussions are—and are not—occurring. This information might reveal gaps in the continuity of skills development monitoring between the introductory and the senior-level assignments, grading, and expectations.

Qualitative Analysis

Our initial analysis sought to characterize the four departments in relation to one another. As observers, we found it interesting how similarities and differences ran across each of the focus groups.

We observed that each department seemed to represent its writing in terms of a dominant metaphor that faculty applied both to the writing itself and to how students should approach that writing. The focus group discussions led us to speculate about the relationship between the departmental discussions of writing and how each department's discipline influences student writing.

Departmental Characteristics

During focus groups, the research team found that each departmental group used distinct metaphors for student writing. In this section, we will discuss the metaphors for writing that faculty used to discuss the requirements that their field imposed on writing. These metaphors were the result of focus group dialogue, not a specific question asking participants to use metaphors. In more than one case, one participant would initiate a metaphor characterizing some topic related to student writing and the other participants would extend the metaphor.

Metaphors for writing. Critical discourse analysis has given us a way of considering "stylistic, verbal, syntactic, and figurative structure and the ways in which such discursive and semiotic structures circulate or articulate with ideology" (Hucklin, Andrus, & Clary-Lemon, 2012, p. 118). One of those stylistic features that we found pertinent to our focus group discussions was the faculty's use of metaphor when they described their expectations for student writing. The English department focus group characterized student writing as taking place in silos. Because of the breadth of contextual and textual elements of English studies, they explained, each course that students take requires a different form of literary criticism. They explained that writing in the colonial literature course was very different from writing in the critical theory course. Therefore, both the faculty, as experts in that field, and the students who are studying that field must separate the writing that they do for that field from a more general idea of what the literary essay should be. One participant told us, "our colleagues in the social science have a better ability to say this is what a good history essay is, or this is what a good political science essay is . . . Our discipline certainly has a general sense, but it allows for variations such as a poetry course or other, more politicized courses."

In the Psychology focus group, modelling was the metaphor characterizing the introduction of students to the discipline of Psychology. Modelling was explained as the method of creating the specific written forms that are meaningful to other psychologists. A Psychology department member explained that, "our aim, ultimately, is to get our students to write in exactly the same style that we ourselves write to produce professional journal articles."

During the History focus group, faculty members spoke about teaching students about becoming historians, and the historians' craft. A quote by one participant captures this metaphor: "[Historical research] is looking at materials that are generated in... were generated in the period that you're studying, so that is the stuff of history basically, the primary sources themselves that come from that period." Historians emphasized primary research as a crucial component of History scholarship. The craft, then, is to be able to place that primary research within its larger context in terms of its significance to that context.

Finally, one faculty member in the department of Political Science brought forward the metaphor of a well-prepared meal, and the others quickly took up that metaphor. One faculty member told us that "I always tell students that a research paper is a sort of a five course meal, you have to have the appetizer [introduction] and the soup [case study] and then the main course [body content]." All Political Science faculty agreed that there are necessary components to a good research paper in Political Science—we felt this brought new meaning to 'hamburger essay.'

Descriptions of writing. Besides using metaphors, each faculty group took pains to describe for the researchers how writing relates to the subject matter of their field. In the department of English, faculty described student writing as the analysis of assigned literary texts. One faculty member stated that "prior to the actual writing . . . there is the object that students are writing about, which in our case is always a literary text. And before they can write about it they have to have understood something about it as well."

In the department of Psychology, faculty described student writing as the codification of observations in a formal, standardized format (i.e. the lab report in APA style). One faculty member stated "what we're trying to do is get students to learn APA style writing and then along with that sort of stylistic pattern. I want them to learn to write as precisely and as accurately as possible as to what actually went on, you know, during the course of the study."

In the department of History, faculty described student writing as the discovery and analysis of texts as historical artifacts. A faculty member told us the History department "frames essay assignments as 'what can we learn about the past from this document?' And so in that case the thesis is, 'here's what we can learn.'"

In the department of Political Science, faculty described student writing as the balanced analysis of empirical studies and theoretical texts. A faculty member told us "we expect . . . students to be able to critically take apart what she or he is writing about within the format of setting out the theory, finding evidence, using deduction as well, using logic, and coming to a conclusion."

Disciplinary Characteristics

In considering both the departmental metaphors and descriptions of writing, we wondered whether or how each discipline's epistemological positioning affected how professors engage student writing. Bakhtin posited that there are centripetal and centrifugal forces in a given context that change the parameters of the genre. The centripetal forces are those members of the audience for whom the message is crafted and who have certain expectations of a text. The centrifugal forces are the needs of the writer to convey a particular idea (Schryer, 2011, p. 35). Our work with the focus groups seems to suggest that some disciplines (i.e. Psychology) have more rigid rhetorical strategies because of the scientists' need to provide not interpretation but validation of conclusions to the audience. Some disciplines, like English, on the other hand, admit to different interpretations of ideas and cultural artifacts, and so allow more scope for a creative interpretation of the rhetorical forms of a genre. Validity, it seems, comes from the elegance of the interpretation rather than in the objective demonstration through the presentation of evidence.

We found it useful, then, to situate our four disciplines along two dichotomous, epistemological axes. First we placed each focus group in relation to what we observed to be its disciplinary/departmental stance on knowledge, or epistemological orientation. We divided epistemological orientation into two polarized positions on knowledge: positivist (knowledge is gained by the analysis and understanding of facts) and relativist (knowledge is gained by engaging and interpreting subjective texts). Next we placed each focus group in relation to its disciplinary/departmental stance on student texts, or research orientation. We divided research orientation into two polarized stances on student texts, assigned texts (texts are given to students to be read, analyzed, and understood) and text discovery (students are encouraged to find unique texts or case studies). We are aware these are overly simplified dichotomies, but they nevertheless gave us a useful analytic lens for discussing how potentially tacit disciplinary norms play a role in written assignments.

Departmental/Disciplinary Epistemological Orientation		
Epistemological orientation	Research orientation	
	Assigned texts	Text discovery
Positivist	Psychology	Political science
Relativist	English	History

Figure 2. Departmental/disciplinary epistemological orientation.

Using our epistemological orientation heuristic (see Figure 2), we described the department of Psychology as a having a positivist orientation while assigning student texts. One Psychology faculty member characterized the department as follows:

> For the most part we feed a lot of what we're expecting to the first years, so we give them a major article then we take them through all the major points and then, you know, try to draw it out of them but... for the most part tell them here are some points that you probably want to hang all your stuff on.

As this faculty member states, the department's approach to writing is to assign a major article and take them through the salient, meaningful points. The student's role is to glean objective facts and learn a textual structure.

The department of English also assigns student texts, but we have characterized this department as relativist in its approach to what types of knowledge texts offer students. One English faculty member explains how assigned texts should be "engaged:"

> Two [essay assignments in my class] are very specifically on the text that we are reading, I don't let them use secondary sources, I want them to engage with the text... I want them actually to deal with the text as an object that they can... they can say things about that can be demonstrated from the text rather than just how it makes them feel.

As this faculty member states, students in English must interpret texts rather than simply provide summaries of major points or personal narratives.

While History faculty also allow students to interpret texts rather that summarize, unlike Psychology and English, History students are taught to seek out primary documents as part of their studies:

> I think one of the key things that we emphasize is ... and this may not be a writing question so much as a research question, but... an ability to conduct primary research we'd say, to how to interpret historical documents.

Discussion

Several findings were not in keeping with the findings of Graves et al. (2010). For example, these researchers found that "the frequency of different assignment types is twice as high [in the social sciences] as in the humanities" (pp. 312-313). However, in the information sheets that faculty handed in for the Focus Group Study, History and English faculty listed far more types of assignments than did faculty in Psychology and Political Science. History had the greatest variety of assignments (archival research, historiography, reflection papers, and document analysis). This may be because the first project considered all the Social Sciences and Humanities fields, whereas this project really just compared four disciplines. While the Course Syllabi Project indicated that Psychology has many different assignments, the Focus Group discussion made it clear that the many assignments were actually nested within one type (i.e. lab reports). The Course Syllabi Project seemed to indicate that English assignments were all research essays. The focus group and information sheets showed that English assignments included discovery of and interpretation of poems that have been hitherto unreviewed, creation of scenes in Shakespeare, technical and thematic explorations, group essays, and presentations. In Political Science, the Information Sheets indicated that professors only asked for research essays, but the discussion disclosed that students are also asked to do book reviews and policy papers, all of which were referred to as "essays" in the syllabi.

Naming Assignments

One of the purposes of the focus groups, then, was to generate a discussion about the kinds of assignments that professors gave to students. What we found was that professors used diverse, descriptive names for their assignments in conversation: movie reviews, book reports, policy briefs, edited collection or archive, reflections, literature reviews, etc. when they were speaking about these assignments. However, when they wrote about the assignments on the course outlines, they would invariably describe them as "essay assignments." In the Course Syllabi project, where we generated categories of assignments from what professors called them, we found that most professors named assignments "essays," "papers," and "reports." In the Faculty Information Sheets, however, where faculty had to choose from pre-set names for assignments, 93% chose the term "essay" to describe their writing assignments. They also chose a variety of other genres that did not seem to appear in the Course Syllabi Project (2010). There are two possible explanations for these naming anomalies: (1) because these courses are still designated by administration as "essay courses," this generic course label is transferred to the more specific assignments for each course; or (2) naming anomalies found between the Faculty Information Sheets, the Course Syllabi Project, and the discussion within the focus groups may substantiate the claim by Graves, Hyland, and Samuels (2010). They assert that faculty do not make a clear distinction between assignments when naming them, and that this lack of a shared vocabulary about writing assignments within and between departments could lead to confusion for students who are trying to decipher the expectations linked to an assignment.

The surveys that were completed by our focus group participants indicated that there were five assignment names that were used in several disciplines: research essay, essay proposal, critique, presentation, and commentary. These names were used with such frequency that one might call them cross-disciplinary genres. It is not known, however, if the other professors' purposes in assigning presentations have more to do with students sharing information only (a positivist stance), or to provide an opportunity for them to present and discuss a particular point of view (a relativist stance). This information might emerge in individual interviews and might illustrate clearer differences between the goals of professors in the different disciplines in assigning presentations. Despite lack of clarity with the names of assignments, each discipline seems to adapt the genre to suit the requirements of the discipline: i.e. the content, evidence generation, and critical analysis seem to be discipline-specific. We also found that professors seem to be unaware that students might be confused by disciplinary differences when they approach a genre that they may think they have mastered in another discipline. Further study with students might confirm or expand our knowledge of whether this confusion does exist and how it plays out (i.e. whether, how, and when a student might attempt to write a research essay in English in the same way that she might write a research essay in Political Science).

Implications of Epistemological Differences

Given our characterization of the epistemological underpinnings of each department's expectations regarding writing, how do these differences play out in what is assigned to students at different levels of study? One major difference between the Course Syllabi Project and the Focus Group Study is that in the latter project, we were able to trace essay assignments for all four years of each discipline. In the current project, much of the faculty discussion centred on first year writing practices, even though we tried to move the discussion to focus on the senior years. This may be because first year classes are generally taught by several members of the faculty, so the first year teaching consortium has come to a consensus on what needs to be taught about writing in their field during that first year. They have developed a common vocabulary about writing that conveys their expectations to each other and to the students.

In keeping with a relativist stance as articulated by the focus group in English, first year students learn to write by writing. They are not given the right answers as to how to interpret a text, but are allowed to figure out an appropriate interpretation for themselves. The Course Syllabi Project showed us that each English assignment in first year is longer than the last (500, 750, 1000, 1500), and that reading outside critics is not necessary until the students move on to longer essays of 1000 to 1500 words. In Psychology, faculty talked about modelling good report-writing practice. There again, it is no surprise that the Syllabi Project showed that first year Psychology students are given one major assignment which is broken down into parts and which students practice (i.e. essay proposal, literature review, results section). These nested assignments lead to the final report due near the end of the first year. Psychology is one of only two programs in the Course Syllabi Project where first year assignments were broken down in this way.

In some cases, professors used assignments to teach the students skills that had nothing to do with their specific disciplines, but everything to do with a more generic form of academic writing. This occurs, for example, where the large writing assignments are broken down into several skills-related parts (i.e. the thesis, annotated bibliography, proposal, first draft, final draft). Here again, the relativist-positivist dichotomy seems to lend a method of interpreting the success or failure of these strategies. Faculty in English and in Political Science spoke of the need for students to learn time-management and the hope that this technique would help them. However, both faculties qualified this statement with the caveat that many of the students just do the assignment (big or small) the night before the deadline, and don't seem to learn anything more when the assignments are broken down into smaller pieces. Only in

Psychology did the faculty assert that this was the best (only) way to teach students to do a lab report.

The epistemological position of the disciplines affected not only what the professors teach about writing, but also how they teach it. Where format is rigid, as in the two disciplines that we identified as positivist, the focus group conversations showed that there is little interest among the faculty to pursue in-process feedback strategies for students' writing. Rather, these disciplines have a propensity to use modeling and assignment rubrics to teach students how to approach the genres common to their disciplines. The relativist disciplines tended not to use modeling but instead to use more in-process feedback techniques such as peer reviews, oral consultations, and written comments on a first-draft. The English and History professors both spoke about how students really needed to take advantage of office hour visits with faculty.

Reading Texts as Objects or Vehicles for Discovery

Professors from different disciplines might be doing the same thing for different reasons. All courses have "assigned readings," but these readings serve very different purposes. In English, reading texts are assigned for both written and spoken interpretation, but in Psychology they are assigned as models for students to follow, or to justify for students' own research, in the literature review. In History, reading texts are assigned as vehicles from which students are expected to "discover" other, related texts. In other words, students are encouraged to find their own texts with which to study a particular event. Political Science also expects students to discover texts by using the assigned readings as vehicles for further research. In this, it is closer to History than to English.

Limitations of the Study

Our focus group interviews and information sheets surveyed only those professors who volunteered to be interviewed, which resulted in a small amount of data that may not represent the views of everyone in the departments we targeted. We might have understood more about whether the differences we discovered between disciplines was due to individual personalities or exigencies of the field if we had sent the information sheets to all members of the departments, whether they planned to come to the focus group sessions or not. This shortcoming was mitigated, however, because we were able to use the previous research which used all course outlines to flesh out departmental/personal differences.

When we examined the information sheets, we noticed that no department mentioned their use of marking rubrics, which seemed surprising. However, the Course Syllabi Project showed that Political Science had standardized marking grids on all the course outlines. It may be that our questions on the Information Sheet were not specific enough for professors to identify the standard marking grid that their outlines contained as a "marking rubric." The survey should make this point clearer.

We also discovered that faculty answered questions 9, 10, 11 and 12 about departmental discussions differently for first year and upper year courses. Perhaps these questions should allow different answers for both levels of courses. Looking forward, this might be another area to explore in different contexts. Do larger departments also hold meetings about writing expectations for first year courses but not about upper level courses? Are expectations for these writing assignments clearer, therefore, for first year? Does a lack of departmental discussions seem to have an impact on students' understanding, and ultimately, upon their performance?

Conclusion

The Focus Group Study has both clarified and challenged some of the findings from the Course Syllabi Project. The two together form a powerful instrument to help us understand what professors' expectations are concerning writing in their disciplines, how disciplinary requirements vary, and how professors convey their expectations to students about the writing that they are assigned. The two studies raise some interesting questions about the issues they set out to explore:

1. What effect does the use of generic terms such as "essay, proposal, critique, and commentary" have on the

misunderstandings that students may have about a writing assignment?

2. Are the epistemological differences that we discovered truly indicative of distinctions that exist between disciplines or are they due to personal interpretations of those disciplines?

3. How do students interpret the expectations that professors convey about the written assignments within a discipline?

All of these questions require further study in order to be answered.

Acknowledgements

We would like to thank the Social Sciences and Humanities Research Council of Canada for their support (SRG 4102011-1845).

We would also like to thank the faculty and administration at Huron University College for allowing us to conduct this research, in particular Dr. Mark Blagrave, Dean of the Faculty of Arts and Social Sciences.

Upstairs/Downstairs | 199

References

Anson, C. A., & Dannels, D. (2009). Profiling programs: Formative uses of departmental consultations in the assessment of communication across the curriculum. [Special issue on Writing Across the Curriculum and Assessment] *Across the Disciplines, 6.* Retrieved from http://wac.colostate.edu/atd/assessment/anson_dannels.cfm

Beaufort, A. (2007). *College writing and beyond: A new framework for university writing instruction.* Logan: Utah State University Press.

Blumer, H. (1968). *Symbolic interactionism: Perspective and method.* Englewood Cliffs, NJ: Prentice Hall.

Brent, D. (2012). Crossing boundaries: Co-op students relearning to write. *CCC, 63*(4), 558-592. NCTE Press.

Creswell, J., & Plano Clark, V. (2006). *Designing and conducting mixed methods research.* Thousand Oaks, CA: Sage.

Graves, R., Hyland, T., & Samuels, B. M. (2010). Undergraduate writing assignments: An analysis of syllabi at one Canadian college. *Written Communication, 27*(3), 293-317. Hudson, OH: Sage Publications.

Huckin, T., Andrus, J., & Clary-Lemon, J. (2012). Critical discourse analysis and rhetoric and composition. *CCC, 64*(1), 107-128.

Hyland, K. (2008). Genre and academic writing in the disciplines. *Language Teaching, 41*(4), 543-562. doi:http://dx.doi.org/10.1017/S0261444808005235

Hyland, K. (2011). Disciplines and discourses: Social interactions in the construction of knowledge. In D. Starke-Meyerring, A. Paré, N. Artemeva, M. Horne, & L. Yousoubova (Eds.), *Writing in knowledge societies* (pp. 193-214). Fort Collins, CO: WAC Clearing House.

Hyland, T., Howell, G., & Zhang, Z. (2010). The effectiveness of the Writing Proficiency Assessment (WPA) in improving student writing skills at Huron University College. *Report Number 2: RFP 006 Student Services.* Toronto, ON: Higher Education Quality Council of Ontario. Retrieved from http://www.heqco.ca/SiteCollectionDocuments/P3%20WPA.pdf

Lingard, L., Albert, M., & Levinson, W. (2008). Grounded theory, mixed methods, and action research. *BMJ, 337*, A567. doi:10,1136/bmj.39602.690162.47

Paré, A. (2008). Interdisciplinarity: Rhetoric, reasonable accommodation, and the Toto effect. In *Interdisciplinarity: Thinking and Writing Beyond Borders,* Proceedings for the 25th Conference of the Canadian Association of Teachers of Technical Writing.

Ramoroka, B. T. (2012). Teaching academic writing for the disciplines: How far can we be specific in an EAP writing course? *English Linguistic Research, 1*(2), 33-42.

Schryer, C. (2011). Investigating texts in their social contexts: The promise and peril of rhetorical genre studies. In D. Starke-Meyerring, A. Paré, N. Artemeva, M. Horne, & L. Yousoubova (Eds.), *Writing in knowledge societies* (pp. 31-42). Fort Collins, CO: WAC Clearing House.

Strachan, W. (2008) *Writing intensive: Becoming W-Faculty in a new writing curriculum.* Logan, UT: Utah State University Press.

Thaiss, C. & Zawacki, T. (2006). *Engaged writers, dynamic disciplines: Research on the academic writing life.* Portsmouth, NH: Boynton Cook/Heinemann.

Appendix A: Letter of Information & Participant Consent Form

Writing Assignments Across the Undergraduate Curriculum

November 25th, 2011

You have been asked to participate in a research study which is being conducted by Theresa Hyland and Writing Services at Huron University College in conjunction with writing researchers at UWO, the University of Alberta, Wilfrid Laurier University, the Royal Military College, and the University of British Columbia. It is a continuation of a study initially conducted by Roger Graves, Boba Samuels, and Theresa Hyland in 2007/2008 entitled "The Huron University College/University of Western Ontario Writing Project: Writing through the Curriculum." In this study, all course outlines throughout the college were mapped for the number and kind of writing assignments that were required, length of assignments, value per assignment, whether or not marking rubrics and explanations of the expectations of the professor were included in the course outline, and whether there was any in-process feedback built into the writing requirements (i.e. peer reviews, discussion with professor, feedback on thesis statement, or research proposal etc.) The purpose of the study was to try to identify differences and/or similarities in how professors convey expectations of student writing across years within disciplines and across disciplines.

Huron was the original site for this course outline study. The information sheet and data analysis methods we used in the study have served as a model for all subsequent, related studies which have been, or are currently being conducted in the above universities. The findings from this study (Graves, Hyland, & Samuels, 2010) seemed to indicate that the amount of information students were given varied most by professor and not by discipline or academic year. One of the limitations of the study was that the course outlines and any supplemental materials provided by professors were the only materials that were analysed to determine how professorial expectations were conveyed to students. When we presented the findings to the Huron faculty, in 2008, faculty members pointed out that studying the course outlines alone gives a very limited picture of how professors convey their expectations with regard to writing assignments. Clearly, there is a need to investigate further the myriad ways in which professors engage with students in talk about their writing. In this follow-up study we hope to (1) gain a fuller understanding of how professors convey their expectations about writing assignments to their students, (2) contribute to the Canada-wide mapping project, and (3) allow professors the opportunity to critically reflect on their practice.

About the Study

The methodology we will follow is one suggested by Anson and Dannels (2009), whereby we start by having "focus groups" of volunteers from different areas of the college in order to elicit common understandings or differences in expectations for writing across courses and departments. We will then move on to individual interviews with volunteers to elucidate how these common understandings are put into practice by individual faculty. If you agree to participate in this study, you will be asked to (a) fill in a pre-focus group information sheet, (b) participate in the initial videotaped faculty focus groups, (c) fill in a feedback sheet after the focus group, (d) supply supplemental materials that you give to students regarding their writing assignments for all courses you are currently teaching, and (e) you may be asked to participate in an individual interview lasting about ½ hour after the initial focus group sessions.

Important Information Related to your Participation

Participation is voluntary, and you may refuse to answer questions or to be videotaped, or withdraw from the study at any time. If you participate in the faculty focus groups, you will be asked to supply supplemental materials that you given to students for their assignments. You may be asked to attend an interview. The focus groups will take place in late November and early January, and the interviews will take place in January and February 2012, at a time that will be convenient for you. Focus group proceedings and the interviews will be digitally videotaped for the purposes of analysis.

Confidentiality

All information and data provided by you will remain confidential. Neither Huron College, nor you nor your department will be identified in any reports of this study. Transcripts of the focus groups and interviews, along with copies of the supplemental materials, will be kept in a locked drawer in Dr. Hyland's office. These will be coded and a list of participants' names and corresponding coded identification numbers will be kept in a separate, locked cabinet in Dr. Hyland's office. Pseudonyms will be used when reporting data (i.e. quotes) from individual cases. The digital video-tapes will be stored on a secure portion of the Huron public drive and will be encrypted for extra protection.

Risks, Costs, and Benefits to You

There are no risks to faculty for participating in this project. Remarks that you make in the focus groups will only be heard by the other faculty participants, the transcriber, and the research coordination team (Theresa Hyland, Grace Howell, and Allan McDougall) for analysis purposes. You will be invited to make further comments in writing if you so wish. There are many benefits to participating in this study. Focus group participants will have the opportunity to develop collegiality within and between departments and reflection on practice. By sharing practices and perspectives with colleagues and critically reflecting on ways to make expectations more transparent to the students, participants may find ways to hone their teaching skills. The follow-up individual interviews may consolidate those discoveries. Huron College has the opportunity to benefit from information gleaned from the much larger, Canada-wide, SHRCC-funded project, as well as having the privilege of being the smallest liberal arts college to be included in the data collection.

Other Information

The plan for this study has been reviewed for its adherence to ethical guidelines by a Research Ethics Board at the University of Alberta. For questions regarding participant rights and ethical conduct of research, contact the Research Ethics Office at (780) 492-2615. If you are interested in participating in our research project, or would like to learn more about the study, please contact Dr. Theresa Hyland at the Writing Skills Centre, or at 519-438-7224 Ext. 317, or by email at thyland@huron.uwo.ca.

Thank you for your time and interest in our research project. This letter is yours to keep for future reference. If you have any questions about your rights as a research subject, you may contact the Dean of FASS at Huron University College.

Contact Information

Dr. Theresa Hyland
Director of Writing and Cross-cultural Services
Huron University College
519-438-7224 Ext. 317

Writing Assignments Across the Undergraduate Curriculum
Volunteer Consent Form

Dr. Theresa Hyland, Coordinator of the Writing Services at Huron University College, is conducting a study to elucidate findings from an initial Writing Across the Curriculum Study of 2007/08 which categorized the ways in which professors' expectations in writing are conveyed in course syllabi. Data from the syllabi were entered into data sheets and were analysed to see if these expectations are consistent within and across disciplines and from freshman to senior year. The current study supplements those findings through videotaped faculty focus groups and audio taped individual faculty interviews along with the collection of supplemental materials that faculty provide to their students about writing assignments, and pre- and-post focus group information and feedback questionnaires. While the data collected in this way may be used in published papers about the research, all data that is used for research purposes will protect the identity of the participants by withholding the name of the college, obscuring the departments that faculty belong to, and through the use of pseudonyms.

Further information concerning the collection of data, analysis, and/or the research project's goals may be obtained from Theresa Hyland at (519) 438-7224 Ext. 317. Email: thyland@huron.uwo.ca. The plan for this study has been reviewed for its adherence to ethical guidelines by a Research Ethics Board at the University of Alberta. For questions regarding participant rights and ethical conduct of research, contact the Research Ethics Office at (780) 492-2615.

You may withdraw from this study by contacting Dr. Theresa Hyland directly at any time up to and including the date of the videotaping of your focus group.

Please circle all the statements below with which you agree:
1. I have read and understood the description of the nature and purpose of this project.
2. I understand that my participation is voluntary and that I may choose not to answer any questions, and that I may terminate my participation at any time.
3. I understand that every effort will be made to maintain the confidentiality of the data now and in the future.
4. I will fill in the attached information sheet
5. I will participate in the appropriate focus group for my discipline.
6. I agree to being videotaped as part of the focus group data collection procedure.
7. I will fill in the feedback questionnaire.
8. I agree to share any supplemental written materials that I give to my students concerning their written assignments.
9. I agree to an interview about my writing assignments and the preparation I give to students for those assignments.
10. I agree to be audio taped for the interview.

_____

(Name)

_____

(Signature)   (Date)

Appendix B: Faculty Information Sheet

Writing Assignments Across the Undergraduate Curriculum
*This sheet will help the researchers understand the context of
your remarks in the focus group and interview sessions.*

Information about You

1. Your Discipline/ Department at Huron

   _____

2. Courses You Teach (2011/2012)

   _____

   _____

   _____

3. Please indicate your status in FASS: tenured/ contract/ part-time/ sessional

Information about your Assignments

4. What type of assignments do you have your students complete? (tick all that apply):

- Annotated bibliography
- Book Review
- Commentary on an article or chapter
- Critique
- Essay Proposal
- First Draft
- Historiography
- Outline
- Poster
- Presentation
- Research essay
- Reflection piece
- Report

- Summary
- Thesis statement
- Thesis (fourth year)
- Other (please specify)_____

5. Do you provide supplemental material about your writing assignments to the students outside of the course syllabus?
   Yes   No
   i.   If you answered Yes, please tick any and all that apply:
        - In-class, written instructions
        - Web-based instructions
        - Marking grids
        - Out-of-class, written explanations (e.g. answers to email requests)
        - In-class, oral explanations, answers to questions
        - Out-of-class, oral explanations or answers to questions
   ii. For which assignments do you provide this supplemental material?

6. Do you build in a feedback requirement for writing assignments before these assignments are marked?
   Yes   No

   i.   For which assignments? (please list all that apply)
        _____

   ii. What is the form of that feedback?
        ○   Written comments on unmarked first draft
        ○   Written comments on marked first draft
        ○   Voluntary, office hour oral consultations
        ○   Required, office hour oral consultations
        ○   In-class, written peer review
        ○   In-class, oral peer review
        ○   Out-of-class, oral peer review
        ○   Out-of-class, written peer review
        ○   Other _____

7. What is the longest piece of writing that you assign students?
   _____

   i. In which course(s) does this assignment appear? _____

8. What is the shortest piece of writing that you assign?
   _____

   ii. In which course(s) does this assignment appear? _____

Information about your Academic Department

9. Do you participate in roundtable discussions within your department about developing writing assignments? Yes No

10. Do you participate in roundtable discussions within your department about grading assignments? Yes No

11. Do you participate in roundtable discussions within your department about increased expectations for student writing from first to fourth year? Yes No

12. Do you have any other information you wish to share about how you convey your expectations for writing to your students?

   _____

   _____

Thank you!

Appendix C: Focus Group Questions

Writing Assignments Across the Undergraduate Curriculum

1. What writing skills have you, as a department, identified as important for students to acquire?
2. What kinds of assignments and assessments do you pose?
3. How do these assignments address your department's stated outcomes?
4. What difficulties emerge when students attempt to complete your assignments?
5. What teaching strategies do you employ to help students overcome those difficulties?
6. Are there departmental challenges that provide barriers to you as you attempt to overcome those difficulties?
7. Are there departmental challenges that provide barriers to the students when they try to overcome those difficulties?

Chapter 8

Cross-Talk and Crossed Boundaries: Resistance and Engagement when Faculty and Writing Researchers Converse

Theresa Hyland
Huron University College

"Even when we believe we have important observations to make about the discourse practices of those we study, we are often ignored, misunderstood, or even treated with downright hostility" (Segal, Paré, Brent, & Vipond, 1998, p. 72).

I'm sure that many of us have had the experience of conducting research on writing, presenting these findings to faculty at our institutions, and then finding that the information has no impact whatsoever. Sometimes, it is almost as though we have said nothing at all. Yet, at other times, the same information delivered in a slightly different format, or for a slightly more receptive audience, seems to create a great stir. Why does this happen? What are the factors that are at play when faculty and writing researchers converse?

This chapter takes the observations made by Paré et al. (1998) about faculty receptivity of writing research in terms of values and beliefs and adds theoretical and practical support to them. The chapter examines faculty response to reports about three different research projects connected to the Writing Across the Disciplines study that were conducted at a small, liberal arts college in Southwestern Ontario. It analyzes these responses in terms of Stern's

(2000) values-beliefs-norms (VBN) construct and Gifford's (2008) theory of dilemma awareness and cooperation, and theorizes that faculty will accept and act upon research findings that they view as credible, useful and important. The chapter explores ways in which we, as writing researchers, can develop research strategies and presentation protocol that highlight these traits to our colleagues.

Introduction

Segal, Paré, Brent, and Vipond (1998) opened this discussion with an article entitled "Researchers as Missionaries," where they explored receptivity in terms of values and beliefs. This chapter was conceived as a result of three incidents that occurred after my research partners and I presented research to the faculty on what our analysis of their course syllabi told us about writing at our college. Each incident elicited very different responses from the faculty and resulted in very different relationships between the faculty and the writing centre staff. Upon reflection on these incidents, I feel that the main factor in faculty responses was related to the difference in perceptions that faculty had about the research and the way it was presented to them. I believe that in order for faculty to engage with the research that we as writing centre personnel conduct, they must find that research credible, useful, and important. Further, like Segal et al., I believe that because research done for and by writing centre personnel is still a relatively new field in Canada, we need to have discussions about how best to present that research to our faculty colleagues who may be unprepared to accept our findings. If we take into account not only who we are addressing, but also the cultural beliefs held by that group, this research can enhance the professional development of our colleagues in other disciplines as well as our own. In order discuss this assertion, I have looked at two theories of organizational change: (1) Stern's Values-beliefs-norms model (VBN) and (2) Gifford's Social Dilemma Approach to Decision Making. In order to make these theories, which were created to explain social reactions to environmental exigencies, relevant to our own discussions, I will relate them to the Segal et al. (1998) article and to Melzer's more recent (2013) article entitled "Using System Thinking to Transform Writing Programs."

Segal et al. (1998) noted that tropes, topoi, and stylistic values differ from one discipline to the next, but also that most faculty believe that it is possible to convey these cultural differences even when they remain tacit. They argued, however, that if you know how the system works, you can more effectively teach someone how to work within that system (p. 75). Our job as writing researchers is to uncover some of the tacit assumptions about writing that are embedded in disciplinary genres, and as writing instructors it is to help faculty articulate these tacit assumptions and to convey that explicit knowledge to the students. Segal et al. (1998) posit two meanings of "better" when we refer to "better writing." We can mean better in terms of clearer, more organized writing, or better in terms of ideologically better. They note that faculty, and often those of us in writing centres, concentrate on the first without acknowledging the second. The problem is twofold: we need to convince faculty that (1) ideology is reflected in rhetorical and stylistic conventions, and the research that we do on disciplinary practices helps explain these conventions because it explores and exposes the mechanisms that each discipline employs; and (2) this information will not alter these belief systems, but may help faculty change behavioural norms regarding writing practices to make them more effective.

Stern's (1995) model of values, beliefs, and norms (VBN) and their effects on behavioural practices was created to determine why environmentally responsible behaviour occurs in some contexts and not in others despite similar ad campaigns and information being present about the effects of such behaviour. His 1999 and 2000 articles examined how environmentalism works as a social movement, and what the mechanism is which moves people from values and beliefs to action. Stern (2000) argued that there are two types of behaviours: impact-oriented and intent-oriented. Impact-oriented behaviour is behaviour that people engage in because they believe it will have an impact on the target problem. Intent-oriented behaviour, on the other hand, highlights environmental intent as an independent cause of behaviour. Stern asserted that environmental intent will still motivate actions even though these actions may fail to result in environmental impact (p. 408).

While most analyses for environmental behaviours use the impact-oriented behaviour model to convince people that changes in our behaviours are needed in order to create a sustainable environment, intent-oriented models will be more effective in changing target behaviours (p. 408). He posited that, in the environmental sphere, personal values, which are both stable and deep-seated, form a basis for beliefs which affect behavioural norms. Beliefs about the environment include an ecological worldview, the idea that there will be adverse consequences for a valued object if action is not taken, and a perceived ability to reduce the threat. Behavioural norms that are intent-oriented stem from a sense of obligation to take pro-environmental action. These norms can be changed while a person's values and belief systems remain intact.

What is relevant to this chapter is Stern's (1999) assertion that VBN research is generalizable to other social movements. "[Such research] may similarly benefit by distinguishing clearly among committed movement activism, non-activist citizenship behaviours, private-sphere behaviour, and policy support" (p. 407). In terms of writing in the disciplines, we tend to try to encourage faculty through impact-oriented modification of behavioural norms. If the faculty do what we say, the impact will be better student writing. A change to intent-oriented behavioural norms might have more success with faculty: in other words, we need to encourage faculty to change their writing instruction behaviours not because they can expect to see an immediate impact on student writing, but because such changes are important to their own view of themselves as faculty committed to student success. This doesn't mean that they have to become writing activists. Indeed, Stern (1999) makes a distinction between supporters of a movement, "those who are sympathetic to the movement and who are willing to take some action and bear some costs in order to support the movement" (p. 82), and movement activists for whom "the movement becomes an important part of their life and a central element in their identity" (p. 82). For a movement to be successful, he claims, it needs both supporters and activists. This view of writing as a social movement also allows us to move away from Segal et al.'s (1998) idea of "writing instructor as missionary." Our goal is not to convert, but to support good behavioural norms that conform to the faculty's already held personal and public values and beliefs.

Just as we can understand our endeavour to promote good writing instruction as a social movement within the academy, we can also glean an understanding of faculty resistance to the information that we provide from our writing research through Gifford's (2006) Social Dilemma Approach to Decision Making. This theory was also created to understand resource depletion in environmental studies. Gifford (2008) defines a social dilemma as a situation where "their personal interest appears to conflict with the common interest" (p. 266). Here I have adapted the main tenets of the theory to understand why there is resistance to the adoption of effective techniques for teaching writing. Poor writing can be seen as a social dilemma in several ways, but here I will explain it in terms of plagiarism in student writing. For students, the expression of ideas can be a 'scarce commodity,' so students plunder others' ideas and their written texts in much the same way that business plunders scarce environmental resources. Hence, we often use the metaphor of 'stealing intellectual property' when speaking of the inappropriate use of sources. Students transfer their inappropriate strategies from one course to another because what they do in one course affects their view of how things work in the academic community. Professors see this as a dilemma as this student behaviour affects their own disciplinary discourse community as well as the wider university community. Plagiarism undermines academics' ownership of ideas. As these ideas are indiscriminately shared in the community, the academic writer's value as an idea-generating resource is diminished.

Dilemma awareness, Gifford states, is "the degree to which being in a dilemma is experienced as a dilemma, as a crucial influence on cooperation" (p. 269). While faculty may acknowledge this social dilemma, their belief system may prevent them from linking that awareness to an engagement with the generic teaching of writing. This is because they may also believe that if students understand the content of the discipline and read widely in that discipline, they should be able to write effectively in that discipline. In other words, writing doesn't need to be taught because the precepts of good writing are tacitly embedded in the content knowledge. This is how two seemingly conflicting beliefs can co-exist within the minds of some academics: (1) the generic teaching of writing can/should be left to others, but it should be confined to the teaching of essay format and grammatical structures; and (2) this knowledge may not directly help with disciplinary writing, but, nevertheless, disciplinary writing is their domain. These beliefs are compounded by a distrust of writing centre research projects that attempt to understand the ideological and cultural basis of writing in a discipline because they are an encroachment on their territory. It seems that if writing instructors are acknowledged as experts in writing in the disciplines, it somehow decreases faculty expertise in their own discipline. Thus, the 'scarce resource' of faculty expertise is eroded. These perceptions may explain why faculty understanding of the social dilemma of poor writing doesn't necessarily lead to an acceptance of help from writing instructors.

At my institution, there are several channels through which dilemma awareness of writing problems can be fostered. First, all Chairs have been asked to write learning outcomes for each course, including how they are demonstrated and how they are assessed. This is demonstrated for the larger, province-wide community through "dashboard indicators" that each institute must articulate to the government, as a method of ensuring quality control in education. One of the common indicators of the success of learning outcomes is through the assessment of the writing that students do. Students who fail may do so because of writing that doesn't meet the standards of the discipline. A second way of promoting dilemma awareness is through departmental reviews which are conducted every five years and which include both an internal and external review of the programs within that department. In preparation for these reviews, and in response to the reviews, faculty have meetings about how to address perceived problems and develop their programs.

When dilemma awareness occurs, Gifford tells us that decision-maker strategies are devised to address the problem. The specific or generalized exchange of ideas that happens in department meetings often deals with content and its delivery rather than writing strategies. Where that exchange does include writing strategies, one of two things happens: either the department (or an individual member of faculty) accesses writing centre services, or the faculty attempts, as a group, to solve the problem with "disciplinary writing tutorials" which they design themselves, usually without reference to writing theory or genre analysis. Gifford also says that when a strategy seems to work there is a feeling (individually or in the group) of self-efficacy or self-satisfaction. In the case of writing, students may earn higher marks and the department perception is that their strategies have worked. When these strategies don't succeed, the tendency is to blame the students rather than seek the help of writing experts. As students' frustration with their grades increases, they may leave the department and go to one that is perceived to be more student-friendly. There may, then, be financial repercussions to the success or failure of student writing in terms of student enrolment and retention.

Administration-Focused Research

Now that we have mapped out the minefield of conflicting values, beliefs, desires, and exigencies that we enter when we present research to the faculty, let us attempt to understand the dynamics underlying the different reactions in our case studies. In the first instance, two other researchers and I embarked on a Course Syllabi Study and the Dean of the Faculty of Arts and Social Sciences in my college agreed to have this study take place at our institution. We received a grant from the umbrella institution for the project, and the Dean provided us with all of the course outlines from the college. In return for the Dean's cooperation, we were to provide a report to the faculty at the end of the project. The purpose of the project was to provide a context within which writing services could be developed both within the college and in the larger context of academic writing in Canada. Accordingly, all course outlines were codified according to a writing data sheet which collated, for each writing assignment, the marking rubric, length of the assignment, descriptive name for the assignment (i.e. paper, essay, research essay, report, review), time given to complete the assignment, grade for the assignment, percentage of final grade that the assignment represented, feedback included in the writing of the assignment, and nested tasks within a larger assignment. The data that we had collected was aggregate and descriptive. The data was separated out by year for the whole college and by program. The presentation and subsequent report that we gave to the faculty occurred at the end of the academic year at a faculty meeting that covered a variety of "end of year" topics. In that presentation, we simply reported information that we had gleaned from our coding sheets, looking for patterns of engagement.

Basically, we found that within the 179 course outlines, there were 485 written assignments. Most assignments were named "papers" or "essays" (63%), and we found that the most assignments were given in second year, with the fewest assignments, worth the most marks, given in fourth year. However, there was no direct correlation between length of assignment and year level, as many of the open level classes (designed as optional classes and not as foundational courses for the discipline) required long essays of 10 pages or more at the end of the course. We found that only 30% of first year assignments were nested (a larger assignment is broken down into its constituent parts), but 59% and 48% respectively of assignments given in the third and fourth level courses were nested. We also found that learning goals, which were explicit statements of what students were expected to learn from the assignment, occurred in only 34% of all assignments, with the greatest proportion of these (39%) occurring in the level four courses. Finally, we found that 70% of all assignments included no rubrics to describe the elements the assignment should contain or information about how the assignment would be graded. Similarly, 86% of the assignments provided no in-process forms of feedback (e.g. peer review during class, a scheduled office visit, or written notes on a preliminary proposal or abstract). The complete findings for the project can be found in the article by Graves, Hyland, and Samuels (2010), "Undergraduate Writing Assignments: An analysis of Syllabi at one Canadian College."

The reaction of the professors to this information was quite hostile. Some attempted to discredit the categories we had devised on the data sheets. For example, one item we included for tabulation was the inclusion of in-process feedback where students systematically received a critique about their writing before it was handed in for a mark. We were looking for something that was embedded within the assignment itself, in the form of a public (in-class) or private critique that could be consulted before the final paper was handed in. The faculty argued that in-process feedback did not need to be included as a separate activity within the preparation of a writing assignment.

Their reasoning was that all students were given the opportunity to seek help from their professors through the mechanism of standardized office hours, which faculty were required to provide for all courses and which were clearly indicated on the course outlines. Others asserted that rubrics, descriptions of assignments, and grade sheets on the course syllabi were not the only ways that faculty gave information to students about their writing assignments. They argued that they gave that information in many different forms: discussion in the classroom, answering questions in emails, and additional handouts at appropriate times in the course. Therefore, the picture we had painted was limited at the very best. While these reactions were worrying to the researchers, the lack of follow-up engagement with writing centre services was even more worrying. The researchers offered to create a profile for each department from the data we had gathered, but not one discipline accepted that offer. Faculty did not approach the writing centre to establish closer ties; there was no increased buy-in to writing workshops or services; there was no increased student activity in the Writing Centre; and there was no perceptible enhancement of the status of writing researchers among faculty. Because faculty had dismissed the research as flawed and incomplete, there was no reason to engage with writing centre services.

So what went wrong? The most obvious problem was that the belief systems of administrators and those of faculty are often quite different. Davis and Jacobsen (2013) assert that administrators look at solutions within the wider context of how they will work in the whole community of the college, how the board will accept those solutions, and how to measure success of proposed innovations. Professors look at administrative solutions in the more immediate context of how they could be introduced into the curriculum, how students will react to them, and how effective these solutions will be in ameliorating the problem (in our case, poor student writing). The "top-down" approach that we used in obtaining support for our project was at fault. While it is always necessary to get the dean on board with such initiatives, we should probably have solicited more support from the faculty before we started our investigations. Instead, this analysis was thrust upon them out of the blue. Also, although the first presentation that we made gave a lot of descriptive information to the faculty about writing assignments in their programs, in the context of the whole faculty meeting, this information seemed to be challenging faculty beliefs and behavioural norms stemming from those beliefs: in this case, that post-essay feedback and open office hours for individual consultations are effective ways of teaching good disciplinary writing to the students. The very terms with which we analyzed the course outlines presented a number of writing "best practices" that are standard tropes in writing research. However, they were neither apparent nor accepted by the faculty as such. This resulted in feelings of frustration, anger, and surprise in our audience. We seemed to be blaming them for the fact that the students didn't write well! Moreover, there had been, until that time, no well-developed history of collaboration between the Writing Centre and the faculty. The Writing Centre was seen by many as a remedial centre for students who couldn't write, and not a research-based academic service that could help professors in their classroom teaching. Segal et al. (1998) foreshadowed this reaction by saying that rhetoricians need to proceed with respect for the cultural complexity and belief systems of others: not be zealous missionaries in the cause of rhetorical "betterment" among professionals. They suggest focus groups where rhetorical dilemmas are discussed or co-investigations with professionals in the field to create a "middle space" between their discipline and ours. Asking the faculty what they perceived as significant might have induced a more positive reception of our research. Moreover, Segal et al. (1998) cautioned that we should have no broad expectations of overarching change and advised that starting with student surveys within the discipline might be a good way to explore information on the course outlines and how they could be changed (pp. 86-89). Stern would describe this as a change in orientation from impact- to intent-oriented persuasion.

Faculty-Focused Research

As a follow-up to the Course Syllabi Project, and as a result of some of the comments made by faculty during that fateful discussion, we decided to embark on a number of focus groups by department, where we could ask the kinds of questions that the initial descriptive research opened up for us. Specifically, we wanted to engender a conversation about what kinds of information the professors gave to students about their expectations for writing, and how they conveyed that information. We also wanted them to explicitly articulate how those expectations for student writing changed between first and fourth year, and how that increase in scholarship should be demonstrated in the writing. Mindful of the push-back that occurred after our last attempt, we proceeded very carefully in setting up the focus groups. First of all, we approached faculty who were already favourably disposed to the work that we do in the Writing Centre, and asked them if they were willing to engage in a focus group about how they work with student writing. Once we knew that we had two or three people per discipline who would support the focus group, we approached the chair of the department with an email invitation to involve the department in a focus group. Having established which departments were willing to participate, we sent the letter of information, consent forms, and the preliminary survey to the chair to be distributed to the faculty and asked the chair to set a date for the focus group. The Faculty Information Sheet (see Appendix B in previous chapter) explained that the answers to the questions would form a context for their remarks during the focus group. We also had prepared a common list of interview questions with which to prime the discussion. In this way, we were able to engage four departments, two from Humanities and two from the Social Sciences, in the focus group exercise. The focus groups were conducted in the Attic Club, a retreat where faculty could relax, have a coffee, and talk in a casual atmosphere. Present at the Focus Group were three researchers: one to ask the questions, one to take notes on the conversation, and one to videotape the session. Three to four faculty members of each department, including the chair of the department, were present for each session. Faculty freely discussed both departmental views of what disciplinary writing should look like, and how the department had decided to educate students about that writing. They also moved to individual strategies that they had used, successfully or not, and why they felt these strategies were appropriate. The moderator (the Writing Centre director) asked questions and encouraged multiple answers for these questions, but offered no commentary on what was being discussed. After the session, we asked faculty to quickly fill in a Post Focus Group Feedback Form which we then collected and calibrated.

We found the conversations in these focus groups to be extremely lively and, given the hostility of the last experience, surprisingly enthusiastic. One of the most interesting findings for us was the fact that faculty in each department used distinct metaphors for how students should approach writing in their field. These metaphors were usually mentioned by one member of faculty, and taken up throughout the discussion by others in the faculty. These metaphors seemed to be powerful expressions of epistemological thinking within the departments in that they created a consensus not just about what writing was, but also about how it should be taught within that department. Moreover, they seemed to be related to the research orientation of the discipline and how student writing should reflect that orientation. Thus, the discussions around the teaching of writing, descriptions of assignments, and expectations for the writing focused on these disciplinary orientations (Hyland, Howell, & McDougall, 2017). After each focus group discussion, faculty remarked on how useful the session was, and some even spoke of repeating the session at a later date. During that year, and the following year, several things happened that made us feel that we had been accepted within the academic community of the college and that writing was clearly a focus for the faculty. The Writing Centre staff were asked to do more customized workshops; there were significantly more students coming to the Writing Centre; the director was invited to participate in the departmental accreditation discussions; and professors began accepting invitations to come to the Writing Centre to talk about writing in their discipline to our tutors and to the students.

I believe this difference in faculty response can be partially explained through Stern's theory. The focus groups put the dialogue about writing into a safe social context: the meeting consisted only of disciplinary peers and the writing services researchers. The Dean of the Faculty was only involved in the focus group for his department, and he participated only in his role as a faculty member and not in his administrative role. This allowed the faculty to discuss writing in a forum where the academic values and disciplinary beliefs were shared. Faculty values regarding writing generally revolve around an altruistic model of the importance of teaching students to think for themselves and to evaluate everything that they read with a critical eye. These values can be seen to be non-egotistic in that they include freedom of speech, balanced argumentation, evidence-based reasoning, and a respectful acknowledgement of the work that others have done. In addition, each discipline has specific values around epistemological orientations, research orientations, and dissemination of information: what constitute valid questions, valid research methods, and valid evidence. The epistemological orientation towards knowledge seemed to be evidenced by polarized views: *positivist,* i.e. knowledge is gained by the analysis and understanding of facts; and *relativist,* i.e. knowledge is gained by engaging and subjectively interpreting texts. We found that Psychology and Political Science acceded to the former view and English and History, the latter.

The beliefs that faculty hold about how to teach writing are not necessarily common across academia but seem to be subject to disciplinary norms. Thus, the metaphors around the teaching of writing and the relative value of assigned texts versus text discovery could be characterized as beliefs. If we accept that these areas form beliefs, they can be mitigated by individual preferences within the department. For example, Hyland et al. found that, in the specific context of their study, there was a general consensus among the faculty in Psychology and History about not only the need for good writing, but also how that good writing could be elicited from the students. Therefore, faculty designed very specific writing laboratories for the students where the process of writing was broken down for practice by the students. Other departments such as English and Political Science depended less on a general consensus within the department about writing in their discipline and more on the beliefs of individual faculty about what "teaching writing" constituted for their areas of specialization. This individualist stance was articulated by one member of faculty in English who told us "our colleagues in the social sciences have a better ability to say this is what a good history essay is, or this is what a good political science essay is.... Our discipline certainly has a general sense, but it allows for variations such as a poetry course, or other, more politicized courses" (Hyland et al.). In other words, in English, beliefs about good writing were articulated by individual faculty members and not by common consensus. However, text orientation did not follow this general consensus/individual preference continuum. Psychology and English were prescriptive in that they assigned particular texts that students should engage with, but History and Political Science wanted students to discover texts for themselves in order to understand a particular event or episode.

While beliefs seemed to be consistent within the focus group, the discussion allowed the faculty to consider how to change their behavioural norms around teaching writing, student motivation, and preparatory tasks for academic writing. The Writing Centre director, through a series of open-ended questions, provided the impetus for these discussions within the focus groups, without commenting on the discussions that took place. Therefore, she was viewed not as an outsider looking in and criticizing what she saw, but as a facilitator whose aim was to help them articulate and share practices, and solve problems that they brought up. In this way, the discussion seemed to be more intent-oriented: how writing fulfilled the "learning outcomes," how to grade student writing, how much writing each course could reasonably ask students to do, and what constitutes an academic assignment.

The need for these discussions was reinforced by the underlying communal awareness of a significant social dilemma at the college at that time: the declining recruitment and retention of students. These conditions presented risks to the faculty because of the possibility of programming reductions and job insecurity should student enrolments decline within a given department. Professors linked their behaviours directly to these administrative threats. Because the college is a liberal arts college, its reputation is tied to a perception that our students go on to successful post-graduate and professional programs. However, if the writing of the students seems not to meet the standards that the professors have set, this may have detrimental effects on these students' ability to move on after graduation. This, in turn, could negatively affect recruitment and retention, particularly in those disciplines where good writing is essential.

The ability to reduce perceived threats through changes in behaviour can vary within disciplines as well as between them, but it helped that these focus group discussions were held outside of the scrutiny of the administration and of other disciplines. Faculty could discuss what measures they had already taken both in terms of the intent and impact on writing and on the risks they faced, assess whether these options had been successful, and consider strategies that others had tried. For example, one professor in English asserted that nested assignments did not lead to better final products in his experience because students did each segment at the last minute. Another professor felt that her strategy of having students critique rough drafts of each others' essays was sometimes, but not always, successful in producing better final products. These discussions demonstrated that former strategies (i.e. both the trial and error strategies of individual faculty, and writing workshops that focused on format and grammar) had been impact-oriented rather intent-oriented. No discussion about why they were using the strategies or how these strategies fit into their perceptions of what constitutes disciplinary writing had previously taken place at the college either informally or formally. The focus groups gave faculty the opportunity to compare strategies and their intent, and place them in a systematic context of disciplinary writing. This was welcomed by the faculty who were frustrated with the lack of impact that their other strategies had had.

Intent-Oriented Research

Seven years after the first course syllabi project, I was given the opportunity to do a follow-up survey of writing assignments across the curriculum at the same institution. In this study, I found that there were significant changes to the number, kind, and length of assignments students had to do. While the number of courses had risen from 179 to 208 in the seven years between studies, the number of writing assignments had risen from 448 to 741 in the same period. This meant that the average number of assignments per course had risen from 2.5 to 3.6 assignments. While third year course still had the most writing assignments, the number of fourth year courses also increased. Interestingly, the professors' labels for writing assignments had also changed considerably. In 2007, 57% of assignments were labelled as essays or papers. In 2014, 33% were labelled essays or papers, but many had much more descriptive labels: document study, clinical report, marketing report, analytic book review, and summary. The inclusion of assignments labelled as presentations, annotated bibliographies, literature reviews, and theses told us that many larger assignments were broken down into constituent parts, and that some of those parts (i.e. a presentation of material) included feedback before the larger assignment was due.

Remembering the former hostility to the presentation of course syllabi information seven years previously, I carefully crafted the presentation of the data as intent-oriented rather than impact-oriented. The presentation was specifically focused on the "so what" factor: what opportunities did this research data offer the faculty? Because the research findings were comparative, and positively oriented to the current faculty strategies, faculty perceived the findings as beneficial to them in three ways. First, the increase in the number and type of writing assignments over the entire college curriculum provided an indication to administration that faculty were engaged in improving the culture of student writing at the college. Second, dissemination of this information to the students could help solve the numbers issue, because it proved that the college was indeed interested in student success. Third, I suggested that the information contained in the report could be introduced into departmental reviews to show that the departments were carefully considering how their teaching strategies were intended to help students understand disciplinary writing. To my relief, when I presented this comparative research to faculty, there was none of the former hostility, but rather an intense interest in the findings, some congratulatory moves on the part of some of the faculty, and concrete invitations to come and talk to those departments which were currently undergoing accreditation review.

Changing perceptions of the social dilemmas facing the college and how to remedy them were also, I think, responsible for this change in attitude. College-wide retention and recruitment figures were significantly down in the Arts and Social Sciences, and faculty across departments and within departments were wrestling with how to reverse this trend. By the time of the third presentation of data to the faculty, a culture of collaboration between the Writing Centre and the various disciplines had already been established through writing in the disciplines talks, customized workshops, and the regular use of the services of the Writing Centre by the students. Anecdotal evidence showed that some professors enthusiastically encouraged their students to come to the centre because they could see the improvement in the papers of those who used the service. Moreover, several of the disciplines which were in the focus groups were also preparing for their five-yearly departmental review. The research was viewed as credible because it validated faculty beliefs and changing behavioural norms that were congruent with these beliefs. It was regarded as useful because of the message it sent to administration that faculty were working systematically towards learning outcomes for their courses. The presentation not only painted a favourable picture of the past seven years, but it implied a reasonable direction for the future. Faculty and administration could use this report to devise strategies to improve student recruitment to a liberal arts college that valued writing and the development of good writing habits in its students.

Conclusion

I stated at the beginning of this article that writing centre research must be viewed as credible, useful, and important. Research is credible if it comes from current practice, addresses acknowledged needs, and honours faculty values and beliefs while indicating why and how to change behavioural norms. Research in writing can be useful when it helps faculty solve dilemmas that they perceive in their discipline and in the administrative context of the college. Solving these dilemmas helps them retain ownership of their disciplinary writing practices, enhances their personal satisfaction, improves their students' writing, and increases their department's credibility with administration.

We live in an era when Writing Centre practices are held to account by administrations and faculty who are hampered by decreasing enrolments and scarce funding. Many university writing centres are run by people who don't believe in doing research into writing and many administrators are willing to let writing services hold a remedial position within the university community. This seems to be combined with a further misperception that because librarians teach students how to do research, they are capable of teaching them how to write academic papers. This is a dangerous misconception in that it reduces writing instructors to experts in format and grammar. Writing Centre personnel who engage in applied research from a theoretical perspective can be extremely useful in the academic context by providing insights to faculty about their tacitly held beliefs. Western University has just announced the allocation of several million dollars to build an interdisciplinary facility on campus. Writing programs are the epitome of interdisciplinarity. We don't have to be missionaries. We do have to be aware of the audience for whom we design our research and fashion our presentations and make sure that the findings we bring to the table are viewed as credible, useful, and important by that audience. One way we can do this is by including faculty not just as subjects of research, but as co-researchers into their own values, beliefs, and behavioural norms regarding writing. The Course Syllabi Project and the many branch projects it has spawned are just the beginning of that research.

References

Carter, M. (2007). Ways of knowing, doing and writing in the disciplines. *College Composition and Communication, 58*(3), 385-418.

Davis, S. N., & Jacobsen, S. (2013). Curricular integration as innovation: Faculty insights on barriers to institutionalizing change. *Innovation in Higher Education, 39*(1), 17-31. doi:10.1007/s10755-013-9254-3

Gifford, R. (2008). Toward a comprehensive model of social dilemmas. In A. Biel, D. Eek, T. Gärling & M. Gustafsson (Eds.), *New issues and paradigms in research on social dilemmas* (pp. 265-280). New York: Springer.

Graves, R., Hyland, T. & Samuels, B. M. (2010). Undergraduate writing assignments: An analysis of syllabi at one Canadian college. *Written Communication, 27*(3), 293-317.

Hyland, T., Howell, G., & MacDougal, A. (2017). Upstairs/downstairs: Conversations from the attic about the classroom below. In R. Graves & T. Hyland (Eds.), *Writing assignments across university disciplines* (pp. 180-217). Winnipeg, MB: Inkshed Publications.

Melzer, D. (2013). Using system thinking to transform writing programs. *WPA: Writing Program Administration - Journal of the Council of Writing Program Administrators, 36*(2), 75-94.

Parker, P. M. & Quinsee, S. (2012). Facilitating institutional curriculum change in higher education. *International Journal of Learning, 18*(5), 49-60.

Segal, J., Paré, A., Brent, D., & Vipond, D., (1998). The researcher as missionary: Problems with rhetoric and reform in the disciplines. *College Composition and Communication, 50*(1), 71-90.

Stark-Meyerring, D., Paré, A., Artemeva, N., Horne, M., & Yousoubova, L. (2011). *Writing in knowledge societies.* Anderson, SC: Parlour Press & WAC Clearinghouse.

Stern, P. C. (2000). Toward a coherent theory of environmentally significant behavior. *Journal of Social Issues, 56*(3), 407-424.

Stern, P. C., Kalof, L., Dietz, T., & Guagnano, G. A. (1995). Values, beliefs, and pro-environmental action: Attitude formation toward emergent attitude objects. *Journal of Applied Social Psychology, 25*(18), 1611-1636.

Stern, P. C., Dietz, T., Abel, T., Guagnano, G. A., & Kalof, L. (1999). A value-belief-norm theory of support for social movements: The case of environmentalism. *Human Ecology Review, 6*(2), 81- 97.

Endnotes

1   This sheet, as well as the Interview Questions Sheet and the Post Focus Group Feedback sheet are included in the Hyland, McDougall, and Howell article, (this volume).

Afterword

Heather Graves
University of Alberta

This collection of essays and the research project that produced them are unique because they offer insight into the nature and scope of writing assignments required of undergraduate students at post-secondary institutions across Canada, information that has not been available previously. Despite administrators of post-secondary education in Canada such as the Ontario Council of Academic Vice-Provosts (OCAV) and the Higher Education Quality Council of Ontario mandating good communication skills for all graduates as one of six undergraduate degree outcomes (Harrison, 2017), little systematic information has been available on how the goal of good written communication skills might be achieved: what and how much do students write to develop good written communication skills prior to graduation? Which courses and departments incorporate writing instruction into their assigned work? What kinds of supports do departments and instructors provide to help students develop these communication skills?

Disciplinarity and Writing Instruction in Canadian Universities

While not comprehensive, the chapters in this book do offer glimpses into the number, genres, and distribution of writing assignments at a selection of post-secondary institutions in Alberta, Manitoba, and Ontario. They get us started understanding what students at the participating institutions write in a variety of

233

programs in Humanities, Sciences, Health Sciences, and Social Sciences. As the authors in this collection have made clear, once administrators of degree programs and/or writing studies programs know what students are writing and how much, they are better able to decide whether their existing programming is appropriate and sufficient, or whether they should adjust the course or program requirements. In fact, in several cases, including the Faculty of Education at the University of Lethbridge and of Engineering at the Universities of Manitoba and Waterloo, program administrators have used the knowledge from this study of undergraduate writing assignments as a catalyst for program review and renewal.

A key point that Slomp et al., Parker, and Jewinski and Trivett each make in their chapters is that, in the changes made to each program, writing instruction is integrated into a context where it highlights for students the professional value of becoming a skilled communicator in writing while remaining simultaneously something that experienced disciplinary instructors can teach. This is a crucial point because at Canadian universities disciplinary instructors are the predominant purveyors of most of the formal writing instruction that Canadian students receive. Very few institutions have mandatory first year writing courses (The University of Winnipeg is a notable exception) because of the expense of funding such comparatively small courses. Graves (1994) provides detailed insight into some historical aspects of this issue. Graves and Graves (2006) update the history ten years after R. Graves' initial study with a collection of investigations of writing programs and solutions in the first decade of the 21st century. A second factor affecting scarcity of mandatory writing instruction is the relative lack of graduate programs in Writing Studies that would produce qualified instructors (in the form of graduate student teachers [GTAs], sessional instructors, or tenure-line faculty), not to mention the lack of tenure-line or even fulltime continuing positions advertised to employ these graduates.

An additional factor lies in research over the past four decades in writing in the disciplines (WID)/writing across the curriculum (WAC), the rhetoric of science, and genre studies that questions the efficacy of generic writing instruction, as generally offered in mandatory first year writing courses in the USA. My recent work on argument in science has identified the basis for generic writing instruction as, in fact, Humanities-based disciplinary discourse (and sometimes English Studies-disciplinary discourse) (H. Graves, 2014). In the textbooks that R. Graves and I have adapted from American editions, The *Brief Pearson Handbook* (Faigley et al., 2017) and the *Little Pearson Handbook* (both previously, Penguin) (Faigley et al., 2015), we have incorporated this research into the rhetoric sections to highlight for readers some of the general variations in disciplinary writing conventions in Science, Engineering, and Social Science disciplines from Humanities-based disciplines. For example, we have expanded the section on structuring assignments in various disciplines to indicate that the Social Sciences generally take a different approach compared to the Sciences or the Humanities. At the same time, it is unrealistic to make the kinds of structural changes to a textbook like the *Brief Pearson Handbook* that would fully reflect the different approaches to disciplinary discourse. For example, we kept the discussion of free writing as an invention strategy without acknowledging its narrow application to Humanities disciplines; such a strategy will likely not help Science or Engineering students. Those students would benefit from learning a writing process used by expert writers in their fields, who begin by assessing their visuals (that is, their research results) to determine the primary knowledge claims they intend to make (Kresta et al., 2011). However, addressing in a meaningful way the scope of the permutations of disciplinary discourse in a writing textbook would require developing it from the ground up, an expensive proposition that few Canadian students are willing to pay for in 2017.

Historically, undergraduates in Science and Engineering have not been asked to write about their (original) research; however, a clear movement has started among Canadian post-secondary institutions to engage undergraduate students in collaborative research projects with faculty. For example, at the University of Alberta, the Roger K. Smith Award for Undergraduate Research has for several years funded original research collaborations between interested undergraduate students and faculty members. The eventual outcome of such projects is publication, so undergraduate students would benefit from learning some of the argumentative strategies employed in disciplinary genres by disciplinary specialists rather than essay-based argument structures as if they were universal. In fact, essays in English Studies are not necessarily constructed or argued identically to essays written in other Humanities areas such as History or Political Science, a fact that further undermines the generalizability of generic writing instruction focused on the essay.

Discourse and Disciplinary Membership

In this volume, Parker and Jewinski and Trivett both note the importance of teaching engineers to write like engineers, a point that has been made numerous times by researchers in writing in the disciplines about Science, Social Work, and other disciplines (Dias et al., 1999; Dias & Paré, 2000; McLeod & Soven, 1994; Penrose & Katz, 2004; Thaiss & Zawacki, 2006; among many others): disciplinary discourse has peculiar features that generic writing instruction cannot distinguish or deliver. Since the 1980s, research on the rhetoric of inquiry and specifically science has explored how knowledge is created and argued for in numerous disciplines, including Economics (McCloskey, 1987), the Human Sciences (Simons, 1989; Nelson et al., 1990), Physics, (Bazerman, 1988; H. Graves, 2005), Biology (Myers, 1990), science generally (Harris, 1997; Gross, 1996, 2006), among many others. These studies illustrate the ways in which writing and thinking—that is, creating and arguing for new knowledge—are inextricably bound together in these disciplines, a finding that undermines the claims of generic writing courses to achieve their goal of preparing students to write in other undergraduate courses.

Interesting research in genre studies also serves to raise the question of whether students, as well as novice writers in a field, should receive writing instruction from within the discipline rather than from a generic writing course. For example, research in English for Specific Purposes (See the *English for Specific Purposes* journal or *Discourse Studies*) and English for Academic Purposes (See the *Journal of English for Academic Purposes*) conducts critical discourse analysis on various genres including the research article in diverse disciplines to document the move and step arrangement in the IMRD structure of this genre (i.e., Introduction, Methods, Results and Discussion). These studies build on the work of J. Swales in his 1994 and 2004 Create a

Research Space (CARS) models for research article introductions to highlight how the sections are structured in different disciplines. Since 2011, S. Moghaddasi and I have studied the structure of argument in research articles in theoretical mathematics, specifically discrete math. We have shown how research articles in this subspecialty differ structurally from other disciplines (H. Graves et al. 2013, 2015) as well as other subspecialties in mathematics. For example, in our sample, we found that two-thirds of writers in discrete mathematics use strategies to establish a niche for their work (Moghaddasi & H. Graves, 2017), while McGrath and Kuteeva (2012) found in pure mathematics that fewer than half established a niche for their work. This work suggests that there is considerable variation in disciplinary discourse structures across and within disciplines.

When the findings from discourse analysis and genre research are coupled with conclusions from studies by WID and WAC researchers, as well as scholars in the rhetoric of science/inquiry, it becomes clear that writing is not an add-on, undertaken once the researcher has completed his/her empirical study. Instead writing is integral to knowing in a discipline; knowing is at the heart of disciplinary discourse. With writing instruction comes knowledge of ways of thinking, analyzing, and being a member of that discipline (i.e., "writing like an engineer" or scientist or forensic anthropologist). That is, students are best served by learning to write in their discipline, taught by disciplinary specialists, rather than exclusively by writing studies instructors.

The Role of Writing Studies Scholars and Teachers

Up to this point, I have argued that disciplinary instructors have a central role in teaching students to write in their disciplines, but I should stress equally that Writing Studies instructors also have important contributions to make regarding writing instruction on Canadian post-secondary campuses. Writing Studies specialists have the background and expertise in research and theory in Writing Studies that disciplinary specialists usually lack; therefore, the former can provide informed direction for their administrators and institutions and speak authoritatively about best practices for achieving programmatic and institutional outcomes related to effective written communication (this all assumes, perhaps optimistically, that administrators and institutions are willing to consult the expertise they have on campus).

Writing Studies scholars can also provide more general instruction on writing (to be distinguished from 'generic writing instruction'). While generic instruction treats one set of disciplinary conventions (for example, English Studies) as universally applicable, general instruction presents existing instructional material in the context of the extensive variation that exists among disciplines. Therefore, students as well as instructors can focus on assessing the extent to which existing instructional material and strategies apply to their individual disciplines or using it to highlight the ways in which their discourse community departs from the traditional, generic precepts. I use this latter approach in my graduate writing courses, which enroll students from across the disciplines. We use existing instructional materials (e.g., Swales and Feak, 2012; Thomson and Kamler, 2016) to hone the students' analytical abilities to understand the nuances of style and structure in their disciplinary discourse. Students can see the subtle details as they are cast in relief through class discussions and small group activities focused on differing discursive conventions and by comparing their own fields' conventions with other students' as they comment on classmates' drafts of genres from their fields. In addition, I have created instructional materials based on my research that provide alternative models of argument to traditional Humanities structures (based on Toulmin, 1958, and others) that can help students see the extent to which their field uses (or not) these traditional structures. In the course, we also use traditional stylistic advice (for example, Williams & Nadel, 2006) as baseline strategy, but these resources require adaptation to show students how they operate within the stylistic conventions of, for example, science or health science-based discourse practices.

Motivating Student Buy-In and Driving Change

Another key point made by both Parker and Jewinski and Trivett is the necessity of adapting the writing assignments to the needs and disciplinary perspectives of the students. Both chapters highlight the ways in which the writing instruction in these professional programs in Engineering aimed to elicit buy-in from the students by featuring assignments that they could clearly recognize as valuable, increasing their motivation to work hard at improving their writing abilities. While these authors focus on the discipline of Engineering, it is worth considering that this point also holds across disciplines. Writing assignments that students can see the value of and understand how the assignment requirements extend outside of the immediate course are likely to be more positively received and likely undertaken with greater dedication. At the same time, not all undergraduate assignments should be practical and extensible beyond an individual course, but it is a point that instructors should take seriously when designing at least some of their assignments. For example, assignments for whom the instructor and other students in the class are the sole audience, while useful to a point, should not be the exclusive choice in most courses in a program if the goal of the program is to prepare students to communicate ideas to multiple readers using diverse genres and formats.

While professional programs such as Engineering and Pharmacy have long dealt with accreditation boards and assessment review, academic programs in areas in Sciences, Humanities, and Social Sciences have not; however, even these areas have recently begun moving in this direction by identifying course and program outcomes as a precursor to evaluating and measuring how well they achieve their stated outcomes. For example, at the University of Alberta in 2016, instructors from across the disciplines were asked to submit their course learning objectives. Once these were collected, it became clear that instructors could use help to create learning objectives in some cases and in other cases to more clearly and appropriately articulate their learning objectives. It does not require much imagination to see where this initiative is headed: eventually program administrators will be asked to measurably demonstrate that their courses and programs achieve the learning goals set out in the course syllabi and program outcomes. The kinds of research presented in these chapters afford clear paths to assessing and measuring course and program outcomes. In the programs and institutions where researchers have inventoried undergraduate student writing assignments, the results of this work have served as catalysts for meaningful discussion related to teaching and giving feedback in various programs, departments, and colleges. Hyland and McKeown have both illustrated in their chapters the ways in which these conversations have increased morale and built stronger networks among department members who participated in the focus groups. These increased opportunities for instructors to interact and share ideas can provide much needed emotional and professional support amongst instructors and can increase the likelihood of improved instruction, resulting in higher quality learning opportunities for students.

Another aspect of helping students develop good written communication skills lies in collecting information about the scope and nature of the instruction that they receive. The process through which this information is collected, however, must be organized appropriately and handled with sensitivity if its goals are to be achieved. For example, Hyland in this volume describes the radically different responses to her collection efforts depending on whether the request for study was initiated by the unit itself or imposed at the direction of an upper administrator. Hyland notes that when the information collection is undertaken with the avid participation and interest of those instructors whose syllabi are being requested, compliance is much higher and reception of results is much friendlier. The lesson here is that these study projects are politically sensitive and, depending upon how they are handled, can succeed wonderfully or fail miserably. Other researchers or writing program administrators who are inspired to offer a similar environmental scan or writing assignment inventory service at their institutions should pay special attention to how the invitation is issued, to whom, and with what reported goal. The framework for initiating such study directly affects the possibility that it can sponsor useful conversations about teaching, writing instruction, and potential change.

Once degree program and writing program administrators know the extent to which students have access to pedagogical strategies such as scaffolded or nested assignments, grading rubrics that articulate criteria for evaluation, the means to receive formative feedback prior to grading, and so on, they can work systematically to ensure that such strategies are present in classes that are intended to help students learn to write in their disciplines. R. Graves' chapter in this volume highlights how students are writing in nearly every course in the curricula in the programs, departments, and faculties that he studied. It also appears that many of these students receive limited formative feedback on these assignments, yet through completing these assignments they are intended to learn how to produce the discourse of their discipline. Given this knowledge, administrators and program designers have evidence of the need to support their instructors in integrating more explicit writing instruction into their courses. For example, access to GTAs, markers, dedicated writing tutors, etc., as appropriate, will ensure that instructors can develop and execute effective pedagogical activities and assignments that incorporate explicit writing instruction without overworking themselves.

These chapters have given us some surprising answers to the questions of what and how much students write (in most cases, they write many assignments over their undergraduate careers) and of which curricula and programs incorporate writing instruction into their assigned work (many instructors assign written work and evaluate student learning through written assignments). They also indicate the kinds of supports students receive to develop written communication skills (some programs/instructors give more support; some give little support).

They all make clear that writing is or has become an integral part of learning and assessment in post-secondary education at the institutions represented here.

References

Bazerman, C. (1989). *Shaping written knowledge*. Madison, WI: University of Wisconsin Press.

Dias, P., Freedman, A., Medway, P., & Paré, A. (1999). *Worlds apart: Acting and writing in academic and workplace contexts*. Mahwah, NJ: Lawrence Erlbaum.

Dias, P., & Paré, A. (Eds.). (2000). *Transitions: Writing in academic and workplace settings*. Cresskill, NJ: Hampton Press.

Faigley, L., Graves, R., & Graves, H. (2015). *The Little Pearson Handbook* (1st Canadian ed.). Toronto: Pearson.

Faigley, L., Graves, R., & Graves, H. (2017). *The Brief Pearson Handbook* (4th ed.). Toronto: Pearson.

Graves, H. (2005). *Rhetoric in(to) science: Style as invention in inquiry*. Cresskill, NJ: Hampton Press.

Graves, H. (2014). *A new model for argument in science-based disciplines*. Unpublished conference paper at the International Writing Across the Curriculum Conference. Minneapolis, MN.

Graves, H., Moghaddasi, S., & Hashim, A. (2013). Mathematics is the method: Exploring the macro-organizational structure of research articles in mathematics. *Discourse Studies, 15*(4), 421-438.

Graves, H., Moghaddasi, S., & Hashim, A. (2014). 'Let G= (V, E) be a graph': Making the abstract tangible in introductions in mathematics research articles. *Journal of English for Specific Purposes, 36*, 1-11.

Graves, R. (1994). *Writing instruction in Canadian universities*. Winnipeg, MB: Inkshed Publications.

Graves, R., & Graves, H. (Eds.). (2006). *Writing centres, writing seminars, writing culture: Writing instruction in Anglo-Canadian universities*. Winnipeg, MB: Inkshed Publications.

Gross, A. (1996). *The rhetoric of science*. Cambridge, MA: Harvard University Press.

Gross, A. (2006). *Starring the text: The place of rhetoric in science studies*. Carbondale, IL: University of Southern Illinois University Press.

Harris, R., (Ed.). (1997). *Landmark essays on rhetoric of science: Case studies*. Mahwah, NJ: Lawrence Erlbaum.

Harrison, A. (2017). *Skills, competencies and credentials* [PDF document]. Toronto: Higher Education Quality Council of Ontario. Retrieved from http://www.heqco.ca/SiteCollectionDocuments/ Formatted Skills%20Competencies%20and%20Credentials.pdf

Kresta, S., J. Nychka, J. Masliyah, M. Gray, & R. Graves. (2011). Writing well²: Building traction and triumph into co-authorship. *Conference of the American Society for Electrical Engineers.* Vancouver, BC.

McCloskey, D. N. (1987). *The rhetoric of economics.* Madison, WI: University of Wisconsin Press.

McGrath, L., & Kuteeva, M. (2012). Stance and engagement in pure mathematics research articles: Linking discourse features to disciplinary practices. *English for Specific Purposes, 31*(3), 161-173.

McLeod, S. H., & Soven, M. (Eds.) (1992). *Writing across the curriculum: A guide to developing programs.* Newbury Park, CA: Sage.

Moghaddasi, S., & Graves, H. (2017). "Since Hadwiger's conjection . . . is still open": Establishing a niche for research in mathematics. *English for Specific Purposes, 45,* 69-85.

Myers, G. (1990). *Writing biology: Texts in the social construction of scientific knowledge.* Madison, WI: University of Wisconsin Press.

Nelson, J. S., Megill, A., & McCloskey, D. N. (Eds.). (1990). *Rhetoric in the human sciences: Language and argument in scholarship and public affairs.* Madison, WI: University of Wisconsin Press.

Penrose, A. M., & Katz, S. B. (2004). *Writing in the sciences: exploring conventions of scientific discourse* (2nd ed.). New York: Pearson/ Longman.

Simons, H. W. (Ed.). (1989). *Rhetoric in the human sciences.* Newbury Park, CA: Sage.

Swales, J. M. (1990). *Genre analysis: English in academic and research settings.* Cambridge: Cambridge University Press.

Swales, J. M. (2004). *Research genres: Explorations and applications.* Cambridge: Cambridge University Press.

Swales, J.M., & Feak, C. B. (2012). *Academic writing for graduate students* (3rd ed.). Ann Arbor, MI: University of Michigan Press.

Thaiss, C., & Zawacki, T. (2006). *Engaged writers and dynamic disciplines: Research on the academic writing life.* Heinemann, NH: Boynton/ Cook.

Thomson, P., & Kamler, B. (2016). *Detox your writing: Strategies for doctoral researchers.* New York: Routledge.

Toulmin, S. E. (1958). *The uses of argument.* Cambridge, UK: Cambridge UP.

Williams, J. M., & Nadel, I. B. (2005). *Style: Ten lessons in clarity and grace, Canadian edition.* Toronto: Longman.

Index

University of Manitoba initiatives in, 56–58

writing assignments, 62–68

See also ME100; teaching effective communications

Melzer, D., 4–5, 18, 31, 212

mentoring, 137–139, 166–167, 175–176,

mini-unit assignments, 160, 167

Moghaddasi, S., vii, 237

Moran, Katherine E., 4–5

motivating students to write, 92–93, 95, 109

Myers, Greg, 73–76, 236

N

naming assignments

faculty focus groups, 194–195

Life Sciences, 83–84, 93–94

Nelson, J.S., 236

Nesi, H., 5–6, 18, 19

nested writing assignments

about, 19–20

Life Sciences use of, 89, 90, 91, 95

number of assignments

assessing, 10–12

comparing with Mechanical Engineering initiative, 64–65

determining Life Sciences frequency and, 79–83

Nursing assignments

audience for, 17–18

coding, 9

in-process feedback on, 20–21

most common genres for, 13–15

nested assignments, 19–20

number and length of, 10, 11–12, 65

rubrics for, 21–22

O

OCAV (Ontario Council of University Vice-Provosts), 233

P

Paltridge, B., 4

Paré, A., 3, 97, 174, 211–212, 236

Paretti, M.C., 51, 54, 62, 67

Parker, Anne, xi–xii, 16, 22, 50–72, 234, 236, 238

participation in faculty focus group, 203–204

pedagogy

    response to *ME100* writing component, 125–128

    structuring Arts Faculty assignments, 42–44

    student exit survey on, 48–49

peer-review résumé creation, 119–120

Pelech, Sharon, 135–173

Penrose & Katz, 236

Peterson, S. S., 4

Pharmacy assignments, 9

    most common genres for, 13–15

    nested assignments, 19–20

    number and length of, 10–12

Phelan, A.M., 150–152

Physical Education assignments

    audience for, 17–18

    in-process feedback on, 20

    most common genres for, 13–15

    nested assignments, 19–20

    number and length of, 10–12

    rubrics for, 21–22

plagiarism warnings, 40–41, 83, 86–87, 88, 94

Political Science assignments, 9–10

    audience for, 17–18

    in-process feedback on, 20

    most common genres for, 13–15

    nested assignments, 19–20

    number and length of, 10–12, 64–65

    rubrics for, 21–22

Popham, S. L., 18

practice-and-theory perspective, 152, 159

Professional Semesters and practicums

    assignment frequency by semester, 145–149

    organization of, 137–139

    requirements for, 136–137